Policymaking in the European Central Bank

Governance in Europe
Series Editor: Gary Marks

Regional Integration and Democracy: Expanding on the European Experience
    Edited by Jeffrey J. Anderson
A Wider Europe: The Process and Politics of European Union Enlargement
    Michael J. Baun
Between Europeanization and Local Societies: The Space for Territorial Governance
    Edited by Jeanie Bukowski, Simona Piattoni, and Marc Smyrl
A Ruined Fortress? Neoliberal Hegemony and Transformation in Europe
    Edited by Alan W. Cafruny and Magnus Ryner
The New Political Economy of EMU
    Edited by Jeffry Frieden, Daniel Gros, and Erik Jones
Democracy beyond the State? The European Dilemma and the Emerging Global Order
    Edited by Michael Th. Greven and Louis W. Pauly
Common Goods: Reinventing European Integration Governance
    Edited by Adrienne Héritier
Differential Europe: The European Union Impact of National Policymaking
    Adrienne Héritier, Dieter Kerwer, Christophe Knill, Dirk Lehmkul, Michael Teutsch, and Anne-Cécile Douillet
Multilevel Governance and European Integration
    Liesbet Hooghe and Gary Marks
Voices of Europe: Citizens, Referendums, and European Integration
    Simon Hug
Contentious Europeans: Protest and Politics in an Integrating Europe
    Edited by Doug Imig and Sidney Tarrow
Wiring Europe: Reshaping the European Telecommunications Regime
    Giorgio Natalicchi
Transatlantic Governance in the Global Economy
    Edited by Mark A. Pollack and Gregory C. Shaffer
How to Democratize the European Union . . . and Why Bother?
    Philippe Schmitter
The European Parliament: Moving toward Democracy in the EU
    Edited by Bernard Steunenberg and Jacques Thomassen
The Euro: European Integration Theory and Economic and Monetary Union
    Edited by Amy Verdun

Policymaking in the European Central Bank

The Masters of Europe's Money

Karl Kaltenthaler

ROWMAN & LITTLEFIELD PUBLISHERS, INC.
Lanham • Boulder • New York • Toronto • Plymouth, UK

ROWMAN & LITTLEFIELD PUBLISHERS, INC.

Published in the United States of America
by Rowman & Littlefield Publishers, Inc.
A wholly owned subsidary of The Rowman & Littlefield Publishing Group, Inc.
4501 Forbes Boulevard, Suite 200, Lanham, Maryland 20706
www.rowmanlittlefield.com

Estover Road, Plymouth PL6 7PY, United Kingdom

British Library Cataloguing in Publication Information Available

Library of Congress Cataloguing-in-Publication Data
Kaltenthaler, Karl, 1966–
   Policymaking in the European Central Bank : the masters of Europe's money /
Karl Kaltenthaler.
       p.   cm. — (Governance in Europe)
   Includes bibliographical references and index.
   ISBN-13: 978-0-7425-5366-8 (cloth : alk. paper)
   ISBN-10: 0-7425-5366-3 (cloth : alk. paper)
   ISBN-13: 978-0-7425-5367-5 (pbk. : alk. paper)
   ISBN-10: 0-7425-5367-1 (pbk. : alk. paper)
     1. Europe Central Bank.   2. Monetary policy—European Union countries.
   I. Title.   II. Series.
   HG2976.K35 2006
   339.5'3094—dc22

                                                                   2006007403

Printed in the United States of America

♾™ The paper used in this publication meets the minimum requirements of
American National Standard for Information Sciences—Permanence of Paper for
Printed Library Materials, ANSI/NISO Z39.48-1992.

Contents

Acknowledgments   vii

Introduction   1

1   The Origins of the European Central Bank   11

2   The Formation of the European Central Bank's Monetary
Policy Strategy   35

3   The Structure and Strategy of the European Central Bank   61

4   The European Central Bank's Operating Environment   91

5   The Exchange Rate Challenge   123

6   European Monetary Union Enlargement and the European
Central Bank   147

Conclusion   165

References   177

Index   189

About the Author   195

Acknowledgments

This book is only possible because of the help of many people that inspired my interest in the European Central Bank or helped in the process of bringing it to completion. Those who were of most help to me in my many trips to Europe to research the book were Otmar Issing, Josef Kaltenthaler, and Hans and Maria-Theresa Tietmeyer. Their insights were invaluable to making this book a reality. There are several academics who were essential to sharpening my arguments and getting my facts straight. They include Chris Anderson, Jeff Frieden, Ron Gelleny, Larry Hamlet, Randall Henning, Matthias Kaleberer, Peter Loedel, Gerald Schneider, and Andrew Sobel. While they helped me immensely, any remaining mistakes are solely my fault. Research assistance from Sunita Arora and Patrick Schmutte is very much appreciated. The fantastic crew at Rowman & Littlefield deserve a huge amount of my gratitude. Their hard work, professionalism, and patience made the preparation of the manuscript a smooth and low-stress process. Special thanks are due to Janice Braunstein, Jessica Gribble, and Susan McEachern. I would also like to thank some people on the home front. First of all, my wife deserves a lot of the credit for seeing the book finished. She braved my long absences to research the book and my hours at the computer turning it into a manuscript. She deserves a medal for putting up with the whole process. I dedicate this book to my two little reality checks, Phillip and Joseph. My two sons not only served as wonderful stress relievers as I trudged through the writing, but they always keep me focused on what is important in life.

Introduction

It was a momentous occasion for Europe. The heads of state and government of the member states of the European Community were seated at a regal table on 7 February 1992, signing the Treaty on European Union (EU) in the Dutch town of Maastricht. The treaty covered a wide range of integration issues, but the most profound stipulation in the treaty, by far, was the agreement to establish a monetary union by 1999 at the latest. This monetary union would create a common currency for the European Community—soon to become the EU—as well as the European Central Bank (ECB). This was a massive step forward in integration and a pivotal point in Europe's history. European leaders were agreeing to cede an important part of their sovereignty, monetary management, to a supranational European institution. The national leaders sitting at that table were setting a new course in Europe's history.

But the road to the Maastricht Treaty and the agreement on European Monetary Union (EMU) is only a part of the ECB's story. A hugely important part of the story is what came after Maastricht. It is imperative to point out that the Maastricht Treaty said a great deal about what the structure of the European Central Bank was to look like and what its general mandate was to be, but it was silent on the policy strategy the bank was to use to achieve "price stability," as called for in the treaty. Thus, it was up to the decision-makers in the nascent ECB to decide what price stability actually meant in concrete terms and how to reach that goal. As the ECB was created as an independent central bank in the Maastricht Treaty, the European central bankers would be making up the monetary policy paradigm for the Eurozone by themselves as they went along. It was a breathtaking responsibility. The decision-makers in the ECB were being tasked with creating a set of monetary policy strategies and tactics that would steer the economic fate of the 300 million citizens in the Eurozone. They had to create this policymaking paradigm in the context of eleven different national economic and political systems and not cause financial markets to panic in response to their implementing a completely new currency and policymaking structure.

The ECB has handled this challenge very well. It has given the financial markets in Europe and around the world confidence in its ability to manage the domestic and international aspects of the Eurozone's monetary affairs successfully. The ECB has kept inflation low in the Eurozone; made the euro the common currency, which is a competitor to the dollar; and given a large portion of Europeans and others confidence that the EU can become, at some point, an economic counterweight to the United States. Thus, the ECB has become one of the most important economic actors in the world in a very short time.

This book is about the politics of policymaking in the ECB. I seek to identify and explain the factors that shape its domestic and international monetary strategies. The project explores questions such as, What motivates the policy priorities of the central bankers in the ECB? Are the policies driven by the economic ideas of the central bankers? Are they due to pressure from other politicians, from financial interests, or, perhaps, from the European public? What role do institutions and structure play in shaping policy strategy? How does a changing EU stand to affect the policymaking of the ECB?

These questions are immensely important because they touch on the role that the independent ECB plays in democratic European societies. Some have argued that independent central banks, such as the ECB, are inherently undemocratic institutions because their decision-makers can make policy based on their own preferences and are not accountable to either elected politicians or the general public (Berman and McNamara 1999; Verdun 1998). Others have argued that decision-makers in independent central banks reflect the preferences of the society in which they operate, implying that these institutions are not as undemocratic as their critics charge (Vaubel 1993).

I argue that the decision-makers in the ECB are not dogmatic economic ideologues, unconcerned with how their policies impact the citizens of the Eurozone. The policy preferences of an independent central banker are shaped by the policy models that the central bankers find or create for best securing the long-term needs of the macroeconomy. The desire to keep the macroeconomy healthy, meaning maintaining low inflation, low unemployment, and solid growth, is driven by the central bankers' two primary personal preferences: to appear competent to as much of society as possible and to maintain broad political support for their operational independence. For the decision-makers in the ECB, the policymaking model that seems to have offered the best roadmap to keeping the Eurozone economy healthy is that of the German Bundesbank. The Bundesbank's track record of monetary management in Germany since its inception has made it a central bank with tremendous credibility and persuasive power. Thus, to put it simply, the European central bankers who have worked together to shape the ECB's monetary policy strategy have, over the years, come to adopt the Bundesbank's monetary policy model, with important innovations. These innovations to the Bundesbank model have been based on the Bundesbank's experience and the different context present in the Eurozone. The ECB has created this hybrid model as a pragmatic means to replicate the Bundesbank's success at the European level and to lend credibility to its own policies. But as the EU expands to take in countries that were not part of the capitalist world economy until recently and that have had limited contact with the German central bank, one must ponder whether the Bundesbank model of monetary policy will continue to have universal acceptance among the ECB's central bankers.

WHY STUDY POLICYMAKING IN THE ECB?

Although the ECB is a relatively new and unstudied institution of supranational governance in the EU, that, in itself, is not a sufficient reason to study it. The ECB deserves serious scholarly attention because of its importance to both the international political economy and the domestic political economies of the states in which it operates. An independent central bank is, in many ways, the most important macroeconomic policymaking body in the economy. By controlling the levers of monetary policy, an independent central bank can play a huge role in determining the growth of an economy, the rate of inflation, and the unemployment level. Thus, the ECB can control the economic destiny of many countries in Europe.

If the European Central Bank can control the economic destiny of the Eurozone economy, this implies that it can, to a great extent, control the electoral fate of the national executive leadership. As myriad studies have shown, governments get the blame and, to a great degree, the credit for the health of the economy. If a central bank is an institution that is really doing a great part of the macroeconomic steering, then the politicians are largely at its mercy. And, if the central bankers are able to provide, given the economic challenges facing them, an economy on a path of low inflation, healthy growth, and low unemployment, then politicians can be pleased that the central bankers are not ruining their reelection chances. But if central bankers provide economic outcomes that the public does not like, then politicians may find central bankers playing a role in damaging their hopes for reelection. Thus, the ECB is clearly an important factor in determining political outcomes in Europe.

The ECB, while only in its infancy, controls the second largest economic area in the world and could potentially challenge the American Federal Reserve's position of global monetary preeminence. Thus, understanding the sources of its monetary policy decisions helps us understand the causes of very important economic and political outcomes.

THE NEED FOR A NEW APPROACH

We know quite a bit about why European leaders agreed to create monetary union and the European Central Bank. Several groundbreaking studies have shown the importance of economic considerations as well as geostrategic calculations playing a part in the decision to move to EMU (Baun 1995, 1996; Dyson 1994; Dyson and Featherstone 1999; Frieden and Jones 1998; Grieco 1995; Gros and Thygesen 1998; Hasse 1990; Heisenberg 1999; Jones 1998, 2002; Kaelberer 2001; Kaltenthaler 1998; Loedel 1999; McNamara 1998; Moravcsik 1998; Oatley 1997; Sandholtz 1993; Verdun 2002; Walsh 2000; Wyplosz 1997). Thus, we have a fairly good picture of the politics that went into the creation of EMU.

Several scholars have looked at the operations of other central banks in order to make predictions about the operations of the ECB. Emmanuel Apel (2003) has compared the American Federal Reserve and the German Bundesbank's monetary policymaking processes to draw inferences about the types of policies the ECB is likely to make given the type of environment it faces. Jakob de Haan (2000), in an edited volume, takes a similar approach by tracing the history of policymaking in the Bundesbank. He shows that it was not as independent as many have thought and argues that the ECB will face the same types of challenges to its independence. Jerome Sheridan (1996) examines the history of monetary affairs in nineteenth-century America and produces predictions for the ECB based on the American experience.

There is a growing literature on the institutional structure of the ECB. Most of these works critique the structure of the central bank, touching either on the degree of independence that the central bank was granted or the policy powers given to it by European politicians (Antenbrink 1999; Campanella 2000; Canzoneri, Grilli, and Masson 1992; Craig 1999; Crowley 2001; de Haan 2000; Demertzis 2001; Dornbusch, Favero, and Giavazzi 1998; Dutzler 2003; Elgie 2002; Gormley and de Haan 1996; Groeneveld 1998; Kaufmann 1995;

Naudin 2000; Taylor 2000; Verdun 1998; Zilioli and Selmayr 2001). All of these studies point out that the political compromises that were necessary to form the ECB have left it with an imperfect policymaking structure.

Another common theme is how the operations of the ECB will affect politics and economics in the EU. Several scholars have focused on the predicted economic consequences of the operations of the ECB (Belke and Gros 1999; Cohen 1994; Dornbusch, Favero, and Giavazzi 1998; Eichengreen 1998; Gros 1998; Henning 2000a; Jones, Frieden, and Torres 1998; Levitt and Lord 2000; Magnette 2000; Masson and Taylor 1993). Others have looked at the political consequences of what the ECB does in terms of policy (Dyson 1999, 2002; Henning 2000b; Soskice and Iversen 1998; Verdun 1996).

The literature on the policies and operations of the ECB itself is not nearly as large. A small, but growing, body of work examines the ECB after it came into operation. David Howarth and Peter Loedel (2003) have created the most comprehensive and insightful study to date of the ECB. They seek to cover a gamut of topics related to the ECB's operations, but they focus primarily on the question of how the ECB fits into a European democracy. Thus, their concerns center on the issue of the ECB's policymaking independence from government and society.

Surprisingly, very few scholars have actually focused on the politics of policymaking in the ECB since it began its policy operations in 1999 (see Eijffinger and de Haan 2000; Favero et al. 2000 for descriptive economic treatments of the issue). Otmar Issing (2001), chief economist at the ECB, has coauthored a book with Vitor Gaspar, Ignazio Angeloni, and Oreste Tristani on the monetary policy of the ECB. This book is a very useful insider's view of how a key figure in the ECB thinks about monetary policy. But it is not a political analysis of decision-making in the ECB.

Matt Marshall (1999) has written an interesting journalistic account of the ECB. He, too, is taken with the issue of the ECB's immense powers, but his primary contribution is to portray snapshots of the inner workings of the central bank. He provides a rare glimpse into the personalities involved in policymaking in the ECB.

Kenneth Dyson's (2000) *The Politics of the Eurozone* is, as the title suggests, a look at the political factors that affect economic and monetary policymaking in the Eurozone. The focus is not solely on the ECB, but his work provides useful information on what the context of policymaking in the Eurozone is like. The book is more conceptual than empirical, which limits how much information it can give us about what drives policymaking in the ECB.

While all of these works contribute to our understanding of various aspects of policymaking at the ECB, none of them systematically explores all potential sources of policy decisions in the ECB. Thus, we have fragments of a picture of what goes on in the corridors of power at the ECB, most of which are based on conjecture, but we do not have a truly focused analysis of the ECB's determinants of policy. This study is intended to move toward producing such a focus.

How should we go about trying to understand the sources of the ECB's policies? The logical place to look would be the literature on central banking. This should give us analytical insights into what, in general, influences central bankers when they formulate their policies.

For the lay public, there is often a veil of mystery surrounding independent central banks' decision-making. In the popular media, decision-makers in independent central banks have long been viewed as remote high priests who control the economic fortunes of their countries. The title of a popular book on the American Federal Reserve, *The Secrets of the Temple: How the Federal Reserve Runs the Country*, sums up what many people think about independent central banks. They are organizations that make immensely important decisions about the economic destiny of countries, yet how and why their policymakers make their decisions seems very mysterious. They are not institutions where the decision-makers make their policy choices after public debates. Nor are they institutions where the policymakers make detailed explanations of their positions on the decisions that they have made, if they make comment on them at all. Independent central banks remain inscrutable institutions for many in the general public because the commercial media tends to portray them as highly secretive institutions.

The academic community also often seems to find independent central banks mysterious compared to other political institutions. In fact, there has been no dearth of scholarly writing on central banking over the last two decades. Central banks seemed suddenly to become a topic of great interest to many students of political economy during the 1980s. This interest in the political economy of central banking seemed to arise out of the developing conventional wisdom that central bank independence was an important part of fighting inflation in the advanced industrialized democracies during the 1970s. This was a salient argument in the aftermath of the inflationary consequences of the two oil crises. But what is noteworthy about this growing body of work on central bank independence is how little of it is devoted to explaining the sources of policy choices in independent central banks.

The research on central banking has seemed to move in four directions since the 1980s. The first direction entailed case studies of the decision-making of prominent central banks. The central banks that attracted the most scholarly attention were the American Federal Reserve and the German Bundesbank because of their relative importance in their countries' economies and the world economy (e.g., Goodman 1992; Greider 1987; Kennedy 1991; Kettl 1986; Marsh 1992; Woolley 1984). These case studies were primarily directed at describing how these central banks operated, and they were meant to shed light on the politics of policymaking institutions, which had previously been ignored by political scientists. They were inherently devoid of generalizable theories of central bank decision-making as there was no real comparative component to this work. Thus, these studies did not provide any analytical frameworks for understanding the sources of independent central bank policymaking.

The second direction was pursued primarily by economists and looked to see what impact central bank independence had on measures of economic performance, such as inflation, economic growth, and unemployment (Alesina 1988; Alesina and Summers 1993; Cukierman 1992; Cukierman, Webb, and Neyapti 1992; Franzese 1999; Hall 1994; Havrilesky and Granato 1993; Iversen 1998b; Suzuki 1993). This work was much more grounded in theory and attempted to explain why an independent central bank would likely produce particular types of economic outcomes. This work did not discuss, however, why those independent central banks chose their pursued policies.

The third major trend in the scholarly literature on the politics of central banking addressed the question of why governments would choose to make their central banks independent (Bernhard 1998; Clark 1993; Goodman 1991; Maxfield 1994, 1997; Rogoff 1985). This research found several possible answers and is still a major source of debate today. It is important to note that this trend in the literature, which built on the previously mentioned economic literature, assumed that once central bank independence was supplied (in an advanced industrialized democracy), the country with the independent central bank would be on a low-inflation path. This work is based on the major assumption that all central bankers have a normative predisposition against inflation as they are bankers and, thus, are socialized to abhor inflation.

Only the fourth, and most recent, trend in the literature on central banking has addressed the question of what the primary sources of the policy priorities of independent central banks are. These works, which are grounded almost exclusively in the economics public-choice perspective, have developed several alternative answers to this question. It is this work that offers the greatest opportunity to aid in answering the question at hand. But, as will be demonstrated in the next section, this work is insufficient as a generalizable theory to explain the sources of independent central bank policymaking.

This book seeks to develop a theoretically informed, systematic approach to understanding the sources of policy orientations in the ECB. The theory used to comprehend the ECB's policymaking is informed by public-choice thinking in political economy. This book takes as its theoretical starting point the idea that independent central banks are political institutions that compete in a world of finite power. I argue, based on the logic of public choice, that independent central bankers have two primary goals: to appear competent to as large a section of society as possible and to maintain policy-making independence. Central bankers try to achieve these goals by keeping the macroeconomy healthy. Economic ideas help the independent central bankers choose policy strategies that will allow them to maximize the health of the economy.

DESIGN OF THE STUDY

The place to start in this discussion of the design of the study is to define precisely the thing to be explained in this analysis, the dependent variable. The dependent variable in this study is the policy strategy chosen by the central bankers.

The study seeks to identify the factor or factors that shape policy in the ECB by developing a theoretical argument about the sources of independent central banks' policy orientations. This argument will then be assessed against the information presented about the potential sources of ECB monetary strategies. The research strategy employed here relies on a qualitative approach to determining the strength of the argument developed in this book.

Why undertake a qualitative study of the sources of ECB policy instead of a quantitative study of potential policy inputs? The large-N quantitative approach to studying the sources of independent central bank policymaking has produced very mixed results (Woolley 1984). It has neither produced definitive answers as to what drives independent central bank policymaking nor provided much insight into how and why monetary policy decisions are made. The in-depth case study approach allows us to look more closely at the causal connections between the dependent and independent variables than would be possible with a large-N study. Thus, this study is intended to provide a very focused analysis of causality that can serve as a base of knowledge for possible future larger-N studies.

The data for this study will be taken primarily from dozens of interviews with the relevant actors potentially involved in the process of shaping the three independent central banks' policy orientations. I interviewed dozens of central bankers, interest group representatives, and relevant government officials over the period 1999 to 2005 to determine what these actors do to influence the orientation of monetary policy in their specific contexts. The interviews were structured to learn what counts most when it comes to deciding on monetary policy.

The policymakers and others interviewed were asked the same questions to determine the level of consensus on issues and also to ascertain what might account for differences in perspectives among the respondents. Thus, central bankers, politicians, market participants, and others were given a particular set of questions relevant to their work and interests. The aim was to get as broad a sample as possible of relevant opinions on the issues in this study. Asking the questions over a period of six years also allowed for a glimpse at how the politics of policymaking in the ECB may be changing over time.

The advantages of using interviews are that they give a detailed picture of the preferences of the actors in question and allow the interviewee to describe her or his thinking that went into decisions in a way that is only possible in an interview. These interviews provide a rich and detailed base of data for assessing the argument.

There are also potential drawbacks to using interview data. One of the most frequently cited criticisms is that the interviewees may respond to the questions in a strategic and insincere manner. This is often a valid concern and deserves a comment. One can definitely imagine situations where actors would try to inflate the appearance of their importance or try to give their decisions the best possible gloss. It is never possible to preclude such types of responses to interview questions, but it is possible to reduce the likelihood that such responses will be offered. One way is to keep all interviews off the record. That reduces the probability that the respondents will feel compelled to spin their thoughts or actions on a particular issue. The second way to combat the strategic answer problem is to avoid questions that seem to attach credit or blame to the respondent. Questions that are value neutral in their assessment of actions are more likely to attract sincere answers. These two strategies have guided the interviews used in this study.

Aside from interviews, this study will also use other forms of data to assess the argument offered here. Data will be taken from official documents, public-opinion research, and other primary source materials. The objective of the data-collection strategy is to have as rich and varied a base of data as possible to determine the validity of the argument.

ORGANIZATION OF THE STUDY

The study is organized in a way such that the theoretical logic drives the empirical enquiry in a systematic manner. The first chapter outlines the empirical and theoretical puzzle that motivates this book. It succinctly describes the policy behavior of the ECB. It also briefly outlines the book's main argument, justifies the case selection and approach, and gives an overview of the chapters.

The second chapter provides a brief outline of the history of the development of EMU and the creation of the ECB. The chapter is meant to provide an overview of the forces that led European leaders to create the institutions of the ECB.

The third chapter explores the development of the ECB's domestic monetary policy strategy. The ECB has clearly acted as a central bank that takes its inflation mandate seriously. In many ways, it seems to be modeling its monetary policies after those of the German Bundesbank, with important modifications. Why has the ECB adopted this modified Bundesbank-style monetary policy approach? This chapter argues that it was the success of the German Bundesbank in managing Germany's monetary policy that made it an attractive example to emulate for European central bankers. The model has been modified for the ECB due to some failings of the Bundesbank experience as well as the different economic context that the ECB faces compared to that faced by the Bundesbank.

The third chapter examines the ECB's external monetary policy. I argue that independent central bank policymakers' exchange rate policy preferences are shaped with the goal of maintaining price stability in the Eurozone and keeping the Eurozone competitive compared to other economies. Of these priorities, price stability is the most important.

Chapter 4 studies the structure of the ECB. It seeks to determine what role the institutions of the central bank play in shaping its policy strategies—more specifically, the structure of decision-making power in the central bank, its voting procedures, means of staffing itself, and so forth. It is found that these various institutions do play an important part in shaping the context in which policy strategies are formed, but the institutions themselves do not explain the form that the policy strategies have taken.

Chapter 6 examines the central bank's policymaking environment in order to determine where it fits into the story of policymaking in the ECB. The policymaking environment includes the ECB's relationship with various national and EU political entities, as well as civil society in the Eurozone. The chapter concludes that while the ECB is a political institution in the sense that it seeks to maintain the power that it has, it is a highly independent central bank with a broad mandate for monetary policy, but with great latitude to make policy as it sees fit. Thus, one cannot describe the ECB as an institution captured by either governmental organizations in the Eurozone or the economic interest groups of the Eurozone society. The ECB's monetary policy strategies are, for the most part, the result of its own preferences.

The concluding chapter briefly summarizes the argument of the book and its empirical findings. It then examines how the research reflects on the existing body of theory on central banking and points out what more needs to be done in order to better understand the ECB and other central banks. It concludes with further research questions raised by this study.

1

The Origins of the European Central Bank

The European Central Bank (ECB) is the result of several decades of efforts on the part of European policymakers to make a currency union in Europe a reality. The trajectory from the first suggestions of monetary union to the launching of the ECB in 1998 was anything but linear and obvious. Political will, the right economic and political circumstances, and the power of those with a strong interest in creating monetary union were all necessary conditions for creating the common currency and the central bank to manage it.

This chapter traces the political origins of the ECB. It addresses two primary questions: why was the ECB created, and why was it structured as it was? While several good studies trace the history of the process of creating monetary union (e.g., Dyson 1994; Dyson and Featherstone 2000; Moravcsik 1998), it is worth briefly outlining the history of the political road to the creation of the ECB, as it puts the central bank into a context that may allow one to better understand why the ECB looks and acts as it does.

This chapter argues that the creation of the ECB is the result of four factors. The most important factor was the need for Germany to anchor itself in Western institutions in the context of unification. This was imperative in order to placate any fears of a resurgent and aggressive Germany and became particularly important in the context of the possibility of German unification in 1989–1990. Second, agreeing to establish the ECB was a way to overcome the problem of Bundesbank dominance of European monetary affairs, which had become increasingly politically unpalatable for many

European governments by the end of the 1980s. Creating the ECB was the only politically viable way to ensure monetary stability in the European Community (EC), which was necessary for trade and the Common Agricultural Policy (CAP), and not to have the Bundesbank act as the anchor institution of the system. Third, and less important, growth in trade and investment inside the EC made monetary union and the creation of a common central bank a logical choice. Fourth, and finally, several prominent Eurofederalists such as Jacques Delors, Helmut Schmidt, and Valéry Giscard d'Estaing helped push the process along. Of these factors, tying Germany down to European institutions was the most important reason for the creation of the ECB.

This chapter also argues that the design of the ECB shows the centrality of Germany to the process. The ECB's structure was created in the image of the Bundesbank because of the success of the German central bank in monetary affairs, its ability to persuade other central bankers of the superiority of its structure, the desire of central bankers and politicians to borrow instant credibility from the Bundesbank by copying its institutions, and, finally, the power of the Bundesbank to exercise a veto in design negotiations. Thus, the ECB was created in order to tie the Germans down, but it was the Germans who got to say what the structure of the central bank would look like.

THE ORIGINS OF EUROPEAN MONETARY COOPERATION

The idea of monetary union is as old as the idea of European integration. It is a widely held belief among some of the earliest proponents of the idea of European unification that a monetary union would have to be an intrinsic element of the process. Nearly everyone who thought highly of the ideal of a politically unified Europe thought this would have to entail a single currency and a monetary authority to manage it.

It is interesting to note that the first serious political impetus to move to a European currency union came not from Europeans but from the Americans. In the late 1940s, as the American government poured cash into Europe in an attempt to stimulate economic reconstruction, one of its principal concerns was cooperation among the Europeans that would lead toward eventual political integration. The Americans favored an integrated Europe because it would eventually make Europe less dependent on America as it saw the gains of economic integration. They also supported integration because it would make Europe stronger in the face of internal and external Communist threats. Thus, the Americans became important political and economic backers of the launch of the integration process.

One of the first major integration initiatives the American government supported was the creation of a currency union. In 1949, in its plan to reconstruct Europe's economies, the U.S. administrators of Marshall Plan aid in Europe began to push the European recipients to consider moving toward a monetary union and the creation of a central bank. The American-led European Cooperation Authority, the agency responsible for the European Recovery Program, had created a plan for the launch of a monetary union by 1952. Considering the leverage the Americans had because of the aid they were giving to the Europeans, seemingly one could expect the Europeans to agree to make strides toward the creation of a currency union. In fact, the idea was a political nonstarter among European heads of government.

The primary obstacle to the plan of creating a monetary union was the British government. The Americans wanted the British to be part of the nascent development of the integration process, such as the European Payments Union and the European Coal and Steel Community, so it had to take British views into consideration. The British government was opposed to the development of a currency union, which it viewed as too much of an infringement on Britain's sovereignty. The idea also received a mixed reaction from French government circles because some French policymakers also disliked the idea of yielding that much sovereignty. Thus, the idea never really got off the ground in the 1950s.

The currency union idea also did not get far because the economic circumstances in Europe did not seem to warrant such a move. Monetary stability in Europe was fostered by the dollar-based Bretton Woods international monetary regime. The exchange rate regime prevented substantial monetary instability and seemed to work well for both the Europeans and the Americans in the 1950s. There was no compelling economic motivation, from a European perspective, to move to a currency union in the 1950s. The Treaty of Rome did not even mention the goal of monetary union.

This does not mean that some Europeans did not push for monetary union. Some in the European Commission, such as Vice President Robert Marjolin, individuals in some European governments, and Jean Monnet, who was now a private citizen, began to push for monetary union as a way of moving Europe forward toward political integration, but the political will was simply not strong enough among European governments to make the development of concrete plans for such a move possible.

The circumstances blocking the road to European Monetary Union (EMU) seemed to change dramatically in the late 1960s. A combination of political and economic factors converged to give realization of the monetary union its first serious chance.

THE FIRST TRY AT MONETARY UNION

The first major initiative by EC member states to form institutions of monetary integration was the failed attempt to create EMU in the late 1960s and early 1970s. German and French policymakers were at the center of this unsuccessful project, being the principal member state proponents of the

EMU plan. Let us examine the sources of that German-French policy initiative.

Although the idea of European monetary integration had been around since the late 1940s, the member states had not taken any meaningful steps toward monetary integration until the late 1960s. The source of the EC's new-found interest in monetary integration was its notion that serious monetary instability was on the horizon. In the later years of the 1960s, the Bretton Woods monetary regime was beginning to show cracks. Increasing challenges to the dollar from international sources and a growing willingness in the United States, the anchor country in the system, to prioritize domestic economic concerns at the expense of the value of the dollar began to cause both governments and market participants to lose faith in the U.S. commitment to the international exchange rate regime.

The collapse of international monetary stability would have a very negative impact on the European Community. Not only would intra-EC trade face possible disruption if exchange rates among member states were to become unstable, but the viability of the CAP would be threatened. The CAP, which was a cornerstone of Franco-German relations, depended on stable exchange rates in order for its payment and pricing system to function properly. The collapse of the CAP would possibly cause serious damage to the entire common market system as the CAP was a major incentive for French participation in the integration project. Given the gravity of possible exchange rate instability, EC leaders began to think about ways to head off a monetary crisis.

In 1969, the Barre Report, a plan issued by Raymond Barre, the EC commissioner for economic and monetary affairs, was made public. It was a plan for EC monetary integration to culminate in monetary cooperation for the member states, with a common currency as its crowning achievement (Tsoukalis 1997, 84–85).

This plan would not have gotten far without an important state picking up the reins of moving toward monetary union. The German government stepped in to act as the political sponsor of the monetary union project in 1969. Chancellor Willy Brandt had made monetary union the centerpiece of his strategy to deepen West Germany's ties to the European integration project. At the Hague EC summit in 1969, a consensus to move to a monetary union was reached under Brandt's guidance.

But German chancellor Willy Brandt's sponsorship of monetary union belied serious disagreement within German monetary affairs circles about the subject of EMU. It came as something of an unpleasant shock to the Bundesbank and the Finance Ministry, Germany's two principal state actors charged with overseeing monetary affairs, when Brandt openly supported the EMU idea at the 1969 Hague summit. The Bundesbank and the Finance Ministry had often complained that international exchange rate regimes were a threat to the Bundesbank's mandate of maintaining domestic price stability (Kaltenthaler 1998, 43).

So, why would the German government sponsor the monetary union project when West Germany had struggled to support the Bretton Woods system and had foregone a great deal of its domestic monetary autonomy in order to do so? The answer is to be found in the German government's interest in cementing its ties to France, which had been so carefully nurtured after the founding of the federal republic. Those ties were facing a twofold assault around 1969. First, there was the issue of what exchange rate instability would do to the CAP and Franco-German economic cooperation within the EC. The CAP provided very substantial benefits to French farmers and was viewed as a trade-off for German access to French industrial markets. The collapse of the CAP could threaten the Franco-German relationship. The second assault on the Franco-German relationship came in the form of Brandt's *Ostpolitik*, or opening to the Eastern European states. Brandt had made it a cornerstone of his foreign policy to improve relations with East Germany and other Warsaw Pact countries. But this opening to the East was greeted with suspicion in Paris. It seemed to many in the French political establishment that the Germans might be reverting back to their traditional foreign policy of swinging between Eastern and Western Europe, paying attention to each region as its interests dictated. *Ostpolitik* could have been viewed as the start of a decoupling of West Germany from its Western institutional ties.

Brandt, aware of French concerns about the CAP and his *Ostpolitik*, took the initiative to support the idea of EMU to further commit the federal republic to the EC (Dyson 1994, 77–78). If West Germany were part of an EC monetary union, it would give up a substantial portion of its sovereignty to Western institutions. What better way to prove the German commitment to the integration process and to Franco-German reconciliation in particular? This desire to secure the special Franco-German relationship was supported by sectoral interests in the German economy, which knew that Germany needed a good relationship with France or that trade with that country would be disrupted (Kaltenthaler 1998). Industry needed exchange rate stability as well. Thus, Brandt fought hard to see the vision of a European monetary union brought to reality.

At this point, the Bundesbank and the Finance Ministry began to shape the German position on the EMU issue. While these actors did not have the political authority or power to scuttle Brandt's EMU plan, they did have the power to help shape the German negotiating position on the institutional design of EMU. These two state actors had this power because they were backed by German banks and industry organizations, which feared a monetary union that would import inflation into Germany (Kaltenthaler 1998). The Bundesbank and the Finance Ministry both wanted to avoid an EMU that would be inflationary for Germany (Goodman 1992). This meant that they supported the idea that EMU should only start once the other potential member states had proven that they were committed to monetary stability and that their domestic economic situations converged on the German pattern. This position was known as the "economist" position during the negotiations over EMU. The French, who represented the "monetarist" position, wanted the institutions of EMU to be in place as soon as possible, and they figured that economic and monetary convergence would naturally follow (Dyson 1994, 79–80). Even though this German position irritated the French and at times threatened the negotiating process, it won the day as it was the only way to achieve the support of the Bundesbank, the Finance Ministry, and the major organizations of German industry and banking (Kaltenthaler 1998, 44). The plan was finally worked out in the form of the Werner Report, named for its chair, Pierre Werner, prime minister of Luxembourg. Although vague in its details, the report was much more economist than monetarist in nature, principally because of the need to please the German negotiating team (Henning 1994).

The Werner Report was created by a small group of individuals committed to developing a workable blueprint for monetary union. It called for monetary union to be achieved in three stages, which consisted of steps toward fixed exchange rates between member countries. The report called for the creation of a system of central banks to oversee the currency, as well as an institution to coordinate the fiscal policies of the member countries. The planned central bank was to be modeled on the American Federal Reserve (Moravcsik 1998, 262). The report did not say much of anything about the mandate of the planned central bank or its relationship to either national or EC institutions. All of the details were to be worked out in later stages.

Events quickly overtook the plan to move to EMU by 1980. In 1971, the United States went off the gold standard, effectively ending the Bretton Woods monetary regime. EC member states were left trying to move to monetary union without a system to maintain exchange rate stability. Because it would be exceedingly difficult to move to monetary union in the context of exchange rate volatility, not to mention the threat posed to the CAP, European leaders scrambled to create an EC exchange rate regime. What they established was known as the "snake in the tunnel." This was a joint float against the dollar with narrow margins of fluctuation in intra-EC exchange rates.

The snake was a stop-gap measure intended to ease the path toward monetary union. It quickly proved difficult to maintain. Weak-currency countries found it too politically costly to maintain the policies necessary to keep their currencies in their bands with the deutsche mark, which acted as the de facto anchor of the system. For many countries, the economic effects of the 1973–1974 oil crisis made it very difficult to maintain a policy that was both beneficial to the domestic economic situation and, at the same time, supportive of the exchange rate. By 1974, the snake was, in reality, a deutsche mark zone, with only the Germans, the Benelux countries, the Dutch, and the Danes left in the system. With France on the outside, the snake did not have the capacity to act as a major step toward monetary union. Thus, in the mid-1970s, the idea of creating a monetary union by 1980 was shelved. It was viewed as impractical considering the lack of political will needed to make it work.

The first try at monetary union had been accelerated by the imminent collapse of the Bretton Woods exchange rate regime, which threatened the foundations of the common market project. But the plan to achieve monetary union and create a European central bank was also, more importantly, a means to try to anchor Germany further into Western European institutions. It failed because of external economic shocks and the unwillingness of governments to bear the political costs of making it work. This would lead the Europeans to try less ambitious measures to ensure monetary stability in Europe.

THE EUROPEAN MONETARY SYSTEM

One of the most important parts of the EMU plan was the creation of a fixed exchange rate regime for the EC's member states in order to facilitate the process of economic and monetary convergence necessary to achieve EMU. This fixed exchange rate regime, the "snake," was a kind of mini–Bretton Woods for the EC, with the German deutsche mark playing the anchor-currency role as it was the most stable and highly valued currency in the EC. This meant that the German Bundesbank set the monetary policy parameters for all of the snake's member states as they had to follow the lead of the Bundesbank in order to keep their currencies within the agreed-upon exchange rate bands. This proved very difficult to do during the oil crisis period of the mid-1970s as the Bundesbank maintained a very restrictive monetary policy to fight inflation. Many governments found the Bundesbank's monetary policy too tight and chose to drop out of the regime rather than face a political backlash from their publics. One of the most important countries to drop out of the snake was France, Germany's principal partner in the integration process.

The failure of the snake as a viable exchange rate regime for all of the EC presented something of a crisis for the Schmidt government. The collapse of the snake caused some of the same problems for the Schmidt government as the breakdown of the Bretton Woods regime had for the Brandt government. A lack of stable exchange rates threatened the CAP, which in turn threatened Franco-German relations. Also, in the late 1970s, the administration of U.S. president Jimmy Carter seemed to place domestic economic

concerns above the external value of the dollar, causing monetary distur-
bances that were deeply felt in Western Europe (Story 1988). These monetary problems seemed to cause disruption in intra-EC trade as firms faced
the transaction costs associated with currency fluctuations.

Aware of the damage that monetary instability was doing to the EC and
the progress of integration, EC president Roy Jenkins proposed the creation
of a European Monetary System (EMS) in 1977 (Ludlow 1982, 55). As in
the case of EMU, it was the German government that became the principal
political sponsor of the EC proposal. Schmidt was convinced that if the EC
did not create a stable set of exchange rates, the Franco-German relationship
would face even more serious strains. In fact, he viewed his support for
the creation of the EMS as a German responsibility to remedy Germany's
past. The EMS would cement Franco-German ties, which would help heal
the wounds of the past (Carr 1985; Schmidt 1989). Schmidt himself said, "I
see it as an instrument to let the countries of the EEC grow together more
quickly than hitherto" (Hanrieder 1982, 209). Clearly, Schmidt was thinking
in geopolitical terms when he took on the political sponsorship of the EMS.

Schmidt knew that the only way to make the EMS work would be to make
it more symmetric than the snake had been. This meant that rather than have
the deutsche mark as the anchor currency of the regime, a "European unit
of account" would serve as the reference value for the currencies in the
exchange rate regime.[1] This plan received the support of French president
Giscard d'Estaing, and the two leaders set about formulating a plan in secret
(Ludlow 1982). This is very significant for it shows that the two leaders
expected significant domestic opposition in Germany to the idea of the
EMS. In Germany, it was relatively clear that the Bundesbank, the Finance
Ministry, and the organizations of banking and industry would be suspicious
of an exchange rate system that tied the hands of the Bundesbank to control
price stability in Germany.[2]

Schmidt was forced by the pressure that he faced from the Bundesbank-
led coalition to allow the Bundesbank to set the German government's negotiating strategy. The Bundesbank argued for an EMS in which the strongest
currency in the system would play the anchor role. That meant that other
countries would have to set their policies to follow the anchor-currency
country's monetary policies. Thus, the EMS that the Bundesbank favored was
not much different from the old snake system (Dyson 1994, 104–109). But
because the Bundesbank's position was backed by the Schmidt government
as a way to get support for the EMS from the crucial societal organizations
in Germany, the French government acquiesced, and when the EMS was
launched in 1979, it looked very different from Schmidt's original intentions
in 1977. The EMS was not created as a step toward monetary union and the
establishment of a European central bank. It was a stopgap measure to save
European integration from the buffeting of exchange rate turbulence.

This case of German policy toward European monetary integration produces much the same story about the German government's geopolitical interests in monetary integration policy and how they were constrained by domestic economic interests in negotiations over EC monetary institutions. Schmidt, like his predecessor, was driven to support a major initiative in European monetary integration in order to try to secure the Franco-German special relationship. But his plans came to be shaped in a profound way by domestic German economic interests. Those interests did not block his plan entirely; they simply molded it to achieve their own goals.

GERMAN UNIFICATION AND EMU

As stated previously, the EMS that was created in 1979 was not fundamentally different from the "snake" that had existed in the 1970s. This meant that the EMS functioned "asymmetrically." In other words, because of the anchor role played by the deutsche mark, the German Bundesbank made its monetary policy based on monetary and economic conditions in Germany, whereas the other member states of the EMS based their monetary policies on keeping their currencies within their exchange rate bands with the deutsche mark. The burden of policy adjustment in the system was asymmetric: Germany led, and the others had to adjust in order to follow.

This system had led to tensions in Franco-German relations from the onset of the EMS because the French franc came under devaluation pressure from the start. This pressure caused the French and German governments to engage in resetting the bilateral exchange rate for their two currencies several times in the early 1980s, causing the French government embarrassment as it had to explain to its public why the French currency always seemed to depreciate while the German currency always seemed to appreciate.

By the mid-1980s, the French government was committed to a "strong franc" policy, which meant it would do what it takes to keep the franc from depreciating (Goodman 1992). The French government also ruled out any new devaluations of the French franc vis-à-vis the deutsche mark. This put a tremendous amount of pressure on the French government to adjust domestic monetary and fiscal policy to protect the external value of the franc. It also had a political cost for the French government as it had a deflationary effect on the French economy. France seemed to be foregoing some economic growth in order to keep the franc strong by following a tightening monetary policy.

By the later half of the 1980s, French patience with the EMS was wearing thin. There was a growing feeling in French policymaking circles that the EMS rules were unfair in that weaker-currency countries bore all of the burden of policy adjustment, and the anchor-currency country bore none. This led to a feeling that a fundamental change in European monetary affairs was due. Attempts at reforming the EMS in 1987–1988 had led to very insignificant changes in the way the system operated, and attention in Paris turned to scrapping the system and moving to the next step in monetary integration: monetary union.[3] Thus, in January 1988, the French government proposed talks on creating EMU. French finance minister Edouard Balladur issued a memorandum calling for the creation of a "zone of one currency" in order to complete the internal market project.[4] This was significant in that support for EMU, which had been strong in the commission since the creation of the Single European Act in 1985 and among Eurofederalists outside of government, such as Schmidt and Giscard d'Estaing, was now being pushed by a major European government. While the memo did not say anything specific about the shape of a central bank to oversee the proposed common currency, this memo did get the issue of the eventual creation of a European central bank onto the agenda of the Ecofin Council.

The Balladur memo was followed in February by a memorandum from Italian finance minister Giuliano Amato calling for a move toward monetary union among the EC's member states. So, Balladur and Amato were throwing the weight of two of Europe's most important states behind the idea of moving toward a monetary union. This was a development that could not be ignored.

The reaction of the German government to the French proposal and the Amato memo was, at first, guarded and cautious. The German government declared that this was a proposal that they needed time to consider (Kaltenthaler 1998, 71). This cautious response on the part of the German government did not reflect the true preferences of the chancellor, Helmut Kohl, and his Foreign Ministry. The German government was waiting to decide what to do. Both Kohl and Hans-Dietrich Genscher, the German foreign minister, wanted to move toward monetary union (Dyson 1994; Henning 1994; Moravcsik 1998). They believed that monetary union was the only way to overcome the tensions in Franco-German relations caused by the EMS (Kennedy 1991).[5] The problem was that the idea of monetary union was greeted with a great deal of skepticism on the part of the Bundesbank, the Finance Ministry, and the banking and industry communities (Henning 1994, 230–231; Kaltenthaler 1998, 71–72). They saw the French EMU initiative as a way to gain control of German monetary policy and move away from a strict price-stability orientation. Because of these concerns, they voiced their skepticism to the EMU proposal, and the Kohl government dragged its feet on moving toward establishing intergovernmental negotiations on designing the institutions of EMU.

But in February of 1988, Genscher surprised many in Europe by issuing a memorandum in favor of EMU. The memo called for the creation of a single currency and a central bank to manage it. In an effort to preempt the opposition that his memorandum would likely bring from the Bundesbank and its allies, Genscher argued that the proposed central bank should be modeled on the Bundesbank and mandated to preserve price stability, as the Bundesbank was doing in the German domestic context. But it also said the central bank would have a mandate to promote growth. Genscher said the proposed central bank should be designed by monetary experts, the central bankers themselves.

The Genscher memo was followed shortly thereafter by a proposal from the German finance minister, Gerhard Stoltenberg, arguing that monetary union was a worthy goal but only under the right conditions. His principal argument was that for monetary union to be achieved, it needed to come after substantial convergence of the economic conditions of the countries to make up the monetary union. This memo echoed the "economist" line of reasoning that had been such a bone of contention in the discussions surrounding the first attempt at EMU in the early 1970s (Dyson and Featherstone 1999, 332–334).

The Bundesbank reacted to the Genscher memo with guarded support. The central bank argued that it did not oppose the idea of monetary union but that it was a far-off goal and that a great deal of ground work needed to be laid before it could be achieved. Many interpreted this as the German central bank's saying that it did not really support the idea under the present circumstances; therefore, they assumed that the Genscher proposal would go the same way as so many previous calls for monetary union had.

But the German government continued to push forward with the impetus toward monetary union. The German government, at least the Chancellery and the Foreign Ministry, was quite dedicated to moving away from the EMS, with all of its sources of tension with Germany's European partners, to monetary union. At the June 1988 Hannover summit of EC heads of government and state, a consensus was reached to move forward with planning for EMU. The summit leaders agreed to establish a committee, chaired by commission president Jacques Delors, to work up a plan for EMU. The plan was meant to be a concrete blueprint to establish a monetary union. One of the most significant aspects of the establishment of the group to plan for EMU was that, unlike the Werner Committee, this group would comprise almost all central bankers and was to be specific about the design of EMU. The central bankers were to act in their personal capacities and not as representatives of their central banks. At the insistence of British prime minister Margaret Thatcher and Danish prime minister Poul Schluter, the mandate for the committee was not to include the design of a European central bank. This was intended to slow the move to monetary union, which both prime ministers did not fully support (Dyson 1994). It would be up to the Committee of Central Bank Governors, in the future, to draft a statute for the central bank.

The establishment of the Committee for the Study of Economic and Monetary Union, or the Delors Committee, as it came to be known, was important for a pair of reasons. First, the politicians were, in a way, co-opting the central bankers to design the future monetary union. Central bankers, but most importantly the Bundesbank, could not very well snipe at the idea of monetary union and a European central bank if it was their design. Second, the project would have much more credibility with financial markets, which had only grown in importance since the first try at EMU, as the plan was designed by Europe's central bankers.

The Delors Committee consisted of the governors of the central banks of the EC member states, Delors, a commissioner, and three monetary experts. But this was not a committee of equals. The most important person on the committee, by far, was Bundesbank president Karl-Otto Pöhl. Pöhl brought two very important assets to the committee.[6] First, he was the very respected president of the most esteemed central bank in the world. He had tremendous credibility to bring to the deliberations. Second, he held a de facto veto over the monetary union project. The Bundesbank, as an independent central bank and a highly cherished institution in Germany, would be a very difficult obstacle for the German government to circumvent if the central bank came out and publicly opposed the plan for monetary union. For these two reasons, Pöhl was the center of the Delors Committee.

Pöhl took the initiative in the committee by issuing his own design proposal for EMU and the European Central Bank when the committee started in September 1988. The proposal was what one would expect from the president of the Bundesbank: it called for an independent central bank modeled on the Bundesbank with a strong price-stability mandate, but, like the Bundesbank, it was expected to support the general economic policies of the EC member state governments (Dyson 1994, 132). The central bank would be federal, with national central banks coming together, along with a central executive, to make monetary policy for the common currency area. This proposal became the foundation of the work of the committee as there was no real disagreement with this model.

The Pöhl proposal also called for setting up binding rules on how national budget deficits could be financed and what levels of deficit would be allowable. But budget policy was to remain a national policy power (Tsoukalis 1997, 165).

The committee also agreed, although there was more dissension about this, that the path to monetary union should come in three stages. It was a much more "economist" than "monetarist" approach to moving toward monetary union. The first stage would be the liberalization of capital in the EC, which meant the dismantling of capital controls. The second stage was to be the establishment of a European system of central banks to supervise the progression toward full monetary union. The third, and final, stage was to be the introduction of the common currency and the start of monetary policy management by the proposed central bank. Countries would join the monetary union once they had proven that they had achieved a high degree of economic and policy convergence with each other at a prescribed high standard. Once the convergence criteria were met, countries could join the monetary union. This convergence was deemed essential if monetary union was to prove a success.

When the Delors Committee issued its report in April 1989, it was endorsed by the EC's heads of government. This was made official at the Madrid summit of June 1989. There, the EC's heads of government committed themselves to move toward EMU along the lines of the Delors Report and agreed to start the first stage of EMU in July 1990. Most Europeans at the time assumed that the actual negotiations that would hash out the details of the rest of monetary union were years away. They could look back to the first attempt at EMU and see how long and arduous that negotiation process had been.

While the Delors Committee was shaping its plan for EMU, the geopolitical ground around it shifted. The iron curtain began to tear in very important places. Most importantly for the path of EMU, the Communist regime in East Germany began to crumble with the loss of Soviet guarantees and with domestic opposition. In the winter of 1989–1990, the East German regime was clearly tottering, and the prospect of German unification was not nearly as remote as it had been since the end of World War II. How would a unified Germany potentially change the political and economic context in the EC and the efforts afoot to move toward monetary union?

When the East German Communist regime began to falter and the Berlin Wall fell in the fall of 1989, the prospect of German unification loomed as a major political issue for Europe's governments. The potential of German unification was a frightening development for the British and French leaders. There was genuine concern in Paris and London as to how it would affect power relations in Europe (Baun 1996). A reunified Germany would be a much larger and potentially much more powerful country in the middle of Europe than the old federal republic had been. The German population would grow to eighty million people, and the united German economy would be a quarter of the EC's aggregate economic size. The potential for German dominance of Europe seemed real, which neither the French nor the British government could countenance. This could threaten French and British security or economic interests or both.

The French and British governments began to act on those fears by trying to develop support in Europe for slowing the momentum toward German unification. But another very important part of the French strategy for dealing with the issue of German unification was to pressure the German government to agree to a rapid move toward monetary union.[7] Monetary union would tie the Germans down to European institutions in a profound way because Germany would lose economic sovereignty by being part of the single-currency project.

From the perspective of the Kohl government in Germany, a Franco-British coalition to stall unification or try to contain German power was a very real worry. The not-so-subtle signals from London and Paris about their opposition to German unification led the Kohl government to redouble its efforts to convince its European partners that a unified Germany posed no threat to them. The best way to demonstrate this was by anchoring Germany deeply into the institutions of the EC. Monetary union would be a fine way to prove that Germany was inexorably tied to the EC and was willing to lose a great deal of its economic sovereignty in order to prove its good-neighborliness to other European countries. Monetary union moved from a worthy goal of the German government to a strategic imperative. The quicker monetary union was achieved, from the Kohl government's perspective, the easier it would be to realize its primary goal, German unification.

German unification was a bargaining chip played most astutely by the French government. Because the French were an occupying power, they had the ability to block or delay German unification, which they made clear to German government officials.[8] The French leadership made it known to the German government that if it wanted French agreement to German unification, the German government would have to commit itself to a rapid move toward monetary union. The British government, on the other hand, which was rather hostile to the idea of monetary union, did not play the linkage card.

Because unifying Germany would be such a political bonus for the Kohl government in the eyes of the German public, the incentive to agree to EMU in order to achieve rapid unification was very great. Being the party of the chancellor who had unified Germany after forty-five years would likely reap a large electoral bonus for the Christian Democrats, as well as their Free Democrat allies. Thus, rapid unification would bring a political payoff sooner rather than later.

Initially, Kohl had not had a completely free hand to do what he wanted on monetary union. When the idea of monetary union was first broached by the French government in 1988, then supported by the Genscher memo in the same year, as mentioned earlier, the response in Germany had been less than overwhelming enthusiasm. But the prospect of unification changed the domestic German political context as it related to monetary union in an important way. Prior to the shadow of unification's appearance on the German scene, the Kohl government had to worry that it would face serious opposition to its plan to move ahead with monetary union. While some large multinational German firms were enthusiastic about the idea of monetary union because of the gains they stood to make from the reduction in exchange rate–related costs of doing business, the much larger majority of

German firms and banks did not view themselves as potential beneficiaries of monetary union.[9]

But the potential economic gains of unification were such for most German firms that they wanted unification as quickly as possible. Unification would be a huge boost to West German business and banking. An East German market was waiting to be conquered. Commercial banking and industry organizations were willing to move toward EMU if it meant rapid unification, as the economic gains of unification would outweigh the potential problems associated with EMU.[10] Thus, they backed the Kohl government's move to proceed on EMU when it became obvious that the two processes were politically linked.

At the Strasbourg European Council Summit in December 1989, the German government agreed to convene an Intergovernmental Conference (IGC) by the end of 1990 to devise a plan for monetary union (Dyson 1994, 27). This was a German agreement to the French demand to make monetary union a concrete issue to be planned, rather than a mere topic of discussion. This was a very important step in the process of moving toward monetary union. Not only was the German government now deeply committed to monetary union, but it had the support of the very powerful German industry and banking sectors. This would isolate any potential opposition or foot-dragging from the Bundesbank, which would not risk alienating the major firms and banks that it needed for political support. Thus, unlike the first attempt at EMU in the early 1970s, this time the European proponents of EMU could count on the unequivocal support of key German actors. The German government had advanced from bringing up EMU as an issue in EC politics to committing itself irrevocably to the project's creation. The prospect of unification and its potential consequences for European international relations had been the key to this strong commitment at Strasbourg.[11]

THE NEGOTIATIONS

Once the IGC commenced in Rome in December 1990, the German government's usual pattern for negotiating monetary integration agreements became evident. The Kohl government faced a Bundesbank and a Finance Ministry committed to shaping EMU according to their preferences, namely, an EMU geared first and foremost toward price stability as its goal. The best way to accomplish this was to replicate the institutions of the Bundesbank and its price-stability mandate at the European level. This Bundesbank position was backed by the banking and industry organizations that also wanted to avoid EMU's becoming a way to reinflate Europe.[12] The Bundesbank knew it had the support of the German public, which feared that EMU would replace the strong deutsche mark with a new, weaker European currency.

The Bundesbank viewed the IGC with a great deal of mistrust. It feared that German negotiators from the Foreign and Finance ministries might make a deal in order to placate France that would threaten the Bundesbank's vision of monetary union based on price-stability fundamentals. The Bundesbank issued public statements during the IGC declaring what it thought was necessary to make monetary union a success. This was done to constrain what German negotiators would agree to in the face of French pressure.

That meant that in IGC negotiations the German negotiators, the finance minister and his permanent representatives, pushed for an EMU that conformed to a very large extent to the Bundesbank and its domestic allies' institutional preferences (Dyson 1994). But the Bundesbank and its allies were not getting everything that they wanted. German negotiators were giving ground to their Italian and French counterparts on the issue of the timetable of the stages.

At the final point of negotiation for monetary union, the Maastricht summit in December 1991, the result was a victory for both the "economist" and "monetarist" advocates of monetary union.[13] The monetarists got a timetable, calling for the establishment of monetary union by 1 January 1999 at the latest. The economists were able to get a set of rather demanding convergence criteria for debt, deficits, inflation rates, EMS participation, and interest rates in order for a country to become part of monetary union. But this was a mixed victory for the economists in that the agreement contained the possibility for wide latitude in how countries could be interpreted as moving toward the convergence criteria to a sufficient degree to warrant inclusion in monetary union. Room for a political decision on meeting the convergence criteria was not what the economists, like the Bundesbank, had in mind.

While the timetable and the watered-down nature of the convergence criteria were not warmly welcomed by Europe's central bankers, the Maastricht Treaty's provisions about the planned European Central Bank were very close to their preferences. The Maastricht provisions were nearly identical to those laid out in the Delors Committee Report, which so clearly evidenced the influence of the Bundesbank as it was, to a great extent, penned by the Bundesbank. The Bundesbank had been made the unequivocal model for the ECB.

THE CURRENCY CRISES

Not long after the dust had settled from the signing of the Maastricht Treaty in February 1992, the plan for EMU faced its first very serious challenge. In the autumn of 1992, the EMS faced an exchange rate crisis that severely tested the capability of European governments to cooperate deeply enough to make it to EMU.

Many factors led to the crisis, but the most immediate was the pressure on weak currencies within the EMS because of the French referendum on EMU membership. Speculation had been building for some time against weaker currencies in the EMS because several of them looked like they were at untenable exchange rates with the deutsche mark. Speculators figured that if there was a no vote in the French referendum on EMU,[14] there would be a run on the franc and other weaker EMS currencies, such as the Italian lira, the Spanish peseta, and the Portuguese escudo.

There was intense pressure on the Bundesbank at this point to lower its interest rates in order to lessen the pressure on the weaker currencies, which were struggling to keep within their bilateral bands with the German currency. From the Bundesbank's perspective, the timing for lowering German interest rates could not have been worse. Inflation in the wake of German unification was a problem that the central bank was determined to overcome. The Bundesbank made some gestures toward reducing the pressure on the weaker currencies in the EMS, but it would not cut its interest rates for fear of allowing inflation to get out of control in Germany.

As speculators began to bet against the weaker currencies, given the Bundesbank's intransigence on interest rates, it was looking increasingly like the weak-currency countries would be unable to maintain their bilateral rates. One of the major factors in this situation was the free flow of capital in most of Europe as a result of the first stage of EMU in 1990. After 1990, there was nothing to stop currency traders from moving their capital out of Britain, France, and Italy, the main targets of speculation.

In September 1992, the Italian and British governments made the choice to pull their currencies out of the exchange rate mechanism (ERM) as they were no longer willing to support the currencies at the rate necessary for them to stay within their exchange rate bands. The Italian and British pullout did not stop the crisis as it flared up again in the summer of 1993, with the French franc once again becoming a target of speculation. Knowing full well that a French pullout from the EMS would mean the end of the progression toward EMU, European leaders decided in August 1993 to widen the bands of fluctuation in the EMS from 2.5 percent around the central rate to 15 percent around the central rate. While this meant that the EMS ceased to function as a fixed exchange rate in the real sense of the concept, it did save the EMU project from the ravages of exchange rate crises.

THE EUROPEAN MONETARY INSTITUTE

Another important step on the road toward EMU was the foundation of the European Monetary Institute (EMI) in January 1994 as part of stage two of the EMU plan. The EMI was to be the precursor of the ECB, with minimal powers of policymaking but an important role to play in planning the nuts and bolts of the ECB's operations and coordinating the work of various central banks and governments in preparing for EMU.

The creation and location of the EMI was, in itself, a matter of controversy. What powers the EMI would have prior to the introduction of the common currency had been a matter of intense debate in the IGC negotiations leading up to the Maastricht Treaty. The French wanted a powerful EMI, whereas the Germans wanted an EMI unable to dictate to the national central banks. The German position won out, and the EMI gave a great deal of say to the national central bank governors.

Another matter of controversy centered on the location of the institute. The French government wanted it located in Lyon, and the Germans wanted it located in Frankfurt. This was an issue of national prestige for the French government, but it was more than that for the Germans. Kohl wanted to placate domestic German fears about giving up the deutsche mark and seeing the Bundesbank superseded by the ECB. There was also a concern that locating the institute in France, with its long history of political interference in monetary affairs, would spook markets (Howarth and Loedel 2003). The Germans were able to win the argument, and the EMI went to Frankfurt.

The EMI Executive Board consisted of a president and the governors of the national central banks that were members of the European Union (EU). In 1994, this meant that the board had thirteen members. The board was very heavily weighted toward the national central banks, with the president of the EMI playing a relatively minor role.

The first president of the EMI was Alexandre Lamfalussy, a Belgian who had been president of the Bank of International Settlements (BIS). He was a popular and uncontroversial choice to lead the institute as he was highly respected by his fellow central bankers, who knew him well because of their frequent interactions with him at the BIS. He built a staff of around two hundred in Frankfurt to oversee the immense amount of logistical and technical detail that would go into launching EMU. This detail included such issues as designing banknotes and coins, setting up a payments system, and sharing central bank data, to name just a few of the things needed to make EMU succeed.

One of the very important tasks of the EMI was to oversee the convergence reports that detailed how well countries were doing in meeting the convergence requirements in order to enter EMU. This was very important but also very difficult for the EMI. The EMI had to be able to discern which countries were actually meeting the criteria, which were close, and which had created the impression that they were meeting them but were in fact providing misleading data.

The deficit requirement was the convergence criterion with which this was mostly likely to occur. Governments began to employ some very creative means to meet the cutoff of 3 percent of gross domestic product. They sold off some of their assets to raise cash, redefined accounts so that they would no longer count as liabilities, and created temporary taxes to plug holes in budgets. The EMI was joined by the European Commission and Eurostat (the statistical office of the EU) in keeping watch over these practices and raising alarms when they thought a country had gone too far.

The seeming lack of political will to make the really hard political choices necessary to keep debt and deficits low was troubling for many in Germany who feared EMU would lead to imported inflation. Thus, in 1997, with the backing of the EMI, the German government advocated a binding agreement whereby each state would be beholden to keep its deficit limits within the Maastricht Treaty limits after it had joined EMU. This would, supposedly, prevent governments from spending in such a way as to drive inflation in the Eurozone, which would impact all countries, even those with disciplined spending habits.

The result of this push was the Stability and Growth Pact, signed in 1997.[15] This committed the governments to keeping their fiscal deficits within the 3 percent ceiling or face fines if the deficits persisted. There were stipulations for deficits in very bad economic times and, very importantly, a potential way out for governments in that fines needed to be agreed upon by all of the other governments. This lack of automaticity was the result of a compromise to make the pact happen, but it set the course for conflict in the EU, much of which has centered around the ECB, which has been the most consistent in its support for real binding rules on deficits to protect against inflationary spending.

At the time the Stability and Growth Pact was being negotiated in 1996, the EMI took on a new president. Wim Duisenberg, who had been governor of the Dutch central bank, was the consensus choice among the national central bank governors. He had a solid reputation as a central banker and was known as a hard-money advocate, in line with German thinking about monetary policy. This was a very important choice because the national governments seemed to be saying that they were willing to see this person lead the ECB when it began operations in a couple of years.

The May 1998 European Council meeting was to decide the membership of the Executive Board and the countries participating in EMU's launch. Which countries would participate in EMU's launch was decided before the summit, and the announcement was mostly a formality. The eleven EU countries to join EMU on 1 January 1999 were chosen based on which had met the convergence criteria set out in the Maastricht Treaty. Greece was the only EU member country that wanted to be part of EMU but was not able to join because of failure to meet the criteria.

The issue of picking the members of the Executive Board was much more controversial. While Duisenberg was the candidate favored by the central bankers themselves, the French government balked at the idea of keeping the Dutchman at the helm when the ECB began operations. The French government wanted something in return for having agreed to place the EMI and ECB in Frankfurt instead of Lyon. Also, it was a matter of some prestige for the French to have their man as president of the ECB. Thus, the French government had proposed in December 1997 that Jean-Claude Trichet, the governor of the Bank of France, be the ECB's first president.

Most had expected that the French government was just posing with this suggestion for domestic political consumption and would back off from advocating Trichet in the face of opposition from other EU governments that were uneasy about this seeming politicization of the selection process. But, in fact, the French government fought doggedly at the May 1998 summit for Trichet's appointment.[16] It became one of the most contentious EU summits in history, with the Germans and French at serious odds over the issue. In the end, they compromised. Duisenberg was chosen as the president, but he "volunteered" to resign after four years to make way for Trichet as president.

Another very important appointment, which did not garner nearly as much media attention but was, in the long run, possibly more important than who was appointed president, was the naming of Otmar Issing as chief economist of the central bank. Issing, a well-respected German academic economist specializing in monetary economics, had joined the Bundesbank as chief economist in 1990. There, he had established a reputation as a monetary policy hawk and strong advocate of monetarist policy thinking. Issing was chosen as chief economist of the ECB because he represented continuity with the Bundesbank, which was important to calm markets. He was also very well respected in central banking circles. This appointment was so important because his monetary policy thinking is starkly visible in the policy of the ECB.

Shortly after the summit that chose the leadership of the ECB, on 1 June 1998, the EMI was shut down, and the ECB was brought into operation. At this point, the ECB set itself to the tasks of setting up a payment system (to become known as TARGET), getting the logistics in place for the launch of the euro, and formulating a monetary policy strategy as well as the decision-making procedures in the central bank. It was a lot to do in a short time and demanded tremendous effort from the ECB's relatively small staff.

On 31 December 1998, one day before the launch of the euro, the EU's finance ministers met to set the irrevocable conversion rates for national currencies to become part of the Eurozone. On 1 January 1999, the euro replaced the eleven national currencies of those countries chosen to participate in EMU. The ECB began at this point to manage the monetary policy of the euro.

CONCLUSION

To summarize, in the late 1980s four factors played a role in getting the EMU process off the ground and working toward its realization. Two absolutely key factors made EMU and the subsequent creation of the ECB possible. First, there was the widespread European dissatisfaction with the dominance of the Bundesbank in European monetary affairs. It was no longer politically tenable to allow the German central bank to dictate monetary and fiscal policies to Germany's European partners. The move toward a single currency and a central bank to manage it was a solution to that political problem.

Second, the German government perceived that it needed to anchor itself more deeply in the EC and its institutions in order to assuage any fears that it was reemerging as a threat to Europe. The prospect of German unification only heightened this sense of urgency and made it politically possible within Germany for the government to make EMU happen. Without German unification, German agreement to a rapid move to EMU would have been unlikely. It may have been possible over the long run, but it would have been much more rancorous and difficult than it was.

The activities of committed Eurofederalists like Delors, Schmidt, and Giscard d'Estaing formed a third, but less important, factor that helped move the process of monetary union forward. These men all advocated deeper European integration and pushed for monetary union, although they did not represent any national government. Because of their passion and prestige in governmental circles in Europe, with the exception of Britain, they were able to exert some influence on how leaders thought about the process.

Fourth, and finally, there was the growth in intra-EC trade and the consequences of deepening economic integration. While the European Commission held this up as a central rationale for moving toward monetary union, it was not nearly as important as the political factors cited above. But this is not to say that economic integration did not have an impact on the need for monetary union. Transaction cost reductions in trade could certainly be expected once monetary union took place, but never to such a degree as to convince governments to take on the enormous burden of creating a monetary union. Politics trumped economics in Europe's march toward a common currency and its central bank.

In terms of the shaping of the institutions of the ECB, three factors played a central role. First, the success and prestige of the Bundesbank in the eyes of the world's central bankers, and of those in Europe in particular, made it an attractive model for the future European central bank. The perceived success of the Bundesbank meant that its policymakers' views on the issue of the design of the future European central bank would be taken very seriously. As we saw, the Bundesbank leadership, chiefly Karl-Otto Pöhl, was very determined to have its view on the shape of the institutions of this European central bank realized. Thus, prestige, combined with aggressive attempts at persuasion, made the Bundesbank voice on central bank institutional design the loudest and most influential among the central banks in the EC.

Europe's central bankers and politicians also opted for the Bundesbank model for the institutions of the common currency's central bank because a central bank modeled on the German central bank would have more credibility with the financial markets than one based on any other possible institutional model. The EC was embarking on a huge gamble by creating a common currency and a brand new central bank, which would naturally make markets nervous about how this would affect price and financial stability in Europe. Thus, in order to calm fears in the financial markets, it would be wise to convince market participants that Europe would be seeing more of the same monetary policy that it had seen during the days of the EMS. In other words, the new European central bank would look, and hopefully act, just like the Bundesbank, which had immense credibility and respect in market circles. Copying the design of the Bundesbank would give the central bank a degree of instant credibility that European policymakers hoped would avoid painful and costly attacks on the new currency.

Finally, there was the German power to act as a veto player in the negotiations over the shape of the European central bank. The veto was held by both the German government and the Bundesbank. European policymakers knew that either of these entities could stop the move toward monetary union if they wished. While it was unlikely that the German government would want to halt the process of creating a common currency and central bank, especially after the prospect of German unification appeared, there was fear until the Maastricht Treaty was signed that the Bundesbank might use its independence and the strong political support of the German mass public and industry and banking organizations to try to block the EMU process. While this was more important among Europe's politicians than its central bankers, who did not need Bundesbank coercion to agree to the model, it was a significant factor in the agreement to base the ECB on the institutions of the Bundesbank.

NOTES

1. "Interview with Helmut Schmidt," *Business Week*, 26 June 1978.
2. Interviews with Bundesbank, Finance Ministry, Federation of German Banks (BDB), and Federation of German Industry (BDI) officials.
3. The reforms of the EMS were a result of the Basle-Nyborg Agreement of 1987, whereby the member states of the EMS agreed to distribute the burden of intramarginal interventions of the EMS more evenly among appreciating- and

depreciating-currency countries. The operational consequences of the agreement were very limited as the Bundesbank chose to interpret the agreement to mean that there was no *obligation* on its part to intervene intramarginally to save depreciating currencies.

4. President François Mitterrand of France had called in December 1987 for the creation of a monetary union to follow the completion of the internal market, but this was a limited gesture and did not capture much attention from the press or policy leaders.

5. Interview with German Foreign Ministry official.

6. Pöhl had initially balked at the idea of being part of the committee. He did not particularly trust the motives of Jacques Delors; nor did he like the idea that Tomasso Padoa-Schioppa was to be part of the committee. Padoa-Schioppa, an Italian adviser to Delors, was viewed as an advocate of politicizing European monetary affairs (see Dyson and Featherstone 1999, 342).

7. *Süddeutsche Zeitung*, 11 December 1989.

8. Interview with German Foreign Ministry official.

9. Interview with German Chamber of Commerce (DIHT) officials.

10. Interviews with Federation of German Industry (BDI) and Federation of German Banks (BDB) officials.

11. There has been considerable controversy over the importance of German unification to the process of creating EMU. Moravcsik (1998) has argued that the prospect of unification was inconsequential to the process of moving toward EMU because the German government had already committed itself to the process by the time unification became an issue. Most other scholars of EMU, myself included, view the prospect of unification as key to German government support because it weakened any chance the opponents of EMU in Germany had to block the government's commitment to the process. It is important to note that this is also the consensus view among officials in the Bundesbank, the Finance Ministry, and the Foreign Office in Germany.

12. Interviews with Federation of German Industry (BDI) and Federation of German Banks (BDB) officials.

13. The treaty was actually signed on 7 February 1992 after a process of minor editing of the text.

14. The Danes had voted in June to stay out of EMU, and polls showed it was very close in France. If the French did not agree to EMU, it would likely mean the end of the project as it would have made little sense with them on the outside. This would create a grave political crisis within the EC.

15. It was called the Stability and Growth Pact as a way to make it more palatable to the public in countries such as France, Italy, and Sweden, where there was a great deal of sensitivity about the trade-off between stability and growth.

16. This was despite the fact that Trichet himself favored Duisenberg for the position.

2

The Formation of the European Central Bank's Monetary Policy Strategy

The European Central Bank (ECB) has been making monetary policy for the euro area of Europe since January 1999. To most observers, the ECB has developed a reputation as a very anti-inflation central bank, and there is substantial evidence to support this view. The ECB has set a definition of price stability as 2 percent or lower inflation. This is important as the central bank is mandated by the Treaty on European Union (Maastricht Treaty) to prioritize price stability as its top policy responsibility. Also, if one looks at the policy record of the ECB since the introduction of the euro in January 1999, it is apparent that the maintenance of price stability has been the central bank's primary concern. While the Eurozone has grown at a rather anemic pace, the ECB has kept interest rates relatively high in order to fight future inflation. The ECB has certainly acted as a central bank that takes its inflation mandate very seriously.

The structure of the ECB clearly reflects the Bundesbank. In fact, in most ways, the ECB is a nearly complete copy of the Bundesbank's organization. Also, the mandate of the ECB set down in the Maastricht Treaty nearly duplicates the mandate of the Bundesbank as laid out in the Bundesbank Law of 1957. Despite all of the obvious institutional similarities between the Bundesbank and the ECB, the two central banks could behave very differently if the ECB's decision-makers operated on different monetary policy principles than the Bundesbank. The Bundesbank was modeled, to a great extent, on the American Federal Reserve System of the United States,

35

yet it operated on quite different policy principles for much of the postwar period.

There are clear signs that the ECB has adopted the monetary policy principles of the Bundesbank. First, the ECB has adopted the Bundesbank's definition of price stability, which is a 2 percent annual rise in consumer prices. Thus, the ECB, like the Bundesbank before it, seeks to keep inflation below the 2 percent ceiling.

Also, the ECB has adopted the majority of the Bundesbank's monetary targeting strategy. It shares the focus of the Bundesbank (before it joined the European System of Central Banks) on money supply growth as a predictor of inflationary tendencies in the economy. Specifically, the ECB states the amount of growth in the broad money stock (M3) that can occur in a year without threatening price stability. Thus, the ECB sets a target range for M3 growth in the coming year that acts as a general guide, or "reference value," for monetary policy as information about M3 growth comes into the central bank.

Instead of calling the target a money supply growth target, the ECB calls it a reference value.[1] The difference in wording reflects pragmatic considerations rather than the principle of the policy. While accounting for the actual size of the growth of the money supply was difficult in the German sphere, it is even more difficult in the Eurozone, with its much larger size. Thus, the ECB does not want to tie itself to the word target, when measuring that target is such an imprecise affair.[2]

The ECB's monetary policy has resembled the Bundesbank's not just in strategy but also in actual practice. The central bank has been able to keep inflation close to its definition of price stability despite bouts of rising oil prices and the euro's depreciation. For most of the period since its operational start, the central bank has seen inflation around 2 percent.

So, why has the ECB copied most of the monetary policy strategy of the German Bundesbank? Why has it added some innovations to this strategy? These are questions of profound importance not just for the citizens of the member states of the euro area, but for anyone with an interest in the international economy. As the ECB steers the second largest economy (the aggregate Eurozone) in the world, its policy decisions have economic consequences for states around the world.

This chapter seeks to identify and explain the sources of the ECB's monetary policy strategy. I argue that the monetary policy strategy of the ECB is the product of a series of decisions made by European central bankers starting in the 1980s and continuing into the 1990s essentially to copy the German Bundesbank's monetary policy strategy, but also modify it to fit the specific conditions of the Eurozone. This decision to emulate the German model of monetary policy was not coerced by German authorities but rather resulted from the persuasive power of the Bundesbank, the domestic success of the

German model, and the hope of replicating that success on the European level.

This chapter begins by briefly outlining the logic of the argument developed here. The next sections trace the development of the ECB's monetary policy. Finally, the chapter concludes with an assessment of the relative explanatory power of the argument and what this implies for our understanding of central bank policymaking in general.

THE ARGUMENT

How can we explain why the ECB has decided to emulate most of the monetary policy strategy of the German Bundesbank? The dependent variable is the central bankers' monetary policy strategy. A monetary policy strategy is the general approach a central bank takes to achieve its monetary policy goals. The specific monetary policy instruments a central bank uses are not the primary facets of a monetary policy strategy. The strategy will consist of a set of broad guidelines about what to focus on in the economy in order to achieve the central bank's primary policy goal. For example, some central banks, such as the Bank of England, have decided to target inflation, establishing an explicit inflation target, in order to achieve price stability. Other central banks, such as the American Federal Reserve, have a very discretionary monetary policy strategy, in which decision-makers do not have a very explicit or constrained monetary policy strategy.

In the case of the ECB, as stated previously, the central bank has decided to adopt the strategy of closely following the growth of the money supply over the medium and long terms to control inflation in the economy. This is coupled with the policy of assessing how economic activity seems to relate to the prospects for the price-stability situation (see ECB 2001). This policy mix is taken straight out of the German Bundesbank's playbook as the strategy was, until the launch of the ECB, a uniquely German way to manage monetary policy.

So, what accounts for the ECB's decision to adopt the German monetary policy strategy? One possible explanation is that Germany's political power in European Union (EU) affairs led to the adoption of the German model. The argument would be that because Germany is the largest economy in Europe and by far the most important contributor to the budget of the EU, it would have a disproportionate say in the design of EU institutions. The logic of this argument may, on its face, seem enticing since it is saying that if the German monetary policy model was the one adopted by the ECB, it must have been because the German government wanted it that way.

There are several problems with this argument when one looks at the picture a bit more closely. First, it makes the assumption that the German government wanted to force the Bundesbank model on the rest of the EU as it thought it was the best model for German interests. This assumption ignores the lengthy list of battles that German governments have had with the Bundesbank over monetary policy since the inception of the Bundesbank/Bank deutscher Länder (BdL) in 1949. In fact, one of Chancellor Helmut Schmidt's goals in sponsoring the European Monetary System (EMS) was to constrain the Bundesbank's ability to make such a price-stability-focused monetary policy (Katzenstein 1987). The willingness of Helmut Kohl to agree to the idea of the ECB before there was any agreement on the model of monetary policy for the proposed central bank also may indicate a lack of concern about giving up the German model of monetary policy (Dyson and Featherstone 2001; Heisenberg 1999; Kaltenthaler 1998; Moravcsik 1998).

Even if the German government had wanted to impose the German Bundesbank's monetary policy strategy on the ECB, it would have had scant opportunity to do so. First, the general blueprint of the ECB was designed in the Delors Committee, which comprised essentially all of the central bank chiefs in the EU, President of the European Commission Jacques Delors, and a few other monetary experts. It was essentially a committee of central bankers that was given the task of designing the general structure and objectives of a proposed European central bank. As the Bundesbank is an independent central bank, it was not a front for the German government.

Second, the monetary policy strategy of the ECB was not created until the ECB itself was created. The ECB's monetary policy strategy was established in 1998, a year before the actual launch of the euro but several years after the embryo of the ECB, the European Monetary Institute (EMI), had come into being. As the EMI/ECB was an institution independent of government or EU bodies' instructions, it would have been very difficult for the German government to force the European central bankers to adopt the Bundesbank's monetary policy strategy. Thus, it seems evident that the decision-makers in the ECB chose the central bank's monetary policy of their own volition. So, what were their motivations for doing so?

One possible explanation would be that the policy ideas held by the central bankers account for the monetary policy strategy that was chosen. It has been argued for some time in political science that ideas matter to the policy courses chosen by elites. The role of ideas has been shown to be crucial in choosing strategies in foreign policy decision-making (Goldstein 1993; Goldstein and Keohane 1993), domestic economic decision-making (Hall 1986; Sikkink 1991), and international cooperation (Haas 1992; Kapstein 1992).

Several scholars have stressed the importance of ideas in making states cooperate to produce European Monetary Union (EMU) (Collignon and Schwarzer 2002; Dyson, Featherstone, and Michalopoulos 1995; Marcussen 2000; McNamara 1998, 2001; Verdun 1999, 2000a).

These works all argue that ideas allow actors to find ways to achieve their interests. Interests alone do not provide unique strategies for achieving goals (Shepsle 1979). Ideas provide the roadmap to realize the goal.

A number of scholars have argued that the decision-makers who came to lead the ECB approximate an epistemic community on domestic and international monetary policy matters (Dyson 2000; Dyson and Featherstone 1999; Dyson, Featherstone, and Michalopoulos 1995; McNamara 1998; Verdun 1999). Peter Haas (1992, 3) says,

> An epistemic community is a network of professionals from a variety of disciplines and backgrounds, that have (1) a shared set of normative and principled beliefs, which provide a value-based rationale for the social action of community members; (2) shared causal beliefs, which are derived from their analysis of practices leading or contributing to a central set of problems in their domain and which then serve as the basis for elucidating the multiple linkages between possible policy actions and desired outcomes; (3) shared notions of validity—that is, intersubjective, internally defined criteria for weighing and validating knowledge in the domain of their expertise; and (4) a common policy enterprise—that is, a set of common practices associated with a set of problems to which their professional competence is directed, presumably out of the conviction that human welfare will be enhanced as a consequence.

Haas argues that the particularly important aspect of epistemic communities is that they are groups of technical experts who share not only causal beliefs but also faith in remedies to solve problems. This means that the technocratic decision-makers have formed a consensus on what the important policy issues are and how to tackle them (Haas 1992; Kapstein 1992).

There is good empirical evidence that European monetary policy elites agreed on how to manage monetary policy in the Committee of Central Bank Governors and the Delors Committee. Amy Verdun (1999) shows that there was a consensus among the central bankers that the German monetary policy model was the best option for the planned ECB. Interviews with ECB officials conducted by me have shown that those officials believed strongly that such a consensus had existed for some time. Asked about the level of consensus on the problems and strategies of the policymakers in the Governing Council, one member stated,

> There is no difference in philosophy at all on the board. The board members have been pursuing the same policies with the same concepts in order to ensure price stability. They have worked together for years to be in the euro area. You have common views developed by mutual understanding and mutual enrichment.[3]

This consensus allowed for cooperation among the central bankers to move forward. As Verdun states, "There was almost no controversy among

the central bankers about the German 'model' to be the most useful model—
by contrast there was still controversy among national heads of state and
governments" (1999, 317).

We know that the consensus on the usefulness of the German model for
the ECB was developed among European Community (EC) central bankers
and predated the consensus on the model arrived at by the national EC
leaders that allowed the ECB to be formed as it was. This central banker
consensus predates the consensus that Kathleen McNamara (1998) points
out was necessary for monetary cooperation in Europe to move to EMU.

These are important things to know, but there is much that these ideational
accounts do not tell us. Missing in these ideational accounts are the microfoundations of policy model choice. The studies cited above are all "ratio-
nalistic," meaning that ideas are chosen to serve actors' interests. In these
studies, however, there is no explanation of why some ideas are chosen
over others. Ideas are said to serve interests, but the interests are not identi-
fied. The model created in this study identifies the interests of the actors in
question in order to determine how ideas influence policy choice. Knowing
the interests of the actors, we can make general predictions about the types
of ideas they will entertain. Knowing the policy ideas adopted by the actors
allows us to predict the actual policies that decision-makers will choose.

The place to start in understanding the monetary policy strategy choice of
independent central bankers is to identify what matters to them most. Without identifying the microfoundations of independent central banker policy
preferences, this model would not be able to offer predictions of what policies the central bankers would choose. Several scholars of political economy have tried to explain where decision-makers in an independent central
bank acquire their policy preferences. Kenneth Rogoff (1985) makes one
of the most prominent arguments about the sources of independent central
banker preference for price stability. He argues that the policy preferences
of decision-makers in an independent central bank come from their professional backgrounds before they joined the central bank. Decision-makers
in an independent central bank come from the ranks of the financial community, according to Rogoff, and bring with them into the central bank the
financial community's general policy preferences for price stability.

Bruno Frey and Friedrich Schneider (1981) offer a different explanation of
why decision-makers in an independent central bank prioritize price stability. They posit that central bankers do this because those decision-makers
hope to maintain an image of prestige with the financial community, the
central bank's primary peer group. Because the financial community wants
the central bank to produce price stability above other economic outcomes,
the central bankers will prioritize price stability in order to appear competent
to the financial community (see Posen 1993, 1995).

Roland Vaubel (1993) posits that decision-makers in an independent central bank derive their preferences for monetary policy from the general public. These public preferences may vary across countries and across time. Vaubel argues that independent central bankers follow the general macroeconomic preferences of their publics in order to appear competent to them. The appearance of competence is important to the central bankers not only so that they have prestige in society but so that they have political support from the general public when or if the central bank decision-makers face pressure from the government. Thus, Vaubel offers the hypothesis that the policy orientations of independent central banks are shaped by the monetary policy priorities (i.e., growth versus price stability) of general publics.

One line of thinking in the literature on central banking is that policy rules can be very important constraints on the types of policy central bankers may choose (Barro and Gordon 1983; Friedman 1960; Kyland and Prescott 1977). One example of a policy rule is legislation that calls for the central bank to produce certain types of policy outcomes. Some countries' legislators set annual inflation targets for the central banks (e.g., Britain, Sweden, New Zealand). The independence of the central bank and the tenures of its decision-makers are contingent upon meeting this inflation target. Thus, these circumstances very much constrain what the central bankers can do in terms of monetary policy. The policy goal is provided for them; they have discretion only in terms of adjusting their monetary policy tools to reach that goal.

Another type of policy rule is a long-term mandate that may be legislated for the central bank. This mandate will spell out what the policy goals of the central bank must be. Mandates for independent central banks state what the policy priorities of the central bank are in terms of price stability and promoting economic growth. Thus, theoretically, such a rule could dictate their policy choices to the central bankers, leaving them little to no discretion when setting monetary policy priorities.

Several scholars have argued that politicians play the primary role in determining the monetary policy priorities of the independent central bank (Bearce 2003; Chappell, Havrilesky, and McGregor 1995; Friedman 1960; Havrilesky 1988; Havrilesky and Gildea 1992). These theories treat the central bank as the agent of political principals (see Calvert, McCubbins, and Weingast 1989). They argue that despite the nominal independence of the central bank, politicians can get the monetary policy that they want. This is caused by the asymmetry in power resources of the central bank and its political principals. Politicians have the power to punish the central bank by controlling its resources and its nominal autonomy. This means that in order to avoid the wrath of politicians, independent central bankers will not make policy that angers them.

I argue that all of the arguments discussed above fail to identify accurately the mechanism that determines the policy priorities of independent central bankers. Instead, I posit that the most important things to an independent central banker, to her interests, are her image of competence, a sense that she is doing a good thing for society, and policymaking independence (see Toma and Toma 1986).[4]

So, why would the image of competence, a sense of public duty, and policymaking independence be so important to central bankers? An image of competence in the eyes of the public is important to independent central bankers for two reasons. First, it gives them psychological satisfaction. One can surmise that those who take jobs as central bankers are not doing it for the money, which is relatively little compared to private-sector jobs in finance, but, at least partially, for the public recognition that they are doing an important job well. A central banker's sense that what she is doing is improving the lives of the general public would also contribute to a psychological payoff.

An image of competence is also important in the sense that it is political capital. Central bankers who enjoy a great degree of public prestige are less likely to face pressure from politicians to act on their wishes. Politicians will not risk the damage to their own popularity by pressuring central bankers who enjoy an image of competence. So, an image of competence can help protect the independence of the central bankers' decision-making. This independence is important for central bankers because it allows them to be masters of their own organization's resources. Policy independence is also important in that central bankers who are independent will have greater societal stature than central bankers who are simply following the orders of politicians.

So, how do independent central bankers maximize the probability that they will maintain an image of competence and therefore their policymaking independence? They do this by achieving good economic performance in their countries. This may be defined differently across time and across countries. In recent times, in the advanced industrialized states, good economic performance has been defined, in general, as strong economic growth, low inflation, and low unemployment. Thus, independent central bankers prefer these economic outcomes in order to maximize their own interests. A key question to pose is, how do the independent central bankers go about trying to achieve these economic goals? In other words, how do they choose their monetary policy strategies?

Two very important questions arise in trying to establish the role played by ideas in choosing strategies: where do ideas come from, and why are some ideas chosen over others? One person or a group of people might consider several alternative ideas in trying to pick a strategy for achieving his or her individual or common goal. How is it that a person or a group is able to get the rest of the group to agree to adopt his, her, or their ideas about the correct strategy for achieving this goal? Arthur Lupia (1998) has created a theory of persuasion that seeks to explain how certain individuals are able to get others to believe their ideas about what actions to take. He argues that for one to be a persuader, she or he must

1. be perceived as having common interests with the target of persuasion
2. be perceived as trustworthy
3. be viewed as knowledgeable

In other words, people will adopt strategy ideas from those whom they think they can trust to provide the best way to achieve the goal.

How does this argument apply to where central bankers get their policy ideas? The ideas held by central bankers have two plausible sources: professional economists in academic settings and other central bankers. Theoretical ideas from the economics profession on the conduct of monetary policy will play a role in shaping the way policymakers think as the theoretical ideas help frame the interpretation of data and provide policy options. Economists likely have more persuasive power than other individuals because it is assumed that they have more knowledge about monetary issues and are not trying to dupe central bankers into following a policy course for their own economic gain, which could be the case with advice from market participants.

Experienced central bankers who have a reputation for effective policy-making are also a source of ideas for monetary policy. Experienced central bankers with good reputations are more effective persuaders than novice central bankers in general because other central bankers will trust advice from those who have been doing monetary policy for some time and have done it in a way that people think has achieved the goals of monetary policy.

It is important to point out that the ideas persuaders are able to get others to adopt may change or be discarded over time. If policy ideas do not live up to expectations as to how they were to achieve policy goals, decision-makers will look for a new set of ideas. That probably means that a new persuader will be sought as the former persuader will have lost his or her credibility.

So, what specific hypothesis does this model provide to answer the question at hand?

The model predicts that European central bankers would look for the central bank in the international system that seemed to have the best track record of managing good economic outcomes in circumstances similar to those faced by the Europeans. This central bank's monetary policy strategy would thus serve as the model for the ECB. Among all of the world's central banks, the German Bundesbank would be the model of monetary policy success in the 1990s. It had the obvious added attraction of being a success in Europe, which meant it had faced the same challenges that the other European central banks had faced, and it had mastered them better than the rest. Also, as the model predicts, the Bundesbank would be an attractive persuader because it had a common interest with other EMU-member central banks in making EMU work well. Its decision-makers were well known to the other European central bankers and thus would be viewed as trustworthy. Finally, to reiterate, because of its unsurpassed economic success, the Bundesbank would be viewed as knowledgeable.

The sections to follow demonstrate how the German monetary policy strategy was developed and came to be viewed as a model in Europe. The chapter continues with insights from ECB decision-makers themselves into how they perceive their choice of monetary policy strategy.

FROM BANK DEUTSCHER LÄNDER TO ECB: THE EVOLUTION OF A MONETARY POLICY STRATEGY IN EUROPE

The monetary policy strategy of the ECB had its origins in the immediate postwar period in Western-occupied Germany. It took a long and winding path through the BdL, the Bundesbank, the EMS, and the Delors Committee, into the Governing Council of the ECB.

The Development of the German Monetary Policy Strategy

It was clear in 1948 that the western zones of occupied Germany were in need of a new currency and a monetary authority to manage it. Thus, the BdL was founded and given the task of managing the new German currency, the deutsche mark, which had been created out of the currency reform.

The BdL was motivated by one overarching principle of monetary policy: the primary responsibility of the central bank was the maintenance of price stability. No other goal for the central bank was to come close to this priority. Not only was this the stated goal of the central bank, but there was also a strong and pervasive consensus among the staff of the BdL that the central bank's most important mission was the maintenance of price stability in the western part of Germany.

What generated this fixation on the need for the central bank to maintain price stability? There were two sources: the experience of the central bankers who came to manage the BdL and a shift in thinking in the German economics profession. There was a great deal of personnel continuity between the Reichsbank and the BdL. Thus, many of the central bankers in the early days of the BdL had been at the wheel of the German central bank when the hyperinflation of 1923 hit. They had also been in the central bank when it became a pawn of Hitler's regime and financed the Nazis' inflationary war spending. These events were devastating to the average German. They pauperized a major portion of the German populace and, in the case of the hyperinflation, bred extremism in German politics. Thus, even the old hands of the Reichsbank who had been hired to steer the BdL saw that a return to inflation in Germany would be a potential disaster. They had learned their lesson well by 1945.

The other source of the emphasis on price stability came from change in the German economics profession during the 1930s and 1940s. Traditionally, the economics profession in Germany had been a relatively strong supporter of economic nationalism and a strong state role in the economy. It did not support the kind of French-style statism but backed collusion between the state and industry on behalf of the German nation. The central bank was viewed as an extension of the state to foster national goals (Allen 1989).

The disastrous consequences of the hyperinflation of the 1920s and the experience with the Nazis led a group of German economists, many who had been at the University of Freiburg during this period, to reject traditional German notions of the economy and to call for a new manner of economic management. This "Freiburg School" of economics, which was most notably represented by the likes of Alfred Müller-Armack, Wilhelm Röpke, Wilhelm Eucken, and Ludwig Erhard, stressed the need for price stability in the economy and as little government intervention as possible. The group also stressed the need for the government to establish clear rules for economic actors and to provide a social safety net for its citizens. While the members of the group differed over the breadth of the rules for the economy and the size of the social safety net, none of them argued with the notion that price stability was an absolute imperative for the economic health of a state. In fact, all of the Freiburg School prioritized price stability, arguing that a noninflationary economy would make countercyclical intervention on the part of the government unnecessary (Allen 1989, 281).

The Freiburg School of German economists was very important to the development of the guiding principles of postwar German monetary policy for two reasons. First, it became the dominant paradigm in German university economics curricula and thus influenced the thinking of nearly all of Germany's economic technocrats educated after the war. Second, the Freiburg School's theoretically based emphasis on price stability buttressed the experiences of the older monetary policy technocrats in Germany. Thus, a confluence of theory and experience molded a consensus among German monetary policy decision-makers that the primary goal of economic management was the maintenance of price stability.

Not only was the price-stability norm an informal consensus among German central bankers, but it came to be institutionalized in the central bank with the passage of the Bundesbank Law of 1957, which established the Bundesbank as the permanent central bank of West Germany, replacing the provisional BdL. Section 1.3 of the Bundesbank Law "assigned the Deutsche Bundesbank the task of regulating the quantity of money in circulation and of credit supplied to the economy with the aim of safeguarding the currency" (Deutsche Bundesbank 1989, 111). The Bundesbank Law also stipulated that "without harm to the performance of its functions, the Deutsche Bundesbank is required to support the general economic policy of the Federal Government" (Deutsche Bundesbank 1989, 115). Thus, the German Bundesbank Law gave the central bank a mandate to make price stability its primary goal. This reflected not only the consensus among the German central banking community about the primacy of price stability, but it also showed that a majority of German politicians supported the notion that the Bundesbank should be an independent central bank with the primary mission of maintaining the stable value of the currency.

It is important to note that no serious challenger arose to threaten the postwar orthodoxy among German central bankers, or politicians for that matter, about the primacy of price stability (Henning 1994; Kennedy 1991; Marsh 1992). Statism was so discredited by the Nazi experience that it did not stand a chance of gaining a significant following. Even Keynesianism never developed a significant following in Germany, making Germany relatively unique among the advanced industrialized states. Keynesianism found little fertile ground among German economists and policymakers because it had within it the potential of prompting inflation and political intervention in the economy, taboos in the German economics profession and among the postwar policy elite (Smyser 1993).

While the Freiburg School's emphasis on price stability became the dominant norm among German central bankers following 1945, it was not the end of new economic ideas affecting the theory and practice of German central banking. The most notable idea to find resonance among German central bankers after the Freiburg School's ideas came from monetarism, an idea founded by Milton Friedman (Friedman 1960; Friedman and Schwartz 1963). Monetarism stressed how measured control of the growth of the money supply was the best way to manage the economy because it maintained price stability and kept massive fluctuations in the business cycle from occurring. Not only did monetarism make demand management unnecessary, but it also limited the range of policy options available to central bankers. Central bankers would decide on a target for noninflationary growth in the money supply, then tailor monetary policy to hit that target. Thus, monetary policy was not about fine-tuning the economy; it was about hitting the money supply growth target.

Monetarism found a receptive audience among German central bankers, who already agreed that the dynamics of the money supply played an important role in what happened to the economy. Rather than supplanting the

Freiburg School's ideas about the primacy of price stability, monetarist thinking came to complement the Freiburg's School's precepts. In the early 1970s, Helmut Schlesinger, the Bundesbank's chief economist, came to introduce monetarist tactics into the central bank's repertoire. The most noteworthy example of this was that, starting in 1974, the Bundesbank began the practice of monetary targeting. Monetary targeting not only gave the Bundesbank a yardstick with which to guide policy, but it also allowed the central bank to signal to participants in wage negotiations what the limits to inflationary wage deals were (Hall and Franzese 1998; Iversen 1998a; Von Hagen 1999).

It is important to note that the monetarism adopted by the Bundesbank in the 1970s was a pragmatic tool to make price stability easier to maintain (see Johnson 1998). When asked about the role of monetarism in the policy-making thinking of the Bundesbank, a directorate member gave this typical answer to the question:

> The price stability mandate was what guided us. Policy ideas such as monetarism only mattered in that they were a way to achieve the goal of price stability, which was our mandate. We had a very pragmatic view toward monetarism. The mandate always came before monetarism. We had no set policy rules determined by monetarism, such as advocates like Friedman have called for.[5]

A Land Central Bank (LCB) president had this to say:

> The Bundesbank generally had a theoretical basis for its deliberations, but it made decisions in a pragmatic way. Monetarism was one of the policy ideas that people brought into deliberations. Less than half of the Central Bank Council (CBC) members were convinced monetarists during the 1990s. We were aware that theory and practice did not always match. What was important was that we got the practice right. Price stability always came before money supply targeting.[6]

The adoption of monetarism in Germany never signaled a fundamental shift in the scholarly doctrine in German university economic programs or among the central bank technocrats (Deutsche Bundesbank 1989, 100–101). In fact, the Bundesbank missed its annual money supply targets about 50 percent of the time between 1974 and 1999, when the Bundesbank handed monetary policymaking power over to the ECB. Despite this record of hitting the money supply targets, no one in- or outside of the Bundesbank questioned the central bank's commitment to price stability. The missing of these money supply targets had to do with the vagaries of measuring the money supply and nothing to do with the central bank's desire to keep inflation in check.[7] No one could question the Bundesbank's price-stability goals, as the central bank defined price stability as a less than 2 percent annual rise in consumer prices—a very tight definition of price stability by international standards.

Thus, the ideas that originated among German central bankers and economists in the 1930s and 1940s about the correct course for monetary policy became entrenched in the BdL and further entrenched and institutionalized in the Bundesbank. Monetarism only complemented and built on these ideas. But all this was made possible because these ideas found general acceptance among the financial sector, the general public, and politicians. Therefore, the policy strategy of the Bundesbank was possible because it did not meet active resistance from any powerfully organized quarter of German society.

Having examined how the Bundesbank's monetary policy ideas came to be accepted in Germany, we must now turn to how those ideas came to influence the monetary policy strategy of the ECB. As we shall see, the process of influence started long before there was any notion of a European central bank.

The Monetary Committee and the Committee of Central Bank Governors

The ideas of the Bundesbank came to be disseminated in multiple ways among the ranks of the EU's central bankers. The Bundesbank began to have influence on European monetary affairs from the time of its creation in 1957, partially due to the relative size of the German economy, but also because of the success of the German central bank in managing German economic reconstruction. German central bankers met with their European counterparts in various fora to discuss monetary policy matters. There was frequent and sustained face-to-face contact between the central banks because of the operation of the "snake" monetary regime and then the EMS. Central bankers also often spoke to each other by phone. The Bundesbank's being at the center of both of those monetary arrangements facilitated its ability to pass along its views on how to conduct monetary policy.

European central bankers would meet and discuss monetary policy issues in other fora outside of the EU, which also allowed the Bundesbank's ideas to get a hearing. One of the most important non-EU fora was the Bank for International Settlements (BIS). The BIS, often referred to as the central bank for central banks, held annual meetings about monetary policy issues at which central bankers could trade views on the best course of action. Clubby, like the Committee of Governors, at the BIS central bankers could speak freely and without the interference of politicians or the press.

Another such forum, which moves from year to year, was the Group of Seven (G-7) meetings. Oftentimes, central bankers went along to these occasions to discuss monetary issues with politicians. While a less central banker–only environment than the Committee of Governors (to be discussed shortly) or the BIS meetings, the G-7 meetings were another place to exchange ideas about the best way to manage monetary policy.

The most important of such non-EC-/-EU venues was the monthly BIS meetings, which were an opportunity for the world's central bankers to come together and discuss common concerns and problems and ponder solutions to them. At the center of many of these meetings were Bundesbank officials, who were famous for how seriously the other central bankers took what they had to say and also for the amount of unsolicited advice they gave.

In 1964, another even more important forum was created for European central bankers to discuss common policy issues, the Committee of Central Bank Governors. The committee, which was created by the EC's Council of Ministers, was mandated to exchange information on pertinent policy matters. Although it was created by the Council of Ministers, it was soon obvious that the membership of the committee, the central bank governors, wanted to make it a forum where they could exchange views without pressure from politicians. The most obvious manifestation of this sense of independence was the location for the committee's meetings, the BIS in Basel, Switzerland. Not only was the committee not meeting in an EC facility, but it was meeting in a country that was not part of the European Community. Clearly the members of the committee believed that this location guaranteed them a higher degree of autonomy from political meddling than would have been possible in Brussels. It was also convenient in that committee members could meet right after regularly scheduled BIS meetings.

It is important to note how the committee conducted its business. Decision-making was based on consensus, and formal votes were avoided. The leadership of the committee rotated every year, and the chairperson was chosen based on seniority. The chair was viewed as one among equals (Andrews 2003b, 963).

It would seem that at first the committee would not be very busy as monetary integration had not started yet, but the group did perform a couple of important functions in that it allowed the central bank governors to get to know each other well and develop a personal rapport, and it also offered them the opportunity to begin to develop a common outlook on policy matters.

When the Bretton Woods system began to collapse in the late 1960s and early 1970s, the committee took on a new importance, one heightened with the creation of the Werner Committee in 1970, which planned the road to monetary union, the creation of the snake in 1972, and the creation of the EMS in 1979. These events not only gave the governors much more to handle as common matters of concern, but they also placed the German central bank squarely in the front of monetary matters in the EC.

The Werner Committee, chaired by Pierre Werner, prime minister of Luxembourg, was charged with creating a plan for movement to eventual monetary union. This committee consisted of Werner, the chairman of the

Committee of Central Bank Governors, the chairman of the Monetary Committee, a European Commission representative, and chairmen from related
EC ministerial committees. This committee was heavy on politicians and
light on central bankers. In fact, the chairman of the Committee of Central
Bank Governors was the only member who was a central banker. Thus,
the report that it produced only partially reflected how European central
bankers thought about the move to EMU (Howarth and Loedel 2003, 29–30).
As the plan to EMU was abandoned by the early 1970s, however, the work
of the committee was not to have much impact on European monetary
affairs.

European central bankers had substantial contact with each other regarding the management of Europe's exchange rate regimes. The snake and EMS
operated as asymmetric exchange rate regimes. This means that one country's currency acted as the anchor, and the other member states tied their
currencies to the anchor currency. As is well known, the German deutsche
mark acted as the anchor of the snake and the EMS, with the Bundesbank essentially setting the monetary policy that all other EMS central banks had to
follow (Heisenberg 1999; Kaltenthaler 1998; Loedel 1999). While this caused
some friction, from time to time, among politicians in the member states of
the snake and EMS, central bankers were coming to a basic agreement on
strategies of monetary management (Dyson 2000; Walsh 2000).

The Bundesbank-led strategy on monetary policy focused on keeping
the currency stable and domestic inflation low. Not only would a policy of
loose credit potentially ignite domestic inflation, but decision-makers were
also convinced that it would undermine the credibility of monetary policy
and lead currency markets to start dumping the deutsche mark. Thus, the
Bundesbank maintained a monetary policy that kept domestic inflation very
low and the deutsche mark stable, yet not overvalued vis-à-vis the dollar. The
German central bank's monetary policy was more geared toward domestic
price stability than influencing the external value of the deutsche mark, but
the central bank always kept an eye on the external value to make sure
that it did not threaten domestic inflation or overvalue the deutsche mark
and thus overburden German exporters. But if there was a choice between
domestic price stability and the competitiveness of German exporters, the
Bundesbank always chose in favor of domestic price stability because of
the consensus among German central bankers that allowing inflation into
Germany through a weak currency would hurt German exporters anyway
in the long run, both by raising their production costs and by damaging the
lending climate (Kaltenthaler 1998; Loedel 1999).

The Bundesbank argument that domestic price stability was the best
way to promote long-term economic growth had been accepted by other
European central bankers by the mid-1970s.[8] European central bankers
had seen how the Bundesbank's focus on price stability had spared West

Germany a great many of the negative economic consequences of the oil crisis that had plagued other countries. The meetings of the Committee of Governors and the Monetary Committee showed a great deal of agreement on what the goals and strategies of monetary policy should be. These committees were given such tasks as trying to coordinate the use of credit mechanisms in the EMS and revaluation of exchange rates. The major disagreements over monetary policy were more between member governments in the EC and between those governments and their central banks. The central bankers were on the same page as to the primary goal of monetary policy: price stability. Because most of the central banks in the EC were not independent of government instruction, however, many of the central bankers' thoughts about policy did not translate into concrete policy strategies. Many European governments were not yet convinced of the primary importance of price stability. Only in the 1980s did the so-called neoliberal consensus develop among the European political elites (McNamara 1998; Verdun 1999). Part of this conversion to the neoliberal stability orientation in economic policy was brought about by the public and private admonitions of EC central bankers to prioritize price stability in order to promote sustainable economic growth.

The Delors Committee

The group of European central bankers that made up the Delors Committee saw its most important moment when the idea of monetary union was floated in the late 1980s. Several European politicians advocated the idea of monetary union, but the idea received particularly important support when the French and German governments agreed, in principle, to make it happen. The German government was aware that it would need the support of the Bundesbank in order to make EMU a reality. Without Bundesbank support, it would be very difficult to persuade the German public to accept the idea.

At the Hannover summit in June 1988, the European Council selected the membership of a committee to draw up a blueprint for EMU. Delors, the president of the European Commission, was chosen to chair the committee (hence the name of the committee). He would be joined by the twelve member-state central bank governors, as well as five other experts in monetary affairs.

This committee was, essentially, the Committee of Governors membership chaired by Delors. It was dominated by Delors and Bundesbank president Karl-Otto Pöhl. The central bankers already had a close working relationship because of their frequent interactions, and they did not like the idea that Delors, a politician, would chair the meetings. They viewed this as infringing on their usually independent mode of discussing monetary issues and worried that it could lead them to a plan that they would not have otherwise agreed upon.[9]

Delors was aware of the difficulty of achieving monetary union if it seemed that the EC's central bankers were not on board. He did all he could to facilitate a consensus among the central bankers on the outline for EMU, even if that consensus did not match his own preferences (Andrews 2003b, 964). Thus, he gave the governors autonomy to draft the plan as they saw fit.

The most important voice on the committee was that of Bundesbank president Pöhl for the same reason that the president of the Bundesbank always had more influence in the Committee of Governors than any of the other governors. The report generated by the governors and supported by Delors created a blueprint for a possible future European central bank that basically copied the Bundesbank's general structure, independent status, and policy mandate. The central bankers, without coercion from the German government, advocated the German monetary policy model for the proposed European central bank (Dyson and Featherstone 2000; Heisenberg 1999; Moravcsik 1998). The EMS central bankers firmly believed that European industry needed a price stability orientation that kept the financial system healthy.

While Pöhl certainly advocated the Bundesbank model, it was not his insistence that led to the final report. There was consensus among the other central bankers that the Bundesbank, being the most successful central bank in the world by some measures, was the logical model for the future European central bank.

Following the issuance of the Delors Report and the political decision to move toward EMU, the Committee of Governors set to work preparing the groundwork. This lasted until December 1993, when it dissolved and reconstituted itself in the form of the Council of the European Monetary Institute, the precursor to the ECB. Thus, the membership of the Committee of Governors came to be the decision-makers of the ECB when EMU was launched in 1999. These individuals had reached a consensus on the goals and strategies of monetary policy for the ECB.

When asked how the consensus was achieved, the interviewed members of the Governing Council agreed unanimously that the close contact among the various central bankers had produced a uniformity of views on monetary policy, a uniformity borne not of coercion but persuasion. A national central bank governor argued,

You know a lot of the board [the Governing Council] members have been pursuing the same policies of price stability for some time now. They have worked together for years to bring this to the euro area. This work has produced a lot of common views.[10]

A member of the ECB Executive Board offered this:

> What happens is what I suppose happens at all central banks. The views may
> be diverse when one enters the central bank, but constant discussions lead
> to a change in views. There may be a majority and a minority but over time,
> because of persuasion, a consensus develops. This is because the people with
> the stronger arguments are able to convince those whose arguments do not
> hold up.[11]

Another ECB Executive Board member spoke more specifically about the
ideas that have come to dominate the thinking of the Governing Council:

> We have come to know that allowing a little inflation to grow will hurt everyone
> in the long run. It will particularly hurt the poor. No central banker thinks now
> that you can let inflation grow to get growth. Inflation will kill growth in the
> future. The academics and policy communities have come to believe that. All of
> the European central bankers have come to believe that. One of the ways they
> have learned this is through working together during the European Monetary
> System experience.[12]

Based on the consensus on monetary strategy that developed in the EMS
over how to manage the priorities of domestic and external monetary policy,
it was very likely that this consensus would carry over into the operations
of the ECB. The Bundesbank lent the ECB its strategy for maintaining price
stability because it is the most credible persuader among the constituent
parts of the European System of Central Banks.

So, why has the Bundesbank become the institutional and ideational
model for the ECB? The most important reason is its success in maintaining price stability and other positive economic outcomes in postwar
Germany. Also, because the Bundesbank became the de facto lead central bank of the EU owing to the anchor role of the deutsche mark in the
EMS, European central bankers viewed the export of price stability from
Germany to other European countries as a positive experience for those
countries. Thus, Bundesbank's economic success both within Germany and
in Western Europe made it an attractive model for the ECB. As one member
of the ECB's Governing Council put it when asked about the model the
Bundesbank presented for the ECB,

> The Bundesbank was the leading central bank before it dominated monetary
> policy in Europe. So, the experience and credibility of the Bundesbank mat-
> tered. The process of disinflation in Europe that started in the 1980s was guided
> by the Bundesbank. Other central banks more or less followed the Bundesbank.
> The price stability dominant in Germany was exported to other European coun-
> tries and finally there was a decisive moment when it finally became entrenched
> in their own thinking. When we started monetary union, there was the common
> conviction that price stability was the most important goal of monetary policy.[13]

When the ECB's design became an issue for discussion between 1989 and 1991, Europe's central bankers broadly agreed that the Bundesbank's structure and principles were the best model for the future ECB. A non-German member of the ECB's Executive Board had this to say about adopting the German model of monetary policymaking: "When we lower or raise rates, some people ask if the Bundesbank would have done that. And it is really important that the answer of the public is yes, the good old Bundesbank would have done it just the way these new people did it."[14]

The Creation of the ECB's Monetary Policy Strategy and Tactics: The Role of the Chief Economist

When the European System of Central Banks, of which the ECB is part, came into operation in June 1998, it may have seemed to many that the famed German Bundesbank had been relegated to an insignificant bit part in European monetary affairs. The Bundesbank no longer controlled the monetary destiny of Europe as it had under the EMS. In fact, the Bundesbank did not even control the monetary affairs of Germany any longer because the ECB ran monetary policy for EMU, of which Germany was a constituent part. The president of the Bundesbank had only one of sixteen votes on the Governing Council of the ECB. It may have seemed like the end of the BdL/Bundesbank's legacy of monetary policymaking, but in fact the ECB is, in many ways, an extension of the German monetary policy paradigm created after World War II. While the institutional structure of the Bundesbank is clearly reflected in the ECB, it is the Bundesbank's monetary policy ideas that are the most important contribution of the German central bank to the ECB.

Although there was consensus among the decision-makers of the fledgling ECB over the goals and general strategy of monetary policy in the run-up to EMU, there were no concrete guidelines for how to formulate monetary policy in the Eurozone. Thus, the members of the ECB's Governing Council had create those guidelines before developing their policy decisions.

The central bankers agreed that inflation needed to be very low in order not to cause inflationary momentum in the Eurozone, which would negatively affect growth and employment. Fighting inflation had to be the central focus of monetary policy, as it was in the Bundesbank. This was stated in the protocol establishing the ECB. The key question was how to formulate policy to do so effectively.

In the run-up to EMU, there had been a series of discussions among European central bankers about what the monetary policy strategy of the ECB should look like. The first set of discussions took place in the EMI, which was the embryo of the ECB created in 1994. The EMI, located in Frankfurt, consisted of an ECB Executive Board and a permanent staff. The

ECB Executive Board was made up of a president (Alexandre Lamfalussy, ex-president of the BIS) and the national central bank governors of the twelve member states of the EU. It was independent of the EU and national institutions and was to act as the precursor to the operational launch of the ECB.

There were two general models of monetary policy commonly used in the central banks in the Eurozone. One model, used by the Bundesbank and others, was to target the growth of the money supply in order to preclude the growth of inflation. This model, based on monetarist economic thinking, is based on the premise that the growth of the money supply is the most important factor in causing inflation. This model called for the central bank to set a money supply growth target for the year that the central bankers thought would allow for economic growth at a noninflationary pace. The central bank would then monitor the growth of the money supply during the year and adjust interest rates in order to keep the money supply growth rate within the acceptable bounds established by the central bank.

This strategy, introduced at the Bundesbank in 1974 by the chief economist Helmut Schlesinger, had the advantage of signaling what the central bank thought were reasonable wage demands in terms of their effect on money supply growth. It was a way for the Bundesbank to contain the demands of the labor unions. The Bundesbank could say that if the unions wanted to make excessive wage demands, the central bank would reduce the amount of growth in the money supply to compensate for the wage demands. The result would be a tightening of monetary policy that could put people out of work, and this would make the unions think twice about their wage demands.

Not only could monetary targeting be a useful signaling device, but it was also political cover for the central bank. Once the annual money supply target had been established, the central bank could argue that monetary policy was no longer discretionary as the central bank was merely creating policy in order to meet its target. The Bundesbank decision-makers could present themselves as caretakers of monetary policy rather than those who were making the decisions that were slowing the economy and putting people out of work.

Monetary targeting has had a mixed record of success both in Germany and around the world. The main problem with the strategy is that it is exceedingly difficult to get an accurate measure of the money supply. With new types of financial instruments, it became almost impossible, in many cases, to get a clear reflection of the volume and velocity of money in the data available to the central bankers. This was the primary reason why the American Federal Reserve abandoned money supply targeting not long after it was introduced.

The difficulties with money supply targeting led several European central banks to look for another model of monetary policymaking. The second model, used by the Finns and Spanish, was to target inflation. This policy model called for an inflation target to be established each year, and then monetary policy would be created in order to keep inflation at or below the target. The advocates of this strategy considered it more efficacious than money supply targeting because there were better data on inflation than there were on the money supply.

But this strategy had its critics, too. The advocates of money supply targeting argued that their strategy was much more preemptive than inflation targeting because money supply growth preceded inflation. By targeting inflation, the money supply target advocates argued, the central bank was dealing with the problem after it was already too late. Because there is sometimes a two-year lag in the effects of monetary policy, by hitting inflation only after it had appeared, one would be fighting against already well-established momentum in the economy. It would be too late to stop inflation effectively, and the tightening of policy could actually start to have an effect only when the economy was already moving back into a slowing phase.

Each of these models was advocated by its countries' representatives on the Governing Council. It seemed that an impasse had been reached as to how to create monetary policy for the ECB.

The deciding factor in the discussions over which monetary policy strategy to employ was the chief economist of the ECB, Otmar Issing. Issing had been chief economist at the Bundesbank from 1990 to 1994. He had replaced Schlesinger and had a similar view of monetary policy. Both were convinced about the imperative of fighting inflation preemptively and the value of money supply targeting. Issing was a very respected economics professor before joining the Bundesbank and had garnered an international reputation as an effective proponent of the Bundebank's monetary policy strategy.

It is crucial to point out how important Issing's position at the Bundesbank was to the central bank's monetary policy strategy. At the Bundesbank, the arguments of the chief economist were, in many ways, the most important influence on the central bank's monetary policy. The chief economist was responsible for formulating the general monetary policy strategy of the central bank, setting the agenda at Central Bank Council meetings, presenting his view of the monetary and economic conditions in the country, and suggesting a specific policy course of action. This would then be discussed and voted on by the council as a whole. While the president was the public face of the central bank, the chief economist was actually much more important in charting the course of policy.

As the design of the ECB called for its chief economist to play the same role as that individual had played at the Bundesbank, the selection of the chief economist was a very important matter. Issing was chosen by the Eurozone heads of government and state for the position because he would immediately lend the central bank credibility with financial markets. He was a well-known and respected central banker whom markets could expect to advocate the policy line he had pursued at the Bundesbank. As that policy line was held in high esteem by financial market participants around the world, Issing was an obvious choice.

The problem was that Issing's views on monetary policy were not accepted by all of the other members of the Governing Council. While he was universally well respected among the other European central bankers, the inflation-targeting advocates were convinced that while collecting useful data on money supply growth was difficult in their home countries, it would be exceedingly difficult to do in the Eurozone, with its varied national measures and collecting systems.

However, Issing was able to win the argument in favor of money supply targeting due to two factors. The first was his ability to persuade several of his colleagues through the force of his ideas and the credibility he brought to the discussion because of his tenure at the Bundesbank. The second factor was a purely strategic calculation on the part of all in the Governing Council to go with Issing's strategy for purposes unrelated to the content of his argument. These decision-makers reasoned that by copying the Bundesbank's monetary policy strategy to the letter, they would be buying themselves a good measure of instant credibility with financial markets (Marshall 1999, 278). The Belgian central bank governor, Alfons Verplaetse, said of the decision to go with money supply targeting, "We said, 'let's be prudent, we cannot be too pragmatic at the beginning. We have to have monetary aggregates if we want the credibility of past monetary policy" (Marshall 1999, 279).

While the decision-makers in the Governing Council decided to go ahead with money supply targeting as their principal monetary policy plank, Issing insisted that the ECB's monetary policy strategy needed to articulate the reality of monetary conditions in Europe, or it would lose the credibility that it had inherited from the Bundesbank.

The ECB's monetary policy strategy was officially announced on 13 October 1998 by the Governing Council of the central bank. Issing, as the foremost representative of the Bundesbank's way of making monetary policy, was most responsible for shaping the specifics of the modified Bundesbank monetary policy strategy that the ECB adopted. This model was a mix of the Bundesbank model and perceived improvements based on Bundesbank experience and Eurozone realities. In many ways, the ECB's model reflected the practice of the Bundesbank more than the German central bank's publicly announced policy model. The pragmatic use of monetary aggregate data and the addition of other indicators of inflation potential had been part of the Bundesbank policy repertoire since the mid-1970s. Thus, Issing was merely making explicit at the ECB what the policy strategy was based on, whereas at the Bundesbank, the policy strategy had been more opaque for several years.

It is difficult to underestimate Issing's importance to the launching of the ECB's monetary policy. His combination of experience with the Bundesbank, reputation in the financial and central banking communities, and persuasive argumentation were key to determining how the ECB would view monetary policy strategy.

CONCLUSION

This chapter has attempted to understand the sources of the ECB's strict anti-inflation orientation since its creation. I have argued, based on a model of policy persuasion, that the Bundesbank served as the model for the ECB's monetary strategy because of the unmatched success of the German central bank in achieving good economic outcomes in Germany. Through a myriad of opportunities, European central bankers had become familiar with the German model and thus knew it well. It was the model that the central bankers believed would most likely allow them to achieve economic success at the European level.

There was ample reason and opportunities for central bankers in Europe to take ideas from the Bundesbank on how to manage monetary policy successfully. Thus, while the Bundesbank became a regional central bank of the ECB, it is still, by far, the most important national component of the ECB in terms of the influence it has had on the central bank. While the president of the Bundesbank may have a bit more say in the meetings of the Governing Council because of the relative size of the German economy, he would otherwise not be a dominant figure in the ECB. The Governing Council must make monetary policy that is appropriate for all of the Eurozone and not for one or a few countries in particular. But it is indisputable that the stamp of the Bundesbank's monetary policy strategy is very prominent in every monetary policy decision made by the ECB.

The evidence collected through interviews and other sources demonstrates that the logic of the argument is correct. It was found that the central bankers in the ECB have formed an epistemic community that shares the belief that replicating the Bundesbank monetary strategy was the best route to producing good monetary policy outcomes. This epistemic community has developed as a result of the years that the European central bankers have worked together, particularly under the EMS.

What are the implications of this finding for our understanding of central banking in general? The most important implication is that ideas matter in central banks. In other words, the mental models that central bankers have of how the economy works matter a great deal in how they make policy. These mental models may be the product of learning about scientific scholarship or may come from practical experience. In the case of the ECB, the mental model of the economy shared by its decision-makers comes from both practical experience and work done in economics. It is this shared knowledge, not inputs from the political environment, that produced the central bank's policy orientation.

This raises an important question. If the general public, financial community, or politicians were adamantly opposed to the policy orientation pursued by the central bank, would the central bankers continue to follow that policy line? It seems that the answer to that question would depend on the political power of the opposing group to infringe on the independence of the central bank. If one of these groups had the power to constrain the autonomy of the central bank, we could relatively safely surmise that the central bankers would try to placate that group by shaping its policies to conform with that group's preferences.

This means that while the ECB may not be taking its policy orientation lead from societal groups, it has the passive support of these groups. Otherwise, the group or groups would mobilize against the central bank until it changed its policies. Thus, there seems to be a passive consensus that the policy line adopted by the ECB is the correct one to produce beneficial economic outcomes for the citizens of the Eurozone.

NOTES

1. See European Central Bank 2001.

2. It is important to note that one of the main reasons the American Federal Reserve dropped monetary targeting was that it became next to impossible to measure the size of the money supply in the United States accurately.

3. Interview with national central bank governor.

4. These goals are not listed in any particular order. The order of importance of these things may differ across central bankers and across time for individual central bankers. My argument differs from Toma and Toma (1986) because I believe that central bankers do derive a sense of satisfaction from thinking that their policies have helped society. This is a psychological payoff that they do not consider.

5. Interview with directorate member, 25 July 2000.

6. Interview with LCB president, 17 July 2000.

7. Deutsche Bundesbank, 100–101.

8. Interview with ECB Executive Board member.

9. Interview with national central bank official.

10. Interview with national central bank governor.

11. Interview with member of the ECB Executive Board.

12. Interview with member of the ECB Executive Board.

13. Interview with member of the ECB Executive Board.

14. Interview with member of the ECB Executive Board.

3

The Structure and Strategy of the European Central Bank

The European Central Bank (ECB) is in many ways a novel creation. It is the world's first supranational central bank. In other words, it is the first instance of a central bank having the explicit legal power to make monetary policy decisions for multiple independent states. The ECB is not an international organization but one that pools the economic governance powers of multiple states. It is a bold experiment in international integration.

While the ECB is unique in that it is the first supranational central bank, it is hardly unique in terms of its organizational structure, powers, and monetary policy strategy. In many ways, the ECB appears to be a near replica of the German Bundesbank, which is now a constituent part of the ECB. The structure, powers, and monetary policy strategy of the ECB are nearly identical to those of the Bundesbank, but in some important ways, the ECB has been given policy powers and independence that Bundesbankers could only dream of.

This chapter describes the institutions and policymaking strategies of the ECB and the environment in which the ECB operates. It describes how these institutions and strategies were intended to function and how they have indeed functioned. This chapter argues that the ECB is, in most meaningful ways, an institutional and operational copy of the Bundesbank. This means that not only was the ECB designed as a copy of the Bundesbank, but it has operated along much the same policy principles that guided the Bundesbank. This is an important point because it is not always the case that copied institutions operate like the original. It may be that the environment is different for the copied institution relative to the original or that the personnel in the copied institution do not share the preferences or norms of the original institution. Because the ECB has operated very similarly to the Bundesbank, I argue not only that the institutional structure of the German central bank has been copied but that the preferences and norms of the German central bankers have been adopted by their European counterparts, who are the decision-makers and staff in the ECB. This is a remarkable process if one thinks about the enormity of getting more than a dozen states, with sometimes very different national traditions, to converge so completely on the same institutional structure and model of monetary policymaking.

This chapter begins by describing the decision-making structure of the ECB. The next section explores the decision-making process in the central bank. This is followed by an examination of how the central bank recruits its staff and what that staff looks like. The chapter then moves from the organizational institutions of the bank and delves into its monetary policy strategy, in theory and in practice.

THE DECISION-MAKING STRUCTURE

The ECB is, in fact, only one part of the European System of Central Banks (ESCB). The ESCB comprises two parts. One is the member national central banks, which are part of the European Union (EU). The second is the ECB.

There are two decision-making bodies in the ECB. The Executive Board consists of the president and vice president of the ECB, plus four other members. These board members are all appointed by common agreement of EU heads of government and state. The Executive Board prepares the meetings of the ECB's policymaking body, the Governing Council, and also runs the day-to-day affairs of the ECB.

The Governing Council, as mentioned above, is the chief decision-making body of the ECB. It comprises the Executive Board and the governors of the national central banks of the member states of European Monetary Union (EMU). Thus, when the Governing Council meets to make monetary policy, which it typically does every two weeks, present are six Executive Board members and each of the national central bank (NCB) governors, who now number twelve.[1]

The meetings of the Governing Council are chaired by the president of the ECB or, if she or he is not available, the vice president. This gives the president an important degree of control over the meeting agenda. The president of the ECB is also a very important person in the central bank in that she or he is its primary external representative. The president leads press conferences after policymaking meetings of the Governing Council and is also the person who represents the central bank in international forums. The president is, in most ways, the public face of the ECB. How the president presents the ECB and its policies to the outside world can have a major impact on how markets perceive policy and how the public views the competence of the central bank. Thus, the president must be a good communicator and politically astute.

There was serious concern in some corners about the way the first president of the ECB, Wim Duisenberg, represented the central bank to the markets and the public. Duisenberg upset many in Europe with his comments about his lack of concern over the depreciation of the euro. This was of particular concern in Germany, where euro depreciation was followed closely as many Germans feared that the switch from the deutsche mark to the euro was eroding the value of their savings. Duisenberg realized that his comments were having a negative impact on attitudes toward the ECB in Germany, and he changed his rhetoric to assuage German fears about the euro's slide in value.

Duisenberg also broke a golden rule of central banking by commenting on how and when the ECB would intervene in international currency markets.[2] These comments led to the further depreciation of the euro. This was considered such a serious faux pas that some European politicians began to call for his resignation. Former French president Valéry Giscard d'Estaing argued,

> I have always thought that the central bank's first president should be a man whose international authority would be immediately recognized. In fact, contrary to the spirit of the treaty, the club of member-state governors named one of their own from a medium-sized country, the Netherlands, to head the ECB. Whatever the personal merits of Mr. Duisenberg, it was a casting mistake.[3]

Duisenberg refused to resign, but the incidents showed the importance of how the president represents the monetary policies to the markets and the general public.

The experience with Duisenberg's ECB presidency raises an important question about who should become president of the central bank. Duisenberg was chosen because of his monetary policy expertise and because he was someone the central bankers could agree on. In hindsight, some politicians and central bankers came to regret the choice because they had neglected to take into account his experience dealing with the public issues of currency management.

One European central bank governor with many years of experience with monetary affairs and who knew Duisenberg well said this about him:

> Duisenberg is a central banker of great skill. But he was the president of the Dutch bank, which followed German monetary policy for years. He never had to explain monetary policy decisions to the Dutch public. The decisions were

made elsewhere and the Dutch followed them. So he has not had the experience with dealing with the markets and the public. This is the source of the
problem.[4]

Duisenberg himself admitted as much:

> I still have to get used to the intensity with which the world watches every
> word you say or every move you make. I originally thought it was somewhat
> exaggerated. I now realize that I have to watch my words with the same intensity
> as Greenspan. You are so easily misinterpreted, or correctly interpreted on what
> you wouldn't have wanted to say in the first place.[5]

The experience of having Duisenberg as president has been a learning process for European governments and central bankers. It has impressed upon
them the importance of picking an ECB president with a background that
will ease his or her dealing with the markets and the public. This means that
EU member governments will not likely pick a central bank official from a
small country to be president in the near future because she or he would not
likely have the experience with explaining and presenting monetary policy
that a central bank official from a large country would have.

Duisenberg's successor, Jean-Claude Trichet, who was appointed in 2003,
has been a much more successful communicator of the ECB's actions. A
respected former president of the Banque de France, he was used to speaking to his public and even a European audience about his country's monetary
policy actions. Even though the manner of his appointment as president of
the ECB was clouded in controversy (see chapter 4), few doubted his monetary policymaking credentials or his ability to represent the ECB skillfully
to the outside world.[6]

Another very important person at the Governing Council meetings is the
chief economist of the ECB, who is an Executive Board member. The chief
economist is not only the principal person who lays out the economic and
monetary picture for the Governing Council but the leading advocate of
monetary policy strategy suggestions for the central bank. In a way, the
chief economist is the chief strategist of the ECB. She or he presents the
economic and monetary picture of the Eurozone to the other members of
the Governing Council at their rate-setting meetings. The chief economist is
the most important person among the Governing Council members in terms
of determining the monetary policy priorities at particular council meetings.

While the chief economist is the most important strategist in the ECB,
this individual does not have a high public profile since it is not the
chief economist who appears at press conferences explaining the ECB's
monetary policy, but the president. Thus, a bit of insulation protects the
chief economist from having to defend the central bank's monetary policy
strategy.

The ECB's first chief economist, the German Otmar Issing, was the central figure in devising the central bank's general policy strategy before the launch of the ECB. The importance of the chief economist position at the ECB is another idea taken from the Bundesbank model. Just as at the Bundesbank, at the ECB, the chief economist position entails more than it does at most other central banks. At the Bundesbank, chief economists such as Helmut Schlesinger and Issing were the most influential individuals in shaping the policy framework of the central bank. They may not have influenced the specific tactics of monetary policy decisions more than any other members of the Central Bank Council, but they devised the strategy into which the tactics fit. The ECB not only brought the ideas of the chief economist from the Bundesbank, but it brought the Bundesbank's chief economist into the central bank as well.

The choice of Issing as chief economist at the ECB is instructive for several reasons. First, by picking Issing, the ECB sent a strong signal that it endorsed the types of policies he advocated as chief economist at the Bundesbank. Thus, it is one more sign that the ECB was adopting the Bundesbank model. Second, Issing was an individual well known by market participants, if not the general publics in Europe. His favorable reputation among the markets would give the ECB an instant quotient of credibility.

Issing's selection as chief economist tells us that the ECB would likely choose as his successor someone known to the markets as a highly regarded monetary policy thinker. Therefore, the ECB's chief economist is likely to remain someone who has had substantial central bank practical experience, an esteemed academic career, or, like Issing, a mix of both. The chief economist's position is one through which the ECB needs to instill confidence in its strategic guidance among market participants.

Now that we have discussed the decision-makers in the ECB, let us turn to the processes of decision-making. The ECB makes its monetary policy decisions at the first meeting of every month. The second, and final, meeting of the month concentrates on other policy issues facing the ECB.

The voting rules outlined in the Statute of the ESCB are quite simple: one person, one vote. Every member of the Governing Council is to have exactly the same vote, and decisions on monetary policy matters are to be taken by simple majority vote. Only in the case of a tie in the council vote does the president's vote count twice. This voting system is set to change as the size of the Governing Council grows. This will be discussed in great detail in this chapter.

It is important to note how opaque the deliberations and voting in the ECB are. There are no published transcripts of ECB deliberations and votes. In fact, no one in the Governing Council will even talk about the generalities of voting in the body. Council members claim that no formal vote is taken, but, rather, all decisions are made by consensus after an exchange of ideas.

While the president and others in the Governing Council will attest after the meetings of the monetary policy–setting body that disagreements were expressed during the meeting, they persistently claim that a consensus was achieved by the end of the meeting.[7] This is a different decision-making procedure from those one finds at the American Federal Reserve or the Bank of England, where formal votes are taken, and dissenters can go on the record with their negative votes and reasons for them.

Why the emphasis on consensus rather than majority votes? It is an important distinction in decision-making because consensus building can take much longer to achieve than a simple majority vote, and deadlock can occur more easily. Thus, there are definite downsides to the consensus-based system.

The reason consensus is so important to the decision-makers in the Governing Council is that this body has a dozen national representatives alongside the Executive Board. The Governing Council does not want votes to appear to break down along national lines. If voting were to become a national issue, there could be substantial pressure on NCB governors, in particular, to uphold the national interest on monetary policy. The Governing Council wants to "Europeanize" the outlook of the council as much as possible and to avoid battles between council members over defending their specific country's economic interests.

One indication of the importance of breaking down the national perspectives of members of the Governing Council is the way they meet. Originally, the Governing Council was arrayed with the Executive Board on one side of the meeting table and the NCB presidents on the other side. Also, the NCB presidents had name cards in front of them that included their countries. President Duisenberg quickly changed this arrangement by placing the members of the Governing Council in alphabetical order and taking country names off the name cards.[8] Now, it is taboo to refer to a Governing Council member as person x from country y.[9]

This does not mean that national interests do not creep into discussions of Eurozone monetary policy. The member countries of EMU do not all operate on the same business cycle, and a single monetary policy can be a good fit for some but not others. This has been very evident in how the fast-growers (Ireland, for example) and the slow-growers (principally Germany) have quite different monetary policy needs. The Irish have had a problem with containing inflation in their economy because of their rapid economic growth, whereas the Germans have had anemic growth and next to no inflation. This led the president of the Bundesbank, Ernst Welteke, to state publicly in 1999 and 2000 that no new rate hikes were needed in the Eurozone.[10]

This public display of national interest among the governors in the ECB's Governing Council damaged the credibility of the central bank's monetary policy and caused the value of the euro to fall in international currency markets. One currency market analyst said, "There has been a feeling in the market that the ECB has talked too much and that the range of opinions expressed has been greater than in the US Federal Reserve or in the Bundesbank. The spectre of ECB officials running back into the arms of a rapacious media after the summer recess at the end of the month must be jangling the nerves of those who are bullish on the euro."[11] This became obvious to the members of the Governing Council, some of whom made open expressions of national positions on monetary policy.

A very important norm of the Governing Council is that no member of that body is to reveal the positions taken by members during policy meetings. The body represents itself to the public as a monolith, and there is a distinct logic to this approach. The idea is that airing the deliberations of Governing Council meetings will put pressure on the individual members of the Governing Council and could also spook the markets by revealing divisions within the body.

All of these aspects of the institutional structure of the ECB are nearly identical to those of the German Bundesbank. The Bundesbank is based on a two-tiered system with a directorate (equivalent to the Executive Board in the ECB) and Land Central Bank presidents. Each member of the Bundesbank Central Bank Council has one vote, and decisions are based on the majority. Monetary policy decisions in the ECB are also conveyed to the public in the same way as in the Bundesbank. One difference between the Bundesbank and the ECB is that the president of the ECB can break ties, while the president of the Bundesbank only has one vote. Thus, the governing structure of the ECB is nearly a complete replica of the Bundesbank's.

REFORMING THE GOVERNING COUNCIL

The EU could grow to twenty-seven members by 2007. This means that the number of NCB governors in the Governing Council could grow from thirteen to twenty-eight if all decide to join the Eurozone and meet the criteria for membership. Combine this with the six Executive Board members, and the Governing Council would have thirty-three members. This is simply too many decision-makers in a body already plagued by its size. If all members of the Governing Council were given the right to speak at their meetings, the result would be long drawn-out affairs (see Bofinger 2003; Gros 2003; Lommatzsch and Tober 2002; Mangano 1999).

Also, without reform of the structure of voting in the Governing Council, small economies would have much more voice than the large economies that make up the bulk of the Eurozone economy (Lommatzsch and Tober 2003). Thus, economies with less aggregate impact on the lives of people living in the Eurozone would have a disproportionate say in their economic fortunes.

There is near unanimity in the EU and in the new member states that reforming the Governing Council will be necessary because of EU expansion.[12] The Governing Council of the ECB has argued that reform is necessary to have efficient decision-making.[13] It also has argued to keep the representative nature of the Governing Council. The controversy centers on how to accomplish this reform. The key question is how to streamline the Governing Council and keep it representative of all EMU member states.

In February 2003, the ECB presented its proposed solution to the Governing Council issue. The ECB decided on a concept of rotating membership in the council. The new Governing Council structure sets a limit of fifteen NCB governors with voting rights. The plan is to be implemented in two stages as EMU expands.

In the first stage, when the number of EMU members is greater than fifteen but less than twenty-two, the governors will be divided into two groups, determined by their country ranking. The country ranking is based on a composite number with two components: its gross domestic product, which makes up 5/6 of the ranking, and the total assets of the aggregated balance sheet of monetary financial institutions (TABS-MFI), which measures the size of the country's financial sector. The TABS-MFI is the total aggregated balance sheet of the monetary financial institutions that are part of EMU.

The first group of governors in the first stage will comprise the five governors of the euro-area countries that occupy the highest country rankings. This group gets four voting rights. The second group of governors comprises all of those remaining. They share eleven voting rights. The Governing Council may delay the introduction of the rotation system until the number of EMU countries reaches eighteen.

The second stage of the system will commence when the Eurozone counts twenty-two members. At this time, the governors will be divided into three groups. The first group will be the five governors from the highest-ranking Eurozone member countries (according to the TABS-MFI), and is half of all of the governors taken from the subsequent positions in the country rankings. This group of governors will have eight voting rights. The third group of governors contains those who remain, and it has three voting rights.[14]

The ECB presented this plan to the EU Council in order to have the ECB's statute amended to include these new rules. The plan faced scrutiny from the European Commission and European Parliament (EP), which could make suggestions about the draft reform. The European Commission endorsed the "general idea" of the reform but offered the following amendments:

1. Lower the number of governors with voting rights from fifteen in order to increase decision-making efficiency.
2. Make population a part of the country ranking.

3. Clarify how the system will be put into operation.
4. Clarify the precise starting point of the rotation system.

The EP's reaction to the ECB's proposed reform was much more negative. The EP adopted a resolution rejecting the proposed reform because the rotation model was too complicated. It proposed an alternative plan that reform should be undertaken by the Convention on the Future of Europe. The EP plan called for operational decisions to be made by an enlarged Executive Board and for general and strategic monetary policy decisions to be made by the Governing Council.

On 21 March 2003, the EU Council adopted the ECB's original plan, but the EU Council did call for the issue of ECB decision-making to be examined at the next Intergovernmental Conference.

The reform of the Governing Council created a hierarchy of countries within EMU that had not existed previously. Larger and richer countries have more say in the making of the Eurozone's monetary policy than smaller and poorer countries (Bofinger 2003). This is a fairly important departure in the decision-making norms of the central bank. The locus of de jure economic decision-making power in the ECB has shifted dramatically, and there is nothing the new member countries can do about it. The reform of the Governing Council means that the new member countries' chances of making their economic priorities a central part of the monetary policy agenda are somewhat small. Even if the new member state central bank governors were to coalesce, they would not likely be able to dominate the voting in the Governing Council. Thus, while the transition economies, in particular, may have strong preferences to achieve greater incomes, the reform of the Governing Council's voting rules means that such preferences will have a harder time finding a voice within the ECB.

But one must ask if the reform of the Governing Council voting structure will really accomplish its aims. The reform, on the face of it, does not really seem to indicate that meetings of the Governing Council will be made more efficient. If all Executive Board members and NCB governors have a right to participate in the meetings, albeit maybe not to vote, what makes the process more efficient?

Some have questioned whether the reform makes the NCB governors less accountable for the policy of the ECB (Bofinger 2003). Since those voting are not directly responsible for the policies made by the ECB, what would make them defend or take the blame for such policies?

One must wonder if the real aim of the reform was not to make de jure what was already the de facto method of policymaking in the ECB. This refers to the fact that not all NCB governors in the Governing Council carried the same weight when they participated in its deliberations. Interviews with members of the Governing Council, both Executive Board members and NCB governors, about the modalities of voting on the council have indicated that there was already a de facto hierarchy of importance placed on the views of big-economy governors as opposed to small-economy governors.[15] This hierarchy was not contested by the members of the council as they saw it made sense to give more weight to the economies that made up the bulk of the Eurozone's aggregate economic size. Thus, the reform of the Governing Council's voting procedure was simply an institutionalization of what had been the practice of deliberation in the body.

THE INDEPENDENCE AND ACCOUNTABILITY OF THE ECB

One of the most important aspects of the ECB is its policymaking independence from all political and societal authorities. Like the Bundesbank, the ECB has been granted nearly complete operational independence. In almost all indices of central bank independence, the ECB is ranked as the world's most legally independent central bank, while the Bundesbank runs a very close second (Howarth and Loedel 2003).

It is quite clear that the statutory independence of the ECB is based on the rules protecting the independence of the Bundesbank. Both the Bundesbank Law of 1957 and the Treaty on European Union (the Maastricht Treaty) state quite explicitly that the central banks are not to take instructions from governments. The Maastricht Treaty is even more explicit than the Bundesbank Law about who the ECB will not take instructions from because the ECB deals with more layers of government than does the Bundesbank.[16] The Bundesbank Law, Part III, Article 12, states, "Without prejudice to the performance of its functions, the Deutsche Bundesbank is required to support the general economic policy of the Federal Government. In exercising the powers conferred on it by this Act, it is independent of instructions from the Federal Government." The ECB Statute is even more explicit. Article 108 of the ESCB Statute of the Maastricht Treaty says,

> When exercising the powers and carrying out the tasks and duties conferred upon them by this treaty and the Statute of the ESCB, neither the ECB, nor a national central bank, nor any members of their decision-making bodies shall seek or take instructions from Community institutions or bodies, from any government of a Member State or from any other body. The Community institutions and bodies and the governments of the member states undertake to respect this principle and not to seek to influence members of the decision-making bodies of the ECB or of the national central banks in the performance of their tasks.

Aside from this clear language proscribing political pressure on the ECB, there are two other institutional safeguards for the independence of the ECB. One of these safeguards is that the Treaty on European Union, which contains the language cited above, would require the consent of all countries party to it in order to be amended. This would be a very difficult task to accomplish as only one dissenter could prevent change to this statute. It would only take a simple act of the German parliament to change the Bundesbank Law.

Second, there is the nascent European Constitution. While it has not yet been ratified, the constitution states clearly that the ECB is to be independent of political pressure. Article I-29 (3) states,

> The European Central Bank is an Institution, which shall have legal personality. It alone may authorize issue of the euro. It shall be independent in the exercise of its powers and in the management of its finances. Union Institutions, bodies, offices, and agencies and the governments of the member states shall respect that independence.

While its future is still not set, the European Constitution will only serve to strengthen the institutional guarantee of the central bank's independence from political interference in its operations.

This very high degree of independence is quite controversial among some European politicians and commentators. Some worry that the independence of the ECB means that the central bank is not accountable to the European public (See Antenbrink 1999; Berman and McNamara 1999; Verdun 1998). If the ECB does not have to answer to politicians or the public, what is to keep it from making policy that does not reflect the values of the society in which the central bank operates?

The founding statute of the ECB in the Treaty on European Union was meant to assuage the fears of those who find the central bank's autonomy troubling. The ECB, since its founding, has argued that for the central bank to remain operationally independent, it must be accountable (Issing et al. 2001). The ECB claims that it seeks to be both accountable and transparent (ECB 2001, 56). It is accountable in that it is held responsible for the monetary policy it makes. It is transparent in that it allows the public to know why it made the monetary policy decisions it did.

According to the Maastricht Treaty, the ECB is accountable to the European public as a whole. This means that it reports to the EP, which represents the European public. The ECB is required to report to the EP each quarter about its monetary policy and economic conditions in the Eurozone. The EP has no power to demand any policy changes of the ECB: it can merely ask questions of the ECB and expect the decision-makers to provide responses. But even to the EP, the central bank will not reveal the individual positions of Governing Council members.

The ECB does several things to explain why it makes the monetary policy decisions it does. First, after every Governing Council meeting, there is a press conference, at which the president and vice president of the ECB present a short version of the logic behind policy action or inaction.

They then take questions from the press. These can be very enlightening exchanges when it comes to understanding the rationale behind policy.[17]

Also, the ECB publishes a monthly bulletin, which describes economic conditions in the Eurozone and explains the central bank's policy stance. These bulletins are a very important source of information about the central bank and are closely scrutinized by the press and economic actors who have an interest in the ECB's monetary policy.

The ECB also makes its positions known to the public through public speeches by the members of the Executive Board at a wide variety of venues. These include speeches to experts on economics, groups of market participants, and the general lay public, important audiences with which the ECB must communicate.

Finally, the ECB issues an annual report that summarizes the year's economic picture and describes the major personnel and institutional issues at the central bank. The annual report details the financial situation at the ECB, which is a matter of great importance to the member central banks and governments. It also explores all of the major operational issues the central bank has faced during the year.

The ECB's communication strategy is another of its aspects that is clearly inspired by the Bundesbank model. The form and style of the ECB's *Monthly Bulletin* closely resembles the Bundesbank's *Monthly Report*, and the annual reports of the two central banks are also very similar.

The ECB and Bundesbank diverge, however, on reporting to the EP. The authorities at the Bundesbank were not obligated to report or testify to the German Bundestag and never did. Having to testify before politicians was considered a form of political pressure. The ECB's obligation to testify before the EP was a concession to those who were concerned about the central bank's high degree of independence. If the politicians could not control the central bank, at least they could understand the reasoning for the central bank's policies.

MONETARY POLICY OBJECTIVES

Equally important to the ECB are the portions of the Treaty on European Union which outline the monetary policy objectives of the central bank. Article 105 of the treaty says, "The primary objective of the ECSB shall be to maintain price stability. Without prejudice to the objectives of price stability, the ECSB shall support the general economic polices in the Community with a view to contributing to the achievement of the objectives of the Community as laid down in Article 2."[18] Article 2 of the treaty lays out the objectives of "a high level of employment, sustainable and non-inflationary growth, a high degree of competitiveness and convergence of economic performance."

The Bundesbank has a more concise monetary policy mandate, which is to "safeguard the value of the currency" (Part I, paragraph 3). Part 111, paragraph 12, states, "Without prejudice to the performance of its functions, the Deutsche Bundesbank is required to support the general economic policy of the Federal Government." The similarities between the two central banks' statements of objectives are obvious. As with the statement of its legal independence, the ECB's statute is more explicit than the Bundesbank's. Both institutions are given explicit instructions, in very similar language, that their foremost priority is to maintain the value of the currency (i.e., to keep inflation low).

MONETARY POLICY STRATEGY

The policy strategy of the ECB was not laid out in the Maastricht Treaty as were the objectives of monetary policy or the rules of the central bank's independent status. The central bank's policy strategy was worked out among the members of the Governing Council not long before the operational launch of the ECB. The monetary policy strategy is geared toward achieving the bank's primary objective of price stability.

The ECB's Definition of Price Stability

If the monetary policy strategy of the ECB is to achieve price stability, this raises an obvious question: how does one know that one has achieved price stability? The central bank obviously had to devise a definition of price stability in order to operationalize its objective. The Governing Council settled on a definition of price stability as growth in consumer price inflation of below 2 percent for the year. This meant consumer prices for the whole euro area, not just a single EMU member state. The ECB uses a measure of inflation known as the harmonized index of consumer prices (HICP), which ensures that the measure of inflation is essentially the same across all EMU member states and that the central bank has a clear picture of price developments in the Eurozone.

The first years of ECB operation showed that the definition of price stability used by the central bank was not without problems. Several people inside and outside of the ECB's Governing Council argued that the ECB should include in its thinking about price stability both the costs of inflation and the benefits of moderate positive inflation. The ECB's initial definition of price stability, as mentioned previously, was "a year-on-year increase in the Harmonised Index of Consumer Prices (HICP) for the euro area of below 2%" (ECB 2004, 16). In May 2003, the Governing Council announced that it had slightly changed its definition of price stability. Now, the Governing

Council would aim to "keep inflation rates below, but close to, 2% over the medium term" (ECB 2004, 10).

What does the change imply? It does not mean that the ECB has gone soft on inflation; rather, it reflects the experience of the first years of operation of the central bank and the perceived need to incorporate the lessons from that experience into its monetary policy strategy. Thus, the first reason given for the redefinition was that deflation could be a real concern for the central bank, as could inflation. Aiming for an inflation rate close to 2 percent would give the central bank room for maneuver to keep inflation low but positive and, thus, would not threaten the Eurozone economy with deflation.

The second argument for revising the definition of price stability was the "possible presence of measurement bias in the prices index, caused by a lack of adequate adjustment for changes in quality" (ECB 2003, 17). In other words, if the price index was saying that inflation was running at 2 percent, but it was actually running at 0 percent, the ECB could be causing deflation in the economy. Thus, measurement problems with the HICP—these were evident to the Governing Council and its staff—created the need for a margin of error in the aim for 2 percent inflation.

The third reason given by the Governing Council was that "a positive rate of change in price level may have a beneficial effect in facilitating the real adjustment of the economy to various shocks in the presence of downward nominal rigidities" (ECB 2003, 17). This means that the ECB was compensating, to a small degree, for the rigidities in the Eurozone product and labor markets.

The final reason for the revision given by the Governing Council was that maintaining a low positive rate of inflation over the medium term would aid economic convergence among the various regions in the Eurozone. In other words, it might help the lesser developed economies catch up with the more developed ones. This was a particularly important consideration in light of the prospect of adding ten new members to the EU in 2004 and their relative economic backwardness.

The ECB's Two Pillars

The monetary policy strategy of the ECB is geared toward preempting inflation rather than reacting to its development. The central bank refers to this as a "forward-looking" monetary policy strategy (ECB 2001, 45). The Governing Council argues that monetary policy must be forward-looking in order to be effective because monetary policy has transmission effects with a lengthy lag time. In fact, the average lag time for policy to have a significant effect on the economy is one year. Thus, the central bank is making policy for a long period into the future.

In order to make a medium-term-oriented policy, as the ECB calls it, the central bank must have a clear picture of what the future holds in terms of monetary developments for the Eurozone. The Governing Council surveys two primary types of information, or "pillars," when it considers its policy decisions. The first is what the central bank calls "monetary analysis." This means that the central bank analyzes the growth of the money supply, largely but not exclusively the broad money stock, or M3, in order to forecast how inflation will develop in the medium to long term. The idea of using money supply growth as a predictor of future inflation is based on the monetarist logic that there is a solid relationship between the size of the money supply and inflation. (This will be discussed in much greater detail in chapter 4.) The thinking is that rapid and large growth in the money supply in an economy will lead to inflation.

Strict monetarists would argue that the way to manage inflation is to set a money supply target and gear monetary policy toward hitting that target. The ECB has chosen not to go this route. Rather, the ECB developed what it calls a "reference value" for money supply growth over a specific period of time and uses that to assess the inflationary threats caused by money supply growth. It is crucial to note that the reference value is not a money supply target; rather, it is more like an alarm indicator. If money supply growth is grossly exceeding the reference value, this indicates to the Governing Council that inflationary pressures are probably building. There is nothing automatic about responding to the reference value for the ECB; the Governing Council uses its discretion to decide how to respond to the data on the reference value. Thus, the reference value is a monetarist device in that it is based on the idea that there is a strong relationship between the money supply and inflation, but it is not what most strict monetarists would recommend because it does not call for automatic policy responses to missing a money supply growth target.

At the start of ECB operations in 1998, the plan was to conduct a formal review of the reference value on an annual basis. On 8 May 2003, the Governing Council, as part of a partial reformulation of the monetary strategy of the central bank, decided to abandon the formal annual review of the reference value. Instead, the members of the Governing Council decided to focus on the longer-term behavior of money supply growth in the Eurozone (ECB 2004, 19). The monetary analysis pillar would be used to "cross-check" the data coming from the "economic analysis" pillar.

The economic analysis pillar for the ECB is a wide array of economic and financial data, which can indicate price developments in the future. This range of data looks "at the interplay between supply and demand of goods, services, and labor markets" (ECB 2001, 50). This means that a very wide range of price factors is surveyed, from wages to asset prices to the exchange rate. The central bank then tries to create a projection of what the aggregate consumer price situation will look like in the short to medium term based on this wide-ranging overview of economic and financial factors.

As one can imagine, it is immensely difficult to develop a clear picture of the first and second pillars of the ECB's monetary policy strategy. It is notoriously difficult to obtain a good view of the money supply situation in a single country, let alone in an economic area spanning more than a dozen countries. Many of the countries, which are now part of EMU, do not have a tradition of collecting data on money supply growth, and it is a struggle for them to do so now. Even countries that have done it for years have a very difficult time with this task. Germany is a good case in point. The Bundesbank was the first central bank in Europe to make money supply growth a central part of its monetary policy strategy and has been using it since the mid-1970s. Despite all of this experience, it is still a tremendous challenge to come up with reliable figures for money supply growth in Germany because money is constantly flowing in and out of the economy, sometimes going to offshore accounts where it becomes nearly impossible to track. This situation is even more pronounced when one looks at the Eurozone as a whole.

Developing a clear picture of the supply-and-demand situation in the Eurozone is also very difficult. One of the principal reasons this is a challenge is that there is a wide variation in the quality and reliability of the data the ECB receives from the EMU member states. Some of this variation in the quality of data is due to the uneven quality of the data collection done by the national central banks, but a good deal of it is caused by the volatile nature of the data themselves. The data are moving targets as they can sometimes be in a state of sustained change, making a snapshot of the economic or financial situation very difficult to develop.

The fact is that the data the ECB uses to make monetary policy decisions are complex and sometimes ambiguous, which leads the central bank to base its policy decisions on two pillars rather than just one. The two pillars give a more complete view of macroeconomic developments than only one could provide. But it is not simply that more data is better than less. The reasoning is that both money supply growth and supply-and-demand developments are good predictors of future inflation.

The next element in the ECB's monetary policy strategy, after it has collected data and assessed their meaning, is to formulate policy. The Governing Council makes policy aimed at the medium term. Why not the short term or the long term? The short term makes little sense as the effects of policy do not register in the economy for, on average, one year. Aiming monetary policy to correct immediate concerns in the economy can lead to a great deal of volatility and uncertainty in the economy as policy changes frequently.

The short term is also not the correct perspective for monetary policy for the ECB because the ECB operates in a financial environment dominated by bank-based financing. In other words, if firms need to raise financing, they depend primarily on bank loans to do so. All of the present EMU member countries have bank-based financial systems, with relatively less-developed equity markets. If the system were equity market–based, capital would be relatively liquid compared to a bank-based system. It would also mean that the equity market would be quite sensitive to monetary policy decisions. In a system where industry depends mostly on the equity market for financing, the central bank is more likely to be short-term oriented rather than medium-term oriented in order to keep the equity market on an even keel. In contrast, in a bank-based system, in which loans are the principal instrument of finance, the central bank will be more interested in the medium-term outlook for inflation, rather than the fluctuations in the market, because the banks depend on the real value of the return on their loans for profits (Henning 1994; Posen 1993).

The long term is not a viable perspective for the ECB either in that it involves too much uncertainty in the data. The economic and financial picture becomes too murky for the central bank at a certain point, and the frame of prediction must be narrowed. This leaves the medium term as the only viable time frame for policy.

THE INSTRUMENTS OF MONETARY POLICY

Central banks use different instruments to affect monetary conditions depending on the type of economic and financial environment in which they operate. The American Federal Reserve uses open-market operations in the form of the federal funds rate to control the monetary situation in the United States. The Bundesbank used control of the discount credit and Lombard loans to regulate the money supply in Germany.

The ECB controls the Eurozone money supply, hence inflation, through a series of open-market operations. It depends most on main refinancing operations to control the amount of funds in circulation. These are essentially short-term (two-week) loans to banks given at a set interest rate. This interest rate is the most important one in the Eurozone as it signifies the central bank's stance toward the monetary situation, and it is the primary factor in shaping the money supply situation. Although the ECB began its operations by offering the bid rates for its refinancing operations at a fixed rate as of July 2000, it began to offer them at a variable rate to better fit market conditions.

The other levers of monetary policy that the ECB uses are not open-market operations but what are known as standing facilities. These are the marginal lending facilities and the deposit facilities. The marginal lending facility provides overnight loans to banks at a set interest rate. The interest rate on these loans is usually much higher than the main refinancing rates;

thus, these loans are used much less frequently. The deposit facility allows banks to make overnight deposits with the ECB at a set interest rate. This operation is meant to reduce liquidity in the financial system when needed.

FINANCIAL MARKET SUPERVISION

One area of policy authority in which the ECB is weak relative to some other central banks is financial market supervision. The ECB was given three tasks to perform in this area according to Articles 105.4 and 105.5 of the Maastricht Treaty and Article 25.1 of the ESCB Statute. The tasks are financial stability monitoring, provision of advice, and the promotion of cooperation.

Financial stability monitoring refers to the function of monitoring "cyclical and structural developments in the euro-area/EU banking sector and in other financial sectors" (ECB 2004, 1). The ECB is to do this along with the other members of the Eurosystem (i.e., the national central banks of the member countries of the Eurozone and the various national financial supervisory agencies). The monitoring is done to assess how vulnerable the financial sector is to shocks and how likely it is that the financial sector can withstand those shocks. This supervision is coordinated in the ESCB Banking Supervision Committee. The ECB publishes three reports a year that outline its assessments of the stability of the EU financial sector. The reports are *EU Banking Sector Stability, Structural Analysis of the EU Banking Sector,* and *ECB Annual Report.*

The ECB's provision-of-advice function refers to the technical expertise that the ECB is asked to provide when EU-level or national-level authorities are designing rules and regulations for financial supervision. The ECB also reserves the right to contribute advice on these matters even when it is not requested. The ECB can make its views known through many avenues. Among them are the Basel Committee on Banking Supervision, the European Banking Committee, the European Securities Committee, and the Committee of European Banking Supervisors (ECB 2004, 1).

The promotion-of-cooperation function means that the ECB has taken on the task of increasing cooperation between central banks and supervisory authorities in the EU. This work is carried out by the ESCB Banking Supervisory Committee. These meetings can lead to memorandums of understanding that iron out the details of cooperation between the interested parties.

These financial-sector supervisory powers are noteworthy in that they are rather limited. The ECB has relatively weak powers of financial-sector supervision relative to many other central banks. This may seem somewhat perplexing given the attempts to create a more integrated and efficient European financial sector, which today remains somewhat fragmented along national lines.

One must ask why the ECB was given such limited powers of supervision over Eurozone financial markets. The answer lies in the unwillingness of national governments to yield control of the oversight of their own financial sectors. During the negotiations that went into the Treaty on European Union, a majority of governments would not entertain the idea of ceding such a politically important power as financial market supervision to the ECB. Because the nature of the financial market is important to governments in terms of how they finance their deficits and allocate politically sensitive credit in the economy, they are loathe to abandon control of financial-sector oversight. The EU member governments have publicly supported this decision by saying that it is in line with the concept of subsidiarity.[19]

In fact, Europe may be heading away from more centralized ECB control of financial market supervision rather than toward more ECB control. The German government created a Federal Agency for Financial Market Supervision, which stripped the Bundesbank of its financial-sector supervisory powers. The German government has also been pushing for more intergovernmental cooperation on EU-level banking supervision, and the ECB is not part of these plans. Thus, the ECB's powers in the realm of financial market supervision are likely to remain limited in the foreseeable future.

The ECB has been troubled by its relatively weak powers to supervise the Eurozone financial sector (see Padoa-Schioppa 2003, 2004). Clearly, the ECB has an interest in the health of the Eurozone financial sector as crises in that sector will certainly have a negative effect on monetary conditions in the Eurozone. In other words, there is a direct link between the ECB's monetary policy duties and the health of the Eurozone financial sector. Thus, the ECB wants to preclude financial crises though its monetary policies rather than deal with them once they have started. Right now, given the present structure of financial-sector supervisory power, it has very limited ability to do that.

EXCHANGE RATE POLICYMAKING

One of the most confusing aspects of the ECB's powers and obligations is its role in exchange rate policymaking. The Treaty on European Union is not very clear on the breakdown of responsibility for exchange rate policymaking in the EU. The provisions in the treaty that refer to exchange rate policymaking powers reflect a compromise, which is open to different interpretations.[20]

The issue over who would control exchange rate policymaking in the Eurozone divided European policymakers into two camps. On one side were EU-member governments who wanted to keep exchange rate policymaking authority at the intergovernmental level because the exchange rate could be such an important factor in their country's economic health and therefore could affect their chances of reelection.

On the other side were the European central bankers and some EU governments who believed it was dangerous to give politicians the power to set exchange rates and obligate the central bank to maintain them. The key concern was that the operations to maintain such rates could undermine the central bank's ability to protect domestic price stability. This had been a perennial issue at the Bundesbank, which chafed at the idea of having to intervene in international currency markets to maintain the deutsche mark's exchange rate with other currencies, be it in the Bretton Woods system, the "snake," or the European Monetary System (EMS). These intervention obligations were always viewed as threatening to the German central bank's price-stability mandate. The Bundesbankers would have much preferred a floating exchange rate system.

The compromise that was worked out gives exchange rate policy power to the ECB's Governing Council, the European Commission, and the Council of Ministers together. Thus, many have concluded that the exchange rate policy needs to be made by consensus among the three bodies. Also, the treaty, in an attempt to placate the central bankers, says that any exchange rate policy made may not jeopardize price stability in the Eurozone. The ECB assumes that it will determine if the exchange rate policy is a threat to price stability, although this is not explicitly stated in the treaty.

Since the launch of the ECB in 1998, there has been no attempt to create an exchange rate policy per se. This means that no explicit exchange rate target or zone has been set for the central bank to maintain. European politicians have suggested that there would be merit in creating exchange rate zones for the euro–dollar exchange rate; however, the ECB has criticized this as a bad idea as it would limit the central bank's room for maneuver on domestic monetary policy,[21] and there was no widespread political support among Eurozone governments to adopt exchange rate zones. Thus, for the foreseeable future, the ECB will not have an exchange rate policy.

There is one minor example of where the ECB has maintained an exchange rate policy, and that is with the Danish krona because the Danes are part of the new exchange rate mechanism (ERM), or ERM II,[22] a fixed exchange rate regime that replaced the old ERM/EMS. The ERM II is not an obligation burden for the ECB because there is only one country in the ERM and the regime's fluctuation margins are ±15 percent around the bilateral exchange rate. The ECB and the Danish central bank have not needed to intervene to maintain the exchange rate since the inception of the ERM II. Even if the central banks had had to intervene, it would not have been of any consequence to the general monetary policy operations of the ECB as the volume of intervention would be minuscule, and there would be no impact on the domestic monetary situation in the Eurozone.

This does not mean that the ECB does not take the exchange rate of the euro vis-à-vis other major currencies into account when it makes monetary policy. If the exchange rate threatens domestic price stability, the central bank will do what it can to change that exchange rate to end the threat. Chapter 4 explores just how important the exchange rate has been to the ECB since it commenced monetary policy operations.

THE ECB OUTSIDE OF THE EUROZONE

Another confusing aspect of the ECB's policymaking powers and responsibilities is its role in international forums outside of the Eurozone. As is the case with exchange rate policy, there was an attempt to make the ECB part of a team of EU institutions when it came to this policy area. When it comes to issues of monetary policy in the Eurozone, the ECB shares the duties of representation with Eurozone finance ministers.

The ECB has observer status at the International Monetary Fund (IMF) and the Organization for Economic Cooperation and Development (OECD).[23] The primary representatives of the Eurozone are the finance ministers of the various member states. Because the ECB does not represent a state, it is oddly situated to participate in the meetings of those organizations.[24]

At the Group of Seven (G-7) meetings, the president of the ECB and the finance ministers of the Eurozone member states represent the Eurozone. Suggestions to develop a single representative for the Eurozone finance ministers have not been successful as governments have not been able to agree on how to accomplish unified representation.

The complicated and limited nature of the ECB's role in fora outside of the Eurozone means that the ECB does not have as powerful a voice in monetary affairs that bear on the Eurozone as it would wish. Eurozone governments could not agree to give the ECB significant power to represent the Eurozone in international fora because of the potential loss of control over agreements that could have serious political consequences in the domestic polities of Eurozone members. As was the case with exchange rate policymaking power, the Eurozone governments could not bring themselves to grant the ECB policymakers all of the powers they wanted. It remains to be seen if the status quo will persist, as the shared responsibilities of representing the Eurozone do not lend themselves to efficiency or clarity of position in G-7 meetings (McNamara and Meunier 2002).

But the leaders of the member states of the EU have recognized that the lack of a single voice speaking for the Eurozone governments weakens their aggregate ability to be heard. Thus, as part of the deliberations over the European Constitution, an agreement was reached to create a "Mr. Euro," who would be a Eurozone member-state finance minister selected by his or her peers for a period of two years. This individual would represent the Eurozone at the G-7 and IMF meetings, as well as in bilateral meetings.[25] She or he would also chair the Eurogroup meetings over the same period (see chapter 4 for a discussion of the Eurogroup). The governments of the Eurozone argued that they could appoint a Mr. Euro before the ratification of the constitution as the Eurogroup is an informal group, and, therefore, there was no need for formal ratification of the constitution to name the group's new head.[26]

Even though the European Constitution remains unratified, European governments decided to go ahead with the plan for Mr. Euro because of the perceived pressing need for effective representation in international fora. After some initial wrangling over who would be appointed, on 10 September 2004, Luxembourg prime minister Jean-Claude Juncker was named to the post. Thus, Juncker, along with ECB President Trichet, will represent the Eurozone at meetings dealing with international monetary affairs.

The creation of the post of Mr. Euro is not without its potential ramifications for the ECB. While it is not problematic for the central bank to have Mr. Euro accompany it to international monetary fora, the aims of some Eurozone governments for the position are a source of concern for the ECB. Nicolas Sarkozy, the French finance minister, called the Eurogroup "an embryo of a European economic government." A long-term, more powerful president would strengthen that group's ability to hold sway over the ECB.[27] Obviously, the ECB would not welcome such an institutional development.

RECRUITMENT AND STAFFING

Another very important aspect of the central bank that is crucial to understanding its operations is who actually runs the ECB. This means that we need to know who the top decision-makers and their staff are. Knowing what type of people are recruited to manage the euro area's monetary policy tells us a lot about why that monetary policy looks the way it does.

The issue of recruitment of the management of the ECB is laid out in the Treaty on European Union. The treaty deals with the appointment of members of the Executive Board but not with the appointment of the governors of the national central banks. The governors are appointed by their own governments under national statutes. Article 11.2 of the Treaty on European Union says that members of the Executive Board are appointed by the agreement of the national governments of the EMU member countries. The people nominated by the national governments must also be vetted by the EP and the Governing Council itself. Once the national governments, the EP, and the Governing Council have agreed to the nomination, the Executive Board member is appointed for an eight-year, nonrenewable term.

Article 11.2 is also important because it states that "members of the Executive Board shall be appointed from among persons of recognized standing and professional experience in monetary and banking matters." This is directly inspired by the Bundesbank Law, which says the members of the directorate must have special professional qualifications. The aim of the ECB statute, as was the case with the Bundesbank Law, is to ensure that individuals who are informed of the complex technology of monetary policy are appointed as the decision-makers in the central bank and not political hacks who simply take policy guidance from their political mentors.

If we examine the backgrounds of the members of the ECB's Executive Board in 2003, we find that all of them had a significant background in economics education and a great deal of practical experience as well. There is a distinct technocratic pattern in the background of the Governing Council members. Of the eighteen members of the Governing Council in the summer of 2003, eleven had Ph.D.s in economics. Only one had no educational background in economics, but this person had substantial experience as a member of the staff of his national central bank. By far the most common occupational background for either NCB governors or members of the ECB Executive Board is experience working in the ranks of the national central banks. In 2003, twelve of the eighteen had come up through the ranks of the staffs of their national central banks to reach their present positions. An academic background is the second most common occupational background. In 2003, nine of the eighteen had backgrounds in academics. Working in the finance ministry of their countries was less common, with six of the group having done that during their careers. Only three of the eighteen had backgrounds in business, specifically commercial banking.

The vast majority of the decision-makers come from the central banking profession and academics. Only a small number have been part of the business, and more politicized, world of the finance ministry. Thus, just by looking at the backgrounds of those in the principal decision-making structures of the ECB, we can conclude that, in general, the Governing Council is a body that represents neither the world of commercial banking nor the world of politics; rather, it comprises individuals who have spent their careers principally devoted to the issues of monetary policy, either in practice or theory.

The staff of the ECB below the level of the Governing Council is hugely important to the running of the central bank. The staff collects and filters the economic data and prepares the reports that members of the Governing Council present at their meetings. The staff can shape, or at least reinforce, the thinking of the people for whom they work. This is true in any central bank; thus, it is important to know who the staff is.

The staff of the ECB comprises three groups of individuals. There are those who are direct support staff for the Executive Board members. This includes technical support staff like economists and secretaries. The direct support staff of the Executive Board members usually comprises people whom the board members knew before they came into the ECB and whom they wanted with them in the central bank. Thus, most of them are drawn from the national central banks where the Executive Board members were prior to going to the ECB. Therefore, the Executive Board members' thoughts about monetary policy prior to coming into the central bank are reinforced by having much of the same staff with them in the ECB.

There is also the staff of the national central banks of the ESCB who support the governors. This group is not really a formal part of the ECB, per se, but its members do influence what goes on in Governing Council meetings as a result of the influence they exercise over the NCB governors and the information they provide to the ECB.

This group dwarfs the ECB staff. There are slightly more than 1,000 staff members at the ECB headquarters in Frankfurt. There are approximately 55,000 staff members in the national central banks. The Bundesbank alone has over 15,000 staff members.[28] Why is the ECB staff so small compared to the NCB staff? Indeed, part of the answer is that some NCB staffs are unnecessarily bloated, and the ECB uses its staff more efficiently. But a much bigger part of the answer is that the ECB staff builds on what the NCB staffs do for it. In other words, the NCB staffs are, in large part, support staffs for the ECB staff. The ECB and NCB division of labor is based on the notion of decentralization of operational tasks. Thus, the implementation of monetary policy and the operation of the payments system are handled at the NCB level. The ECB sees itself as the coordinator of the operations of the NCBs.[29] The one major operation that the NCBs are not involved in implementing is intervention in the foreign exchange markets. This is done solely by the staff of the Executive Board members on their orders. The NCB staffs create the reports of national economic pictures that the ECB staff uses to create the broader Eurozone view of what is going on in the economy. Without the NCB staffs, the ECB staff would have to grow substantially.

The NCB staffs are not all of equal quality, which becomes an issue when having to depend on them for economic data and analysis. The standards for staff hiring differ substantially between EMU member states. This is a product of the professionalization of the bureaucratic culture in the EMU member states and the experience of the central bank with such tasks. In the days when the European central banks, for all intents and purposes, followed the policy lead of the Bundesbank, there was not much need for small-country central banks to develop big professional staffs or to collect great quantities of economic data. Now, some central banks are having to catch up in data collection and hiring quality staff.

The third group of staff at the ECB is the general support personnel who are not assigned to a particular Executive Board member. These are individuals who work on data collection and analysis, as well as the day-to-day issues of running the central bank, but not on the specific policy issues being considered by the Governing Council. These individuals are hired through an open selection process, and all EU member state nationals are eligible.

One issue of central concern in hiring the staff for the ECB was the national makeup of the personnel. This was important to the politicians who created the ECB, as well as to the Governing Council members themselves. There was agreement that the staff of the ECB should think of themselves as working for Europe and not as representatives of their home countries. Thus, there would be no national quotas for hiring, no focus on national origin in the workplace, or no signs in the workplace to designate one's country of origin. The ECB does not even keep records of the breakdown of its staff by national origin.[30]

THE MONETARY POLICY OPERATIONS OF THE ECB

We have seen so far that the ECB is a central bank with a clear mandate to achieve price stability, a very high degree of legal independence, and a strict set of self-imposed rules about how to conduct monetary policy. Also, the ECB operates in a more complex economic and political environment than most central banks in the world face. But the political and economic environment the central bank faces actually works in its favor, making it easier for the ECB to maintain its operational independence. Let us turn to the record of how the ECB has made monetary policy since January 1999.

The main issue that we want to address is whether there is consistency between the stated policy strategy of the ECB and the actual policy actions of the central bank. Has the ECB followed its defined price-stability mandate, or does it seem to have made other issues, such as promoting economic growth, a priority? Rather than exploring specific monetary policy decisions, it seems that the trends in the economic data should tell us which picture emerges.

The picture for inflation in the Eurozone since the launch of the euro in January 1999 has been relatively positive for the ECB. As stated earlier, the ECB defines price stability as annual growth in the HICP of below 2 percent. Figure 3.1 shows inflation from January 1999 to March 2003.

As figure 3.1 shows, there was a steady rise in inflation from July 1999 to March 2000, with the general trend peaking in June 2001. We can see that for about half of the period under investigation, the ECB did not keep inflation within its price-stability range. From April 2000 until May 2002, the ECB was operating in an environment where inflation was above the central bank's

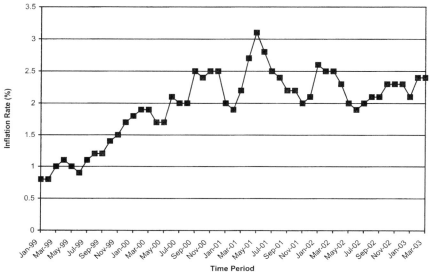

Figure 3.1.   Inflation (HICP)

stated allowable limit. Was this because the central bank was not pursuing its price-stability-oriented monetary policy or because of some other factor?

If we look at the history of interest rate decisions made by the ECB during this period, we see that the central bank started a trend of pronounced tightening in the fall of 1999. Interest rates were raised in 25 and 50 basis-point increments from October 1999 until November 2000. Main refinancing operations bids rose from a level of 2.5 percent to 4.75 percent. Figure 3.2 shows the trend of ECB interest rates from January 1999 until April 2003.

This not only kept real interest rates higher in the Eurozone than in the United States during this time, but it was done during a period of slumping growth. Figure 3.3 shows the trend in real growth in gross domestic product from January 1999 until December 2003.

As we can see, the growth picture in the Eurozone turns sour in the second quarter of 2000. There is a steady decline in real growth rates for two years, until the first quarter of 2002. Thus, if we look at the overall picture of inflation, interest rates, and growth rates, we see that the ECB has seemed to make a very strong effort to maintain Eurozone price stability. The central bank raises rates substantially and keeps them high in response to a rise in inflation and despite the clear slump in growth rates. Thus, looking at the inflation rate alone does not tell us if the ECB really pursued a price-stability-oriented policy. When combined with interest rate and growth trends, the inflation picture shows a central bank very intent on curbing growth in consumer prices. As chapter 4 will show, the ECB began its monetary policy

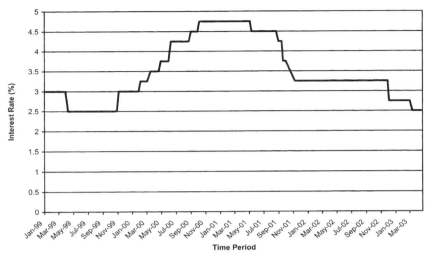

Figure 3.2.   Interest Rates: Main Refinancing Operations

operations under difficult circumstances as the depreciation of the euro on foreign exchange markets led to a difficult inflation scene in the Eurozone. Rather whether the ECB has remained true to its monetary policy strategy, the question has been raised quite often whether the ECB should not move away from that strategy to aid growth in the Eurozone. As long as the decision-makers in the ECB remain convinced that price stability is the foundation for economic growth, there is little chance of a change in strategy.

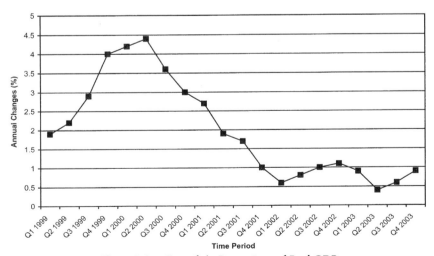

Figure 3.3.   Growth in Percentage of Real GDP

CONCLUSION

This chapter has set out to describe the structure and operational principles of the ECB. It has shown that the ECB is a highly decentralized central bank, operating with multiple nodes of decision-making power. The shared policy responsibility between the Executive Board members and the NCB governors is a close replica of the German Bundesbank's structure, albeit at the supranational level. Like the Bundesbank, the ECB is a central bank that places a premium on ensuring that it be kept independent of political or societal pressure. This structure, combined with a societal and economic environment that does not challenge the operations of the ECB, means that the central bank has great discretion to implement its operational principles as it sees fit.

Because the ECB has so much policymaking autonomy, in many ways it is an interesting experiment in how technocrats can implement economic ideas as they see fit. Not even the Bundesbank had the ability to make policy so independently of political or economic pressures. Thus, the ECB could be an important incubator of new monetary policy ideas.

NOTES

1. The ECB General Council comprises the president, the vice president, and the national central bank governors of all EU member states. The General Council does not make monetary policy decisions but rather shares information on the European economic situation and helps prepare the way for EU member states eventually to adopt the euro and become part of EMU.

2. "Duisenberg under Fire over Euro Remarks," *Financial Times*, 11 July 2001.

3. "'Mr. Euro' Takes Charge of Tricky Balancing Act," *Financial Times*, 22 September 2000.

4. Interview with an EMU member state central bank governor, June 2000.

5. "Builder of the Euro Team Spirit," *Financial Times*, 7 December 1998.

6. "Trichet's Chance," *Financial Times*, 6 November 2003.

7. "Inside the ECB: Consensus and Europeanism Rule," *Financial Times*, 22 October 1999.

8. "Builder of the Euro Team Spirit," *Financial Times*, 7 December 1998.

9. Interview with Executive Board member.

10. "Germany Urges Caution on Interest Rates," *Financial Times*, 7 March 2000.

11. "Bankers' Silence Is Golden for Euro," *Financial Times*, 17 August 1999.

12. This is a more pressing concern in the large, older member states because of what they may lose in terms of relative voting power in the expanded Governing Council.

13. *European Central Bank Monthly Bulletin*, May 2003.

14. The composition of the groups will be adjusted when there are changes in GDP and TABS-MFI data, as well as when the number of national central bank governors increases due to EU expansion.

15. Interview with members of the ECB Governing Council.

16. See Bundesbank Law (1957) Part III, Paragraph 12, and Article 108 of the Treaty on European Union.

17. The ECB has ruled out using code words, which it had done previously, to indicate which way it was leaning in interest-rate policy. This would give the central bank more leeway to make policy as it sees fit. "ECB Rules Out Smoke Signals on Interest Rate Moves," *Financial Times*, 3 August 2004.

18. See Article 105, Treaty of European Union. It goes on to say, "The ESCB shall act in accordance with the principles of an open market economy with free competition, favouring an efficient allocation of resources, and in compliance with the principles set out in Article 4."

19. *Subsidiarity* refers to the concept that power to make policy decisions should be decentralized to the national level unless such decisions can only be taken effectively at the EU level.

20. See Howarth and Loedel (2003, 105–107) for an excellent discussion of the confusing nature of the treaty on this matter.

21. "Issing Rejects Euro Target Zones Call," *Financial Times*, 30 December 1998.

22. ERM stands for "exchange rate mechanism." It was the formal name of the intervention rules of the European Monetary System (EMS).

23. See Howarth and Loedel (2003, 112–114) for a description of the ECB's role in the IMF and OECD.

24. The ECB's relationships with the IMF and the OECD have not been without tension as these two organizations have both criticized the ECB for having an overly tight monetary policy. See "OECD Hits at Operations of European Central Bank," *Financial Times*, 1 March 2000, and "Duisenberg Hits at IMF over Criticism of Monetary Policy," *Financial Times*, 14 April 2000.

25. "Austria Threatens Plan to Delay Plans for 'Mr. Euro' Post," *Financial Times*, 7 September 2004.

26. "Ministers Delay Decision on Creating Job of 'Mr. Euro,'" *Financial Times*, 6 July 2004.

27. "Ministers Delay Decision."

28. "Central Banks Slow to Fight the Battle of the Bulge," *Financial Times*, 29 January 2001.

29. Interview with an official of the Human Resources Directorate at the ECB.

30. There has been some talk of the ECB's being an "Anglo-Saxon" institution because of the use of English as the working language in the central bank. The *Financial Times* made a point of this in 1998, stressing that 10 percent of the staff at the central bank was British, even though the United Kingdom was not part of EMU. See "Anglo-Saxon Face of Bank for Europe," *Financial Times*, 28 July 2003. This may be wishful thinking on the part of the British newspaper as one could point out that none of the senior policy officials at the bank are British.

4

The European Central Bank's Operating Environment

The operational principles and structures of the European Central Bank (ECB) certainly affect the way it makes policy. In order to understand the functioning of the ECB, however, we need also to explore the external environment in which the central bank operates. This means we need to look at the kinds of economic and political forces outside of the bank that condition both how and why the ECB makes the policy that it does.

The ECB is a central bank that faces a unique political, societal, and economic environment among the ranks of central banks. The ECB is the only central bank in the world that is truly supranational. This means it is the only one that does not interact with a single national government but with multiple national governments and supranational political authorities as well.

Not only does the ECB not operate in a unified political system or national society, but it also does not make policy in a single national economic realm. While the economies of the European Monetary Union (EMU) member states are treated as a single entity by the ECB when it makes policy, there are some important national differences between the economies. Thus, the ECB operates in a world of economic complexity like no other central bank and also has to make policy for multiple societies with different histories, traditions, and values.

The key question raised by examining the political and economic environment in which the ECB operates is, does it aid or hinder the ECB's ability to fulfill its mandate to maintain price stability in the Eurozone? The answer to this question is that, for the time being, the economic and political environments do help the central bank achieve its stated goal. This is because these two facets of the ECB's operational environment give the central bank policymaking autonomy, either because the relevant actors in the environment agree with the central bank's policies or because those who oppose the central bank's policies cannot coalesce to pressure the central bank sufficiently to change its policy course.

This chapter begins with an exploration of the political context facing the ECB. This includes the national, European Union (EU), and international levels of political authority. Next, it describes the societal context in which the ECB functions, treating both the organized and nonorganized aspects of European society. Finally, the chapter delves into the economic environment confronting the ECB. It describes and analyzes the nature of the economic and financial structures in the Eurozone and how they could constrain or shape ECB policy.

THE POLITICAL CONTEXT

The political context in which ECB works is unique. No other central bank is a supranational organization operating in the economic space of fifteen (soon to be many more) sovereign states. The ECB does not operate in a unitary political system but in one characterized by multiple levels of policy authority. The ECB must contend with not only the several national governments but with EU institutions as well. Thus, the political space in which the ECB operates can best be characterized as complex and, to a degree, confusing.

National Government Appointment Powers

The national governments of the EMU member states are important to the central bank principally for their appointment powers. The national governments have the power to appoint not only their national central bank (NCB) governors but also the members of the Executive Board. This is an important power in that who sits in the bank has a lot to do with the types of policies that will be pursued. But national governments have no powers to recall the decision-makers once they are appointed. Nor do they have any powers to issue instructions to the central bankers once they are in the central bank. Thus, legally, the powers of the national governments vis-à-vis the central bank are extremely circumscribed.

The power of appointment over who sits on the Executive Board, especially who is to be president, is of immense political importance to some of the national governments for a couple of reasons. First, it is a matter of national prestige to have one of your nationals sit on the Executive Board. The top honor is to have your national act as president. Politicians can take credit at home for having "their man or woman" named as president of the bank. Second, the national government may hope that having its national on the Executive Board could mean that its preferences for monetary policy will get a more sympathetic hearing. Thus, every government hopes that it can successfully get its people into the positions on the Executive Board.

While all of the national governments may hope to get their people onto the Executive Board, there are some obvious constraints on who can be picked. First, there is the rule that the person must have expertise in economics and monetary issues. Second, there is the political reality that excludes certain options for stacking the board. For example, no country will be able to get more than one national onto the Executive Board at a time. While this is not a written rule, it is clear that allowing this to happen would violate the ECB's principle of broad national representation at the central bank.

Another unwritten rule that seems to be developing is that there must be some gender diversity on the board. While the world of central banking is a male-dominated domain, the ECB, since its inception, has had at least one female on the Executive Board at all times. Thus, when the board's one female, the Finn Srikka Hämlinnen, retired in 2003, she was replaced by another female, Austria's Gertrude Tumpel-Gugerell. The issue of gender diversity in the institution is particularly important in the northern European member states, many of which have gender quotas in some political institutions.

By far the biggest appointment issue at the ECB has been the selection of the president. The president from the inception of the ECB was the Netherlands' Wim Duisenberg. Duisenberg was a compromise appointment. He was initially acceptable to both Germany and France, the countries who did the most to get their candidate into the president's job.

The Germans could not nominate a German for the president's job because then it would look like the Germans ran the ECB. As noted earlier, the ECB was in many ways an attempt by many Europeans to get out from under German monetary dominance. An ECB led by a German would make it seem as if such dominance had been institutionalized at the European level. Hans Tietmeyer, the president of the Bundesbank and perhaps the most respected central bank governor in Europe at the time, said, "I have said clearly that I am not a candidate. I do not regard it as the best solution that a German should be the first president of the ECB."[1] Tietmeyer threw his weight behind Duisenberg's candidacy.

The Germans knew and trusted Duisenberg, who as president of the Dutch central bank had a reputation for agreeing with the German

conception of monetary policymaking and the notion of central bank independence. Duisenberg had been president of the European Monetary
Institute (EMI), the institution that acted as a preparatory forerunner to the
ECB. His leadership there had been decided by a vote of the governors of
the central banks that participated in the EMI. Thus, Duisenberg was the
central bankers' choice.

The French government, on the other hand, was determined to get one of
its nationals, specifically, Jean-Claude Trichet, the governor of the Banque de
France, accepted as president of the ECB. French president Jacques Chirac,
who had initially agreed to Duisenberg's appointment, changed his mind
right before the appointment was to be made and nominated Trichet. This
set off a political battle with the German government, which viewed this
nomination as (1) a betrayal of an informal agreement between governments, (2) a French government attempt to gain influence over monetary
policymaking in the ECB, and (3) a threat to the credibility of the ECB as
an independent central bank. While the German government had no problem with Trichet as a central banker as he has impeccable central banking
credentials, it feared that if the French government were so adamant about
having a French ECB president, it must be because it wanted to encroach
on the independence of the central bank. Thus, a compromise deal was
worked out where Duisenberg would serve half of his eight-year term as
president; he then would step down, and Trichet would take over.[2] This
looked to most observers like a political deal that could possibly infringe on
the independence of the central bank.

The French and German governments, in an attempt at damage control,
claimed that there had been no deal to share the term between Duisenberg
and Trichet. Duisenberg, in an effort to salvage his own credibility, also
claimed that he had not been pressured into accepting only half the term
but had decided on this course for personal reasons.[3] At the press conference
where the nominees were announced, they were met by laughter from the
press corps. These assertions simply stretched credulity. The matter was
made worse when President Chirac made the following statement at the
press conference: "One has to defend one's own interests. We are in a
system of Europe of nations where each nation defends its interest."[4] This
overt politicization of the appointment process rattled financial markets and
advocates of central bank independence. Many feared that the infant ECB
was becoming politicized. But the actual ramifications of the presidential
appointment process on the policies of the ECB were negligible. The issue
of Trichet's appointment was really about national prestige and not about
stacking the ECB with a lackey of the Chirac government in France. Trichet
was anything but Chirac's man. As a monetary hawk, Trichet had resisted
very heated criticism about the Banque de France's monetary policy after the
start of its operational independence in 1994. Thus, the only asset Trichet

had for the French government was that he was French, thereby giving France prestige in that one of its own led the ECB.[5]

As noted in chapter 3, Trichet did become president of the ECB in 2003. Thus, it appears that there was, in fact, a secret deal to replace Duisenberg with Trichet midterm. While Duisenberg claimed that he was resigning as president for personal reasons, it was widely believed that he was fulfilling the promise made at his appointment to make way for Trichet midway through his eight-year term. As this had been expected by a number of ECB watchers, it did not have a noticeable effect on markets.

Thus, despite the raucous political battle over the appointment of the ECB president, the appointment process has posed no serious challenge to the principles of the ECB. No government has brought forward clearly unqualified or politicized candidates. In fact, the ECB's Executive Board is much less politically tainted than the American Federal Reserve's Board of Governors is or even the Bundesbank's Central Bank Council was.

Politicians and the Operational Independence of the ECB

National governments' lack of power over the ECB is only exacerbated by the fact that the national governments would find it very difficult to achieve a consensus to pressure the ECB in a certain direction on policy. Not only is there a strong tradition of central bank independence in some countries, foremost in Germany, but there have been different economic interests among some of the national governments at various times. Also, and perhaps most importantly, all EU member states would have to agree to any change in the Treaty on European Union (Maastricht Treaty) that could limit the independence of the central bank. This is exceedingly unlikely to happen because it would be nearly impossible to get all EU governments to agree to such a departure from the spirit of the ECB's original design.

The ECB also faces relatively weak EU institutions. The Treaty on European Union calls on the ECB to report regularly to the European Parliament (EP). While it may be troublesome and annoying for the president and vice president to testify before the EP, there is no threat to the ECB's independence inherent in such testimony. The EP has no power to amend the Maastricht Treaty, and it has no operational leverage over the central bank, such as controlling its budget.

The European Commission has little interaction with the ECB on policy matters. The EC commissioner on monetary affairs has no direct power in ECB affairs. She or he may state what the commission would like to see happen in terms of financial or monetary issues in Europe. This position has not been used to pressure the ECB since its inception but rather to guide European governments to work toward greater financial and fiscal policy coordination.

The more important EU institutions for the ECB are intergovernmental institutions dealing with monetary affairs. Of the two, Ecofin and the Eurogroup, the Eurogroup is by far the more important.

Ecofin is the Economic and Financial Affairs Council in the EU. It comprises the finance ministry as well as economics ministry officials from all of the EU member states. Ecofin is chaired by the finance minister from the country that holds the EU's rotating presidency at the time. It is the formal representative body of the EU member states' finance ministers, and it has significant EU statutory authority over financial and economic matters. It has been where EU governments have hashed out agreements on much of the EU's financial and monetary rules and institutions. The ECB can participate in Ecofin's meetings, but it rarely does.

Since the inception of the ECB, Ecofin has been supplemented by what is now known as the Eurogroup. The Eurogroup is an informal grouping of the EMU member states' finance ministers, plus the economic affairs commissioner and the president of the ECB. It excludes those EU member states that are not part of EMU. At the present, it is intended to be a forum where the finance ministers and the ECB can discuss the pertinent financial, economic, and monetary issues in the EMU. It has no statutory authority to make any decisions but is merely a forum to discuss matters of mutual concern.

The Eurogroup has been altered slightly since its inception by the decision of Eurozone governments to appoint a weightier president to lead the group. In September 2004, as discussed in chapter 3, the Eurozone governments appointed Luxembourg prime minister Jean-Claude Juncker president of the Eurogroup starting in January 2005. This new position, dubbed "Mr. Euro," is meant to give the Eurozone a more unified and coherent voice in international monetary fora by having one person, rather than the separate national representatives, represent the Eurozone finance ministers. The creation of Mr. Euro does not signify that the Eurogroup is gaining power on the ECB.

When the idea of the Eurogroup was floated by the French government in the run-up to EMU, it was not meant to be a talk-shop about EMU-related topics. The French government envisioned the group as a form of economic government to act as a political counterweight to the ECB.[6] The German government primarily resisted this idea under pressure from the Bundesbank, among others, and the French were forced to agree to the Eurogroup as an informal grouping within Ecofin.

The Eurogroup plays an important role in that it is a forum for an exchange of information between the ECB and the finance ministers. The finance ministers can tell the ECB president of their domestic economic and financial concerns, and the ECB president can relay what the central bank would like the EMU member governments to do to facilitate EMU monetary and financial operations. Such issues would include fiscal policy, budget deficits, and the euro exchange rate. These are matters of mutual concern, where an exchange of information is helpful to all in the group.[7]

It is important to note that despite the French government's desire, the Eurogroup has no power to control the monetary policy of the ECB.[8] It has no power under EU law and contains nothing like a majority of finance ministers who would agree to try to pressure the ECB on monetary policy issues.[9] Thus, the Eurogroup is far from being an economic government or political counterweight to the ECB.

The Stability and Growth Pact

The lack of a unified political authority has one very important downside for the ECB. Crucially, there is no single fiscal policy in the Eurozone, but fifteen separate policies. This makes it difficult for the ECB to operate in an environment of convergent economic conditions across the Eurozone. Also, it is important that EMU member states not make fiscal policies that act counter to the monetary policy of the ECB. Specifically, if some member states enact very expansionary fiscal policies, those policies could work against the ECB's price-stability-oriented monetary policy and introduce inflation into the Eurozone.

There were major discussions among academic and practicing economists about the issue of EMU as an optimal currency area. The key issue at the heart of this discussion was whether the various national economies of the EMU member states were operating on roughly the same business cycle, thereby creating an optimal currency area, or operating on very divergent business cycles, making a common monetary policy a very difficult thing to formulate. Which business cycle should the central bank focus on if several moved in opposite directions?

The optimal currency area problem was complicated by the fact that governments could make fiscal policy on their own within EMU under the Treaty on European Union. Divergent fiscal policies, without any degree of coordination, would belie the notion that the Eurozone was a single economic area. The ECB, in an environment of nationally controlled fiscal policies, would be trying to make one monetary policy for myriad national economies. But trying to get the national governments to give up such an important economic tool and symbol of national sovereignty as fiscal policy was an impossibility in the negotiations over EMU (Dyson 2002).

In addition to the issue of how to make monetary policy for an economic area in which governments moved in divergent directions on fiscal policy was the issue of imported inflation. In a currency union, it is very possible for one country's inflation to spill over into other countries in the union. So, if one government does not exercise fiscal policy discipline and causes inflation in its economy, it can lead to inflation in the other members of the currency union as their products are denominated in the same currency.

The issues of a lack of a common fiscal policy and imported inflation were of particular concern in Germany after the Maastricht Treaty was finalized. The German Bundesbank was a particularly vociferous critic of the idea of having a common monetary policy without any mechanism for coordinating or constraining spending. It was not long before the German Finance Ministry joined the Bundesbank in calling for measures to ensure that governments could not abandon fiscal discipline after joining EMU. In 1996, the German government brought this proposal before the EU Council of Ministers in order to get a formal agreement on the matter.

The idea of such an agreement was not universally popular among the EU member governments. It would tie the hands of governments in fiscal policy matters, making it very difficult to spend on rising social policy costs. The main issue was how the agreement could become a political liability for governments with their domestic constituencies. Being forced to cut social programs or not being able to offer fiscal stimulus in an economic downturn could hurt governments come election time. Yet, despite the reservations of some governments, the agreement was reached and named the Stability and Growth Pact.[10] The pact would not be part of the Maastricht Treaty but a separate agreement among EU member governments.

The Stability and Growth Pact of 1997 was an attempt to preclude EMU member states from making inflationary fiscal policies that would then threaten price stability throughout the Eurozone. The pact states that EMU member governments may not have annual budget deficits of more than 3 percent of their gross domestic product (GDP). There is an exception to this rule is if the country in question is facing a serious economic crisis. This is defined as a 2 percent or more drop in GDP in a year or a serious national disaster. A recession with a drop of 0.75 percent or less of GDP in a year would not qualify a country for exemption from the pact's rules.

If a country is deemed to have exceeded the budget deficit limit by the European Commission and the Ecofin Council, there will be a vote as to whether to impose a fine. The decision to levy the fine is not automatic but is to be made by a unanimous vote of the Ecofin Council. The council interprets whether the country in question is in economic crisis or has exceeded the 3 percent limit and must pay. If the country is fined, it must make an interest-free deposit at the ECB ranging from 0.2 to 0.5 percent of its GDP, which is a function of the size of the deficit. If the deficit is reduced to a balanced budget, the money is returned; if not, it stays permanently at the ECB (Van Oudenaren 2000, 189–190).

Thus far, the commission has issued a number of warnings to countries clearly over the budget deficit limit, but it has not levied any fines. The principal culprits have been France, Germany, Italy, the Netherlands, and

Portugal. Portugal has made stringent efforts to keep its deficits below the limit, whereas the French, German, and Italian governments have remained somewhat defiant about the admonitions of the commission, arguing that the pact places undue constraints on governments' ability to manage economic downturns.

The commission has hesitated to issue warnings to Germany, the principal proponent of the pact, even though it has exceeded the deficit limit, because it would be very politically embarrassing to the German government to get such a warning. Thus, the German government has repeatedly promised to keep its finances in order, but it has been unwilling to cause itself the political pain that would come with such measures.

The problems with getting countries to abide by the pact led the commission to suggest that the pact be revised to accommodate short-term deficits in countries with low levels of debt.[11] Ironically, the major obstacle to such a change in rules was the German government. The German government advocated keeping the Stability and Growth Pact rules the same, despite the fact that it had broken those rules for two successive years.[12] The reason for this seeming contradiction in German policy was that the German government could not admit to its public, and more importantly to the Bundesbank, that it could not live up to the fiscal rules that the Germans had demanded in the run-up to EMU. But the German government also could not live up to those rules because of the immense political pain that doing so would cause.

The issue of Eurozone countries breaching the Stability and Growth Pact's rules became a crisis in late 2003. It had become obvious by then that the German and French governments were going to break their promised budget deficit ceilings for 2004. The European Commission began to issue statements about the need to hold all of the countries of the Eurozone accountable to the rules of the pact. The French government responded with defiance.[13]

The ECB weighed in on the issue, stating that further breaches of the pact would undermine the fiscal foundations of price stability in the Eurozone.[14] The ECB feared that if governments continued to flout the rules, markets would lose confidence in the Eurozone's governments' ability and willingness to make disciplined fiscal policies, which would make it more difficult for the ECB to quell inflationary expectations in the Eurozone.

The issue came to a head when the German government, which was clearly going to breach the budget ceiling for the third year in a row in 2004, issued a statement that the pact was only meant to punish governments who refused to work toward keeping budget deficits in line. Hans Eichel, the German finance minister, argued in November 2003 that "the goal is to apply sanctions only against countries that refuse to co-operate."[15] This was a very loose reading of what the pact was intended to achieve. The pact never mentions that countries that try hard to reduce deficits will not be eligible for the sanctions mechanism. Eichel was looking to save face and find a way for Germany to avoid sanctions without seeming to defy the pact's rules.

The commission's reaction was that the German government was trying to avoid sanctions that it now clearly deserved.[16] The German government also came under fire from within Germany. The most prominent critics of the German government's position on the pact were the Bundesbank and the Federation of German Industry (BDI). The Bundesbank warned against any "soft interpretation" of the pact's rules.[17] The BDI argued, "Those who flout the Pact must be punished."[18] This criticism was most embarrassing for the German government, particularly since the Germans had been the pact's principal architects, and there was lingering concern in Germany that the euro would be a weak currency compared to the deutsche mark.[19] Allowing countries to engage in inflationary spending would surely weaken the euro on international exchange markets.

The 25 November Ecofin meeting decided the matter. In that meeting, a coalition of countries led by Germany and France were able to win a suspension of the operations of the Stability and Growth Pact. This group was opposed by Austria, the Netherlands, Finland, and Spain, but to no avail.[20] Essentially, the Ecofin Council had agreed that the pact's rules were no longer binding.[21]

The reaction of the ECB and the commission was scathing. The ECB declared,

> The conclusions adopted by the Ecofin Council carry serious dangers. The failure to go along with the rules and procedures foreseen in the Stability and Growth Pact risks undermining the credibility of the institutional framework and the confidence in sound public finances of Members States across the euro area.... It is now absolutely imperative that effective action be taken to limit negative effects on confidence.[22]

The commission's reaction to Ecofin's decision was to challenge its legality. In the commission's view, the finance ministers had breached the treaty that their countries had signed. The commission chose to bring the matter to the European Court of Justice in order to underpin the notion that European law was binding on all EU member states that had ratified it. The problem for the commission was that even if it were to win the case, there would be no way to force the governments of the Eurozone countries to implement the decision.[23] Thus, the German-led coalition had proven that many European governments were not willing to abandon national sovereignty over fiscal policy and that there was not much the commission could do about it.

On 13 July 2004, the European Court of Justice ruled on the action of the Ecofin Council in November 2003. The court decided that the action was illegal in light of the treaty obligations of the signatory states, but it also ruled that "responsibility for making the member states observe budgetary discipline lies essentially with the council."[24]

The reaction of the EU governments and the commission was actually positive. Hans Eichel, the German finance minister and one of the top offenders of the pact, said, "The Court has confirmed that the Council has room for manoeuvre."[25] This reaction was indicative of a position held by several EU governments that nobody could force them to live by the budget rules that they themselves created and were empowered to enforce. Thus, as long as the Eurozone governments decided not to enforce their own rules, the Stability and Growth Pact would be on hold.

In an attempt to save the pact from oblivion, the European Commission took it upon itself to try to reform the rules of the pact. In September 2004, the commission issued its reform plan, which had five major points:

1. Allows for excessive deficits in times of "sluggish growth" as well as "serious recession"
2. Allows for more time to correct excessive deficits
3. Allows countries with low debt to run higher deficits
4. Encourages "peer pressure" for countries to correct excessive deficits
5. Argues for better use of annual council policy guidelines

The commission argued that these changes to the pact did not require the amendment of the treaty but would be technical changes to the pact.[26] These proposals were to be taken up by the Ecofin Council within a year of their issue.

The ECB chose to undertake a period of study before commenting on the commission's proposals, although President Trichet said he saw no reason to change the wording of the pact. But the Bundesbank, one of the most important parts of the European System of Central Banks (ESCB), sharply criticized the proposals. The central bank stated, "Instead of strengthening the Stability and Growth Pact, the proposed changes would have a detrimental effect. . . . The incentive to maintain a sound budgetary policy in the member states of the monetary union would be undermined, and a false signal would be sent to those countries which have not yet introduced the single currency."[27] It was very likely that the ECB would welcome any weakening of the pact as it is viewed as an important part of the institutional structure of monetary union.

Just such a weakening of the pact came on 20 March 2005, when EU finance ministers reached a deal essentially to change the nature of the pact so that it would still exist but would have little constraining power over EMU member state government finances.[28] The rewritten pact called for governments to keep deficits "close to the reference value." Also, governments were given a range of reasons, some rather ambiguous, as to why they could engage in "temporary" spending that would exceed the deficit ceiling. Most importantly, Germany was able to use unification as a reason to not have to stick to the deficit ceiling. Thus, for all intents and purposes, the new Stability and Growth Pact text meant that governments were no longer constrained by the pact to limit their spending.

The ECB's reaction to the decision was very negative. Immediately after the pact details became public, the ECB issued a statement warning about the potential consequences of the pact's changes to the monetary stability situation in the Eurozone.[29] As the larger, more powerful countries of the Eurozone, namely Germany, France, and Italy, supported the pact changes, the ECB could do little but complain.

The political fallout of the crisis over the Stability and Growth Pact may continue for some time. Some political observers have speculated that it may have cost the president of the Bundesbank, Ernst Welteke, his position. In early 2004, Welteke was accused of having received an expensive hotel stay from the German Dresdner Bank, which the Bundesbank oversees and regulates.[30] But many accused the German government of stoking the media frenzy over Welteke's supposed misdeeds in order to make him resign. The logic behind this reasoning was that Welteke, as a major critic of the German government's handling of the Stability and Growth Pact issue, was a prime target of the government.[31] The pressure was finally too much for Welteke, and he resigned on 16 April 2004. Although this was an embarrassing moment for the Bundesbank, it was interpreted by many in Germany as the consequence of the Bundesbank's embarrassing the government over its suspending the pact.[32]

Clearly, in practice, the Stability and Growth Pact has not been the constraining institution it was meant to be. As a result, the ECB could face a myriad of unconstrained fiscal policies, which could make it very difficult for the central bank to meet its goal of maintaining price stability in the Eurozone.

The European Constitution

One of the most important developments for the ECB could be the creation of a European constitution, which has the potential to strengthen the independence and powers of the ECB, weaken them, or merely maintain the status quo. The European Council meeting in June 2004 produced a constitutional text that seems to protect the institutional status quo of the ECB more than anything else.

It did not always seem that this would be the case. The idea of a constitution for the European Union had been discussed for some years. It made sense to take all of the important principles of EU institutions and place them in one document rather than keep them in several disparate treaties. Therefore, at the Nice European Council in December 2000, an intergovernmental council to establish a constitution was suggested. The Laeken European Council meeting set the process on its way, establishing the constitutional convention process. The convention, led by former French president Valéry Giscard d'Estaing, debated for fifteen months and submitted a draft constitution in June 2003.

The ECB followed this process from start to finish because of its importance for the central bank. It could have potentially changed a huge part of the ECB's power and operations. The ECB's input into the constitution was substantial. The central bank took part in expert testimony, issued comments and drafting suggestions, and sent letters asking for revisions. At various stages of the process, the ECB signaled that the draft was either incomplete in outlining the powers of the central bank or that it was contrary to the views of the ECB on institutional matters.[33]

Nearly every bit of advice that the ECB gave on the constitution found its way into the text. As a testament to the ECB's credibility and power, the central bank was able to change the minds of several members of the convention, who wanted to water down the emphasis on price stability in the mandate of the central bank.

All in all, the constitution reaffirms all of the institutional principles of the Maastricht Treaty concerning the ECB and the Statute of the ESCB. The ECB itself has said of the constitution, "The discussion of the aspects of particular relevance to the ECB and ESCB therefore demonstrates that no substantive changes have been made to the monetary framework of the EU."[34]

While it is not certain that the constitution will actually ever be ratified, given that the French and Dutch national referenda failed to ratify it (with more referenda to come), the constitution itself would only stand to bolster the institutional standing of the ECB in the EU.[35] Merely the process of drawing up the constitution acted as a reaffirmation of the principles that underpin the ECB.

THE SOCIETAL CONTEXT

Just as the ECB does not face a unified political system in the Eurozone, it does not face anything near a cohesive Eurozone society. There are vast differences in the history, culture, and structure of the various national societies within the Eurozone. This diversity offers both challenges and opportunities for the central bankers in achieving their goals.

Three facets of Eurozone society are particularly relevant for understanding the context in which the ECB operates. They are industrial relations, the nature of the financial sector in the Eurozone, and the public. Each of these facets has the potential to influence the manner and goals of ECB monetary policy and therefore merits attention.

Eurozone Industrial Relations

The first important facet is the structure of the organized economic interest group systems in the Eurozone. When we discuss the structure of these systems, we are referring to the interests, organization, and power of economic interest groups in Eurozone countries. Economic interest groups include unions and organizations that represent the interests of capital, such as industry and finance groups.

While there may be a high degree of uniformity across the Eurozone countries in terms of what labor and capital organizations want, there are marked differences in how much power those groups have in their societies. For example, in the northern European countries in the Eurozone, labor and capital are both highly organized and powerful. In these corporatist systems, deals are cut between labor and capital that make disruptions, such as strikes, relatively rare. These deals are also useful for keeping inflation in check by promising workers benefits in exchange for moderate wage demands. The Bundesbank, for example, counted on corporatist wage deals as a way to keep prices stable in Germany (Hall and Franzese 1998; Iversen 1998b).

In the southern European countries, however, where corporatism has not developed to the same extent, cutting such deals is very difficult. Thus, instead of consensus over wages and worker benefits, southern European countries have seen much more conflict between labor and capital. The incidence of strikes is much higher in southern Europe, and unions are not prone to wage moderation when bargaining. Thus, industrial relations in southern Europe have not always helped the central banks in those countries to maintain price stability. Even if the central banks in southern Europe were to admonish labor and capital organizations to cooperate and reach a consensus, this would be very difficult to achieve because those organizations in southern Europe are usually not centrally organized enough to bring such a far-reaching deal into being.

So, what does the difference between the northern and southern European styles of industrial relations mean for the ECB? It means that when the ECB admonishes labor and capital organizations in northern Europe to work for wage moderation, the central bank can have some hope that those organizations will be able to achieve a moderate wage deal. In southern Europe, with its splintered and conflicting labor and capital organizations, the ECB has little hope that its admonitions will lead to moderate deals. Thus, the ECB has a much less cooperative set of social partners in southern Europe relative to northern Europe.

One development that could possibly change this situation over time is the birth of labor and capital organizations developed at the European versus the national level. Labor has created a group of European-level umbrella organizations, such as the European Trade Union Confederation (EUTC), Eurocadres, and the European Confederation of Cadres. European capital has created the Union of Industrial and Employers' Confederations of Europe and the European Association of Chambers of Commerce and Industry.

While some European-level labor union confederations and industry groups have developed, they have very limited powers over their national memberships. The ECB would certainly welcome the rise of a Eurozone-level corporatism, which would aid in fostering wage moderation. This is highly unlikely to develop in the foreseeable future because of the collective-action problems inherent in creating supranational economic interest organizations.

The Financial Sector

One potentially very important aspect of society in terms of influencing the ECB's monetary policy is the Eurozone financial sector. The financial sector, meaning the institutions that provide capital and hold savings, is the central bank's partner in implementing monetary policy. In order for both the central bank and the financial community to operate effectively, they must keep in close contact and be aware of each other's actions. This makes the financial sector the most attentive sector of the economy to the decisions of the central bank (Frey and Schneider 1981; Henning 1994; Posen 1993; Rogoff 1985; Walsh 2000; Woolley 1984).[36] Thus, the financial community is the most likely sectoral interest in an economy to be mobilized to influence monetary policy.

The power of the financial community refers to its ability to reward or punish the politicians and independent central bankers. This ability is a function of several factors. The power of the financial community is determined by (1) the degree of uniformity of the policy preferences of relevant actors in the financial community, and (2) the domestic economic importance of the financial community. The degree of uniformity in the financial community's policy preferences is important because a financial community that has a unified position will be more powerful as a united front on policy matters than a financial community that has fragmented interests on policy issues and thus either cannot coalesce for collective action or works at cross purposes.

So, how do these power resources on the part of the financial community determine how it can act as a source of the policy preferences of decision-makers in an independent central bank? A powerful financial community can influence the policy preferences of central bankers by having some say in the selection of central bankers and their image of competence and policymaking independence.

The type of financial community that a state has will determine, to a great extent, the preferences and power of the financial community over monetary policy (Posen 1993). In industrialized states, there are two principal types of financial communities, universal bank–based financial communities and capital market–based financial communities (Henning 1994; Posen 1993; Walsh 2000; Zysman 1983). Universal bank–based financial communities will be more anti-inflation oriented than a capital market–based financial community. They will also be more powerful vis-à-vis an independent central bank than a capital market–based financial community. Let us explore why this is the case.

A universal banking system is dominated by universal banks as the principal type of financial institution. A universal bank not only takes savings accounts from customers but also lends money to firms and individuals and holds equity stakes in firms. A universal banking financial system is likely to be more anti-inflation oriented than a capital market system because of the relative weights in the two systems of banks holding debt versus equity. When a financial institution derives its profits from lending money at a fixed rate of interest, it has an inherent preference for keeping inflation as low as possible because inflation decreases the real value of the money that it gets back from the borrower. That said, the universal banks would not want an extremely tight monetary policy that could dampen growth to the extent that it damages the performance of the firms to which they lend, either.

A capital market–based financial system is one where firms principally raise their capital by issuing equity or bonds to individuals and financial institutions. A capital market–based financial system will have investment banks that have a different stake in inflation than commercial banks. Investment banks operating in the stock market will be less concerned with inflation, on the whole, than banks in a universal banking system because these financial institutions are more concerned with increasing the returns on their equity stakes. A strict anti-inflation monetary policy may slow economic growth to the extent that the returns on their investments are reduced. On the other hand, investment banks and firms do not want an extremely loose monetary policy that could let inflation grow rapidly and thus cause a collapse of confidence in the investment climate.

Bond market participants, another important part of a capital market system, will have a different interest in inflation from those involved in the stock market. Bonds, which are fixed-income instruments, are more sensitive to inflation than stocks. Thus, a bond holder has an interest in seeing inflation as low as possible and will want a tighter monetary policy from the central bank than those involved in the equity market.

Commercial banks in the capital market–based financial system, as well, will want to keep inflation as low as possible as their main business is maintaining savings accounts and lending to individuals and firms. Thus, commercial banks will want a monetary policy that is primarily geared toward price stability.

The mix of institutions in the capital market–based financial system means that there is not a unified set of preferences among financial institutions for a particular monetary policy orientation. Investment banks and commercial banks can send potentially conflicting signals about what they want from monetary policy as each type of institution has different tolerances for inflation. Thus, on the whole, the primary signal coming from a capital market–based financial sector to politicians and central bankers is that both growth and inflation need to be primary concerns of the central bank.

Therefore, after examining the preferences and likely political power of the institutions in these two types of financial systems, we would predict that, all things being equal, a universal bank–based financial system would be a powerful advocate for a strong price-stability-oriented monetary policy. Financial institutions in the capital market–based system would not be as politically powerful as those in the universal bank–based system, and their rather heterogeneous interests toward monetary policy would be aggregated as a signal for a monetary policy balanced between growth and inflation concerns.

While we know that the financial community is not a primary source of personnel for the decision-making ranks of the ECB, we must explore the possibility that the financial sector influences monetary policy decisions because of its importance as an audience to central bankers. We need to determine, first, if the members of the Governing Council care about their image of competence with the financial community. If they do care about their image of competence, they will then look to see what the monetary policy preferences of the financial community are so that they can maintain their image of competence by following those preferences. That requires that we ask whether the Governing Council perceives clear, coherent policy preferences in the financial community. Finally, we need to ask if those policy preferences are indeed an important guide to monetary policy.

Let us examine what the members of the Governing Council think about these issues. In relation to the image the ECB decision-makers have in the financial community, six members of the Governing Council were asked what they thought of their image in the financial sector. Here is what one of the central bankers had to say:

> I know that there is this critique that central bankers are always thinking about whether the financial sector will applaud or protest what the central bank does. I do not buy this. . . . If I read in the paper that this is the most incompetent

person you have ever seen and has damaged the economy, I certainly would
not want that. But from my perspective as a central banker, I have to work for
what I am here for and that is price stability. This is the benchmark against
which my decision-making is measured. This is, as I see it, a service to the
public at large, to European society.[37]

Here is a statement representative the sentiments of the other members
of the Governing Council:

It is difficult to hold up to criticism. It is difficult for politicians. It is difficult
for institutions. It is difficult for central bankers. Nevertheless, to perform your
duties means you live up to your responsibilities. Your work will not be permanently applauded. Your responsibilities may mean doing things for the medium
or long run that may hurt people in the short term. That is what can get you
criticized.[38]

Another NCB governor echoed these thoughts: "It is not that important
because an independent central banker should not be liable to any community, neither governmental nor private. So from that point of view, what
people think of me is not important."[39]

A member of the Governing Council, who is on the Executive Board,
argued, "You have to care what they think because if you do not, the credibility and efficiency of monetary policy can be damaged. That's why our
image to the financial community is important."[40] Thus, his emphasis was
on the practical importance of what the financial community thinks of the
ECB.

The answers to this question tell us that if the central bankers care about
their image in the financial community, it is only inasmuch as that image
allows them to get the financial community to do what the central bank
wants.

The next thing to explore is whether the financial sector presents its policy
preferences to the Governing Council in a clear and coherent manner. All of
the Governing Council members interviewed claimed that no coherent position on monetary policy emanated from the European financial community.
Here is a representative quote from an NCB governor:

I have never witnessed a coherent position from the financial community, either
coming from the commercial banks or from other groupings that would say
"you should decrease rates, you should increase rates. We are satisfied with
the monetary policy, we are not satisfied with the monetary policy." There are
a lot of voices, a lot of eloquent or vocal positions, but no positions of the
community as a whole.[41]

The others all made the same point. Some stressed that not only was there
not a coherent European financial community, but many of the member

states' financial communities were not coherent in their monetary policy preferences. If there is no coherent position coming from the financial community, it would be very difficult for the central bankers to take guidance from the financial community on how to make monetary policy.

Finally, when asked how important the policy positions of the financial community actors are in the making of the ECB's monetary policy, there was once again unanimity among the six respondents. All six said that the financial community was important as a source of information, but it did not drive the policy of the central bank. Below is a response offered by an Executive Board member:

> It [the financial community] is important because the banks are the channel, and they have the contact with the clients. If the clients complain about the rates, the banks will be able to explain it. So, to a certain extent, the understanding of our actions is channeled through the banks to the final client.[42]

Another Executive Board member said the following:

> They [the banks] are not important in effecting the basic philosophy or basic decisions of the ECB. They, on occasion, may be in the position to provide us with input that is valuable to us. It's more than them trying to get us to do certain things rather than others. The assessment of the situation and the economic and financial picture may be helped by their input.[43]

An NCB governor made this statement about the role of the banks:

> Of course we take them [the financial community] into account because they are the heart of the various capital markets. They have something to tell. So, we take into account their reasoning and what they have to say, but we certainly are not following what they are suggesting, if they are suggesting anything. We take them into account because it is important information. They are part of the transmission mechanism.[44]

European bankers who were interviewed echoed these points made by members of the Governing Council. An economist at a major multinational bank headquartered in the Eurozone had this to say about his bank's influence:

> In principle, they don't listen to anyone. They are well aware of the fact that their economic analysis, also as far as the models are concerned, and the techniques that they use, and the manpower they put into the whole thing is far superior to whatever you get in the markets. On the other hand, there are things that the central bank does not see, at least not immediately, and that is market expectations, which is a very important element. I would say that the monetary policy stance is more or less developed autonomously. Whatever evidence they get from our participants is used to back up and enrich their own opinion.[45]

Another banker echoed this sentiment by saying, "I think the banking community has very limited influence on the central bank."[46]

So, why is the financial sector only important as a conduit of information? Why can it not influence monetary policy? The reasons put forward by the Governing Council's members centered on the financial sector's being only a part of the whole economy. The ECB has to take a broader view so as not to damage the interests of other segments of society. An NCB governor said the following about why the banks do not drive policy:

> They [the banks] are too short-sighted. They do not take into account the longer-term effects of policy. That is the role of central bankers. Central bankers' role is to look beyond the present, what we can see now, and take into account the potential implications for the future.[47]

An Executive Board member gave the following response:

> In some cases the financial sector might be opposed to, say, rising rates. They might see that as against their interests. I could not care less, to be quite blunt. I would not do anything to intentionally make them angry. But if they want us to trade away our mandate, the service we owe to the larger society, for me it is no question. It's easy.[48]

An NCB governor answered the question this way: "We know that they defend their interests. And those interests do not always coincide with those that we have to defend, the interests of the overall population."[49]

The evidence presented above clearly does not confirm the notion that the ECB is captured by the Eurozone financial sector. The inability of the European financial sector to drive policy is the result of its narrow interests. It seems that the members of the Governing Council of the ECB believe that following the policy demands of the financial sector could potentially put the central bankers at risk of making short-sighted policy.

The General Public

When asked about their image of competence among the general public, all six respondents replied that it was very important. None of the six stated that the image was very important to them personally, but all agreed that an image of competence was important for the central bank as a whole. Two reasons were stressed as to why the image of competence is important for the central bank. First, the central bank needs public support in order to remain an institution independent of government control. Second, the central bank needs to maintain an image of competence in order to protect the value of the currency. If the public loses confidence in the central bank, people may not want to hold euros, which would erode the value of the currency. A major fall in the value of the currency would stoke inflation.

Below are the responses of the six Governing Council members when questioned about how important their image in the eyes of general public was. One Executive Board member offered this:

> Our image is very important. This is because most of the efficiency of monetary policy depends on it. If we have a positive image, the effect is our policy can act more quickly and with better impact. But also we can only act independently if the public backs us. We need not only to convince them that we are acting right, but they should support us.[50]

An NCB governor echoed the link between image and the central bank's ability to maintain price stability:

> It's very important in my view. It's really very important because the central bank depends really on how strong its reputation is. That has an effect on the stability of the currency, which means the soundness of the economy.[51]

An Executive Board member stressed the importance of political support for the central bank. He said, "If this was an institution that could be characterized as incompetent, that would completely undermine its general support."[52]

The evidence seems to indicate that an image of competence held by the general public is important to the central bankers, but not because they derive psychic gains from such an image. The image of competence allows them to achieve their goal of price stability and to be independent of government pressure.

What about the public's monetary policy preferences? How clear are they to the members of the Governing Council? The responses to this question were mixed. Some central bankers said that the monetary policy preferences of the European public were clear because of the mandate for price stability laid out in the Maastricht Treaty. Because the treaty was ratified by the member-state parliaments, some argued, the mandate for price stability as the primary goal of the central bank had been publicly legitimized. Here is what an NCB governor said about this: "I think the public's preference has been expressed in the Treaty and in the basic objective which has been entrusted in the European System of Central Banks, and from that point of view I think, yes, the public's preference is stability."[53]

But the ECB decision-makers stressed that it was very difficult to tell what the public's monetary policy preferences were because there is no one European general public. Below are representative responses to the question:

> We are really just getting started. It is very difficult to even define what the general public in this is. It is one of our difficulties.[54]
>
> The problem we have presently is that the general public in Europe is fragmented. To a certain extent, this fragmentation is simply the effect of the fact that

we have different member states that used to have different monetary policies. And it is much more that there are political divisions and regional economic differences. So, one of the many challenges that we have is to try to convince the whole public everywhere that we are the central bank that is taking care of the interests of everybody. But this has to develop and has a long way to go.[55]

This evidence shows that the decision-makers do not view the general public as having coherent or clear monetary policy preferences.[56] The one central banker who believed the public expressed a monetary policy preference thought it was done in an indirect and very general manner. This would seem to make it very difficult for the central bankers to take their policymaking cues from the general public.

The next step is to ask the central bankers explicitly what role the Eurozone general public plays in influencing their monetary policy decisions. All of the respondents agreed that the public is not important as a guide to policy. An Executive Board member argued,

> The problems of monetary policy are very technical. So, public understanding of our monetary policy stance is very vague. It's difficult to get any guidance from public opinion on whether to increase or decrease interest rates. The public just does not know what the likely effect is going to be. Either they trust us, or they don't trust us.[57]

An NCB governor said the following:

> Sometimes you have to go against the dominant view in public opinion. You cannot always follow public opinion. There has to be leadership from the bank. And leadership, of course, means that in some situations, you have to do it even if it is not seen as wanted.[58]

Another NCB governor had this to say:

> It [public opinion] is important if they back our line, but we never fish for public sentiments on what we should do. It is beautiful encouragement if the public follows our line, but we never look for guidance from the general public. Never.[59]

The third NCB governor added this: "When I make policy in the ECB, I only have one thing in mind, and that is how to achieve the objective [price stability] that has been entrusted to me for the whole Eurozone."[60]

This evidence indicates that the public does not act as a guide for the ECB's monetary policy. But the public is crucial as a source of political support for the central bank. A lack of public support would have serious economic and political consequences for the ECB.

It is vital for the ECB, if it is to maintain its operational independence over time, that it enjoy at least passive acceptance by the various national publics in the Eurozone. Several scholars have argued that the key to the Bundesbank's, and to a lesser extent the American Federal Reserve's, substantial operational independence was the support of their respective publics. Any attempt to encroach on the independence of the Bundesbank would have led to a significant public outcry in Germany.

If publics, particularly those of large countries, oppose the EMU project or the policies of the ECB, the central bank could face intense pressure from politicians to mold the ECB's policies to fit the politicians' demands. Thus, the ECB leadership knows it needs to keep the Eurozone publics on its side.

It was clear from the start of EMU that there was wide variation in support for it among the member states. The EMU initiative was a relatively popular idea in the majority of its founding member states. In Italy, France, Spain, Ireland, and the Benelux countries, EMU garnered well over a majority of the population's support. The idea of a common currency was not popular at all in Germany, with less than 40 percent of the public supporting the idea in 1999 (Kaltenthaler and Anderson 2001). This is very important in that Germany is the largest economy, by far, in EMU and is home to the ECB. The German public, which gave up its most cherished postwar achievement, the deutsche mark, when it entered EMU, is probably the most important public for the ECB to have on its side among the Eurozone states. The second most important public would be France, the other portion of the "motor" that drove the EMU idea to fruition.

A German public that actively opposed the idea of EMU and the ECB would be a significant political problem for the new central bank. This is one of the reasons why the ECB has made such an effort to get its message out and to appear accountable and transparent. The ECB has been largely unsuccessful in its attempt to win over the German public (and keep the others favorable) as public opinion in Germany has not warmed significantly to the idea of EMU over time. Table 4.1 shows the breakdown of European public opinion concerning the benefits to respondents' country of being part of EMU.

The table shows the results of a Eurobarometer survey conducted in the spring of 2003, which asked respondents whether they thought that the introduction of the euro would be advantageous or disadvantageous for their country. The results show some interesting patterns of public opinion toward the euro.

The average among the EMU member states' publics polled was largely favorable toward the euro. Of those polled, 53.9 percent said that the introduction of the euro was advantageous overall. Those who thought the euro's introduction was disadvantageous overall were 31.7 percent of the

Table 4.1. Percentage of Citizens of Europe by Country Who Responded Positively, Negatively, Neutrally, or Not At All to the Following Question: In your opinion, for our country, is the adoption of the euro an operation that is advantageous overall and that will strengthen us for the future, or, rather, the opposite, an operation that is disadvantageous overall and will weaken us?

	Country (%)												
	Europe (total)	Belgium	Germany	Greece	Spain	France	Ireland	Italy	Luxembourg	Netherlands	Austria	Portugal	Finland
Advantageous Overall	53.9	72.0	38.8	45.9	62.2	65.0	73.1	57.0	71.9	42.4	52.4	57.2	64.5
Disadvantageous Overall	31.7	15.8	51.7	23.7	18.2	22.5	19.0	29.0	13.7	40.8	24.6	21.9	11.3
Neither (No Change)	7.3	5.7	5.0	17.6	8.3	3.2	2.5	10.8	8.6	7.3	16.6	5.0	16.0
Do Not Know/Not Applicable	7.2	6.5	4.5	12.8	11.2	9.2	5.4	3.2	5.8	9.5	6.4	15.9	8.1

sample. Thus, on the average, the euro is looked upon favorably by Eurozone publics. But this average masks differences between Eurozone countries that could be politically significant.

We see that in every country of the Eurozone, there is a majority that is favorable toward the euro, except for Germany. In Germany, 51.7 percent said the introduction of the euro was disadvantageous for the country. Only 38.8 percent thought the euro's introduction would be advantageous overall for Germans. Only the Netherlands comes close to this kind of negative attitude toward the euro, although even that country has a majority that is positively predisposed toward the common currency (42.4 percent advantageous, 40.8 percent disadvantageous).

How do we explain this, and what might it mean for the operation of the ECB? It is best explained by the perception of the German populace that it had so much more to lose than other Europeans because of EMU. The deutsche mark was not just the anchor of European monetary regimes starting in the 1970s; it was a symbol of Germany's economic success in rising from the ashes of World War II. A German central banker once stated, "The French have their military parades and flag, and we have the deutsche mark. It is what makes Germans proud."[61] The currencies of the other EMU member states did not carry the same emotional weight as the deutsche mark did in Germany.

What does this pattern of favor toward the euro mean for the operations of the ECB? It is certainly good news for the ECB that in only one Eurozone state does the majority of the population look at the euro with disfavor. That is an implicit vote of confidence in the operations of the ECB. People would not say they looked at the euro as advantageous for them if they thought it was being mismanaged. But it must be disturbing for those in the ECB to know that four years after the launch of the euro, the German population still laments its introduction. This means that political support for the ECB cannot be taken for granted when the Eurozone's most powerful population does not have confidence in the currency. It clearly shows that the ECB has a lot more to do in order to win over the German public and to feel assured of its support.

THE ECONOMIC CONTEXT

Another context very important for understanding how the ECB operates is the economic context, that is, the attributes of the Eurozone economy that affect how the ECB makes policy. Certain aspects of the Eurozone economy are particularly important to the ECB: the sectoral breakdown of the economy, the structure of labor markets, the nature of financial markets, and the exposure of the Eurozone economy to trade.

Table 4.2.   Key Real Economy Characteristics of the Euro Area in 2000

	Unit	Euro Area	United States
Population	millions	303	276
GDP (share of world GDP)[a]	percentage	16.0	22.0
Sectors of production[b]			
Agriculture, fishing, forestry	percentage of GDP	2.7	1.4
Industry (including construction)	percentage of GDP	28.8	24.7
Services	percentage of GDP	68.5	73.9

[a]GDP shares are based on a purchasing power parity (PPP) valuation of country GDPs.
[b]Based on real value added. Data for the United States refer to 1999.

When we look at the breakdown of the Eurozone economy by sector (i.e., agriculture, industry, and services), we find that it is very much a service-oriented economy. Table 4.2 shows the breakdown by sector compared with the United States.

The similarity between the United States and Eurozone economies in terms of sector contributions to gross domestic product (GDP) stands out immediately in the table. Both economies have quite small agricultural sectors and large service sectors. Industrial production now makes up roughly one-fourth of the economies in both places. This means that monetary policy is not geared solely toward keeping the industrial sector healthy but instead must take into account the complexity of a service-based economy. Because there is a multitude of different types of service firms in a service economy, generalizing the needs of the sector is quite difficult. This complexity is mitigated by the ECB's policy strategy to focus on price stability, which it asserts benefits all sectors of the economy over the long run.

Labor market structure is also very important to the ECB in how it affects price stability and the ECB's political standing in the EU. How does the labor market affect price stability? If the labor market is fluid and unrestrained, it will keep the price of labor at its market value. If, on the other hand, the labor market is rigid, it will not allocate labor to meet demand efficiently, and this will drive up its price.

Obviously, a central bank with a remit to maintain price stability will not be pleased to see that the labor market in its economy is not market based as this will make it harder for the central bank to achieve its operational goal. This has certainly been the case for the ECB. While not all of the Eurozone economies have the same degree of labor market rigidity, it is quite substantial in some.

Statutes making it very difficult to lay workers off in many of the Eurozone economies have meant that firms cannot really hire or fire based on the demand for labor. Not only does this drive up the cost of labor in sectors of the economy facing a labor shortage, but it can also lead to unemployment in some economies, particularly among younger workers. This unemployment is caused by firms' reluctance to hire workers they may not be able to get rid of when there is a downturn in the economy. This unemployment can be a problem for the ECB in that people may blame the ECB for causing the unemployment, saying that it is so focused on price stability that it does not care enough about growth. Thus, the ECB has every incentive to advocate labor market liberalization, which it has consistently. But it is difficult for governments to heed such calls when they have to worry about voter backlash against the idea of increased job insecurity.

As was pointed out earlier, financial markets are hugely important to the ECB. They are the transmission belts for monetary policy. In the Eurozone economy, firm financing takes place primarily through bank loans. Bank loans to the corporate sector equal about 45 percent of GDP in the Eurozone, whereas in the United States, for example, they account for only 13 percent of GDP. Stock market capitalization was 90.1 percent of GDP in the Eurozone, while it was 192.9 percent of GDP in the United States.

This structure of corporate financing in the Eurozone means that the ECB is concerned primarily with keeping the real value of loans high so that banks will keep the flow of credit going when it is needed. If the real value of the return on loans were to be undermined by inflation, banks would be less willing to lend credit as they would fear real losses on their balance sheets. Thus, European banks will strongly support a stability-oriented monetary policy.

While Eurozone banks will support a stability-oriented monetary policy in the Eurozone, they will not give the ECB carte blanche to make policy as tight as it wants. While banks depend primarily on the real return on their loans for profit, they also depend on the economic health of their client firms to keep the demand for new loans going. If the ECB kills off economic growth, firms will not demand new credit, and banks will suffer. Therefore, we can say that Eurozone banks want price stability, but not at the cost of at least moderate growth. This means that the ECB's support base from the financial sector in the Eurozone is conditioned on its ability to provide both growth and low inflation, a balance that can be difficult to achieve at times, particularly in the short run.

A final aspect of the economic context in which the ECB operates is the Eurozone's exposure to trade. The Eurozone is a more exposed economic area than the economies of the United States or Japan, its closest competitors in size. In 2000, exports of goods and services accounted for 19.1 percent of GDP in the Eurozone, but only 10.7 percent in the United States and 11.1 percent in Japan (ECB 2001, 14). Thus, the Eurozone is roughly twice as exposed to trade as the United States.

What this figure does not reveal to us is the variety of exposure of the national economies within the Eurozone. Table 4.3 shows the relative exposure to the international economy of EMU member states.

Table 4.3.   Exports as a Percentage of GDP

Country	Percentage
Belgium	76.1
Germany	29.4
Spain	27.5
France	26.0
Ireland	90.4
Italy	25.5
Luxembourg	117.5
Netherlands	61.4
Austria	45.1
Portugal	30.4
Finland	37.7

Some of the Eurozone economies are very exposed to trade because of their small population sizes and reliance on foreign markets to absorb their goods. For example, Ireland and Belgium get over 70 percent of their GDP from exports. Others, with large populations, such as France and Germany, are much less dependent on trade. These countries derive about 25 percent of their respective GDPs from exports.

What does the variation in exposure to trade mean for the member states of EMU? It means that they have different interests in how monetary policy affects the exchange rate. For small, very trade-exposed countries, the exchange rate will be a crucial economic factor. These trade-dependent economies will want a low-valued exchange rate to make their goods price competitive in world markets. The larger, less exposed economies will be much less concerned about the exchange rate and more concerned about how monetary policy will affect domestic demand conditions. These different national conditions in terms of trade exposure could lead to domestic firms' exerting incongruent pressures on the various NCB governors. That does not mean that the governors would respond to that pressure when making policy, but they would be aware of the sentiments within their countries.

CONCLUSION

The ECB is an immensely independent central bank, both nominally and in practice. Its statutory independence is unrivaled in the world. The Treaty on European Union bestowed on the central bank more protection than even the Bundesbank enjoyed in Germany before monetary union. But the ECB does not just enjoy de jure independence; it has yet to face a serious challenge to its policies from any corner of Europe.

The reasons for this high level of independence are the general consensus among European policymakers concerning the merits of central bank independence in light of the Bundesbank example and the fact that financial markets in Europe both expect and prefer that the operational autonomy of the central bank remains unthreatened by politicians. Politicians and the markets have generally taken the position that the monetary policies of the ECB are more on the right track than not and that pressuring the central bank would be counterproductive.

It is particularly important that German politicians and financial markets have supported the ECB's policymaking independence as the Germans have the greatest power to change the status quo, if they wanted to. The political and economic weight of Germany relative to the other EU member states is still quite substantial. German support for a continuation of the Bundesbank model means that the ECB has Europe's biggest power on its side.

So far, the publics of the EU have not played a major role in the politics surrounding the independence of the ECB. While there has been no obvious backlash against the ECB among the member states' publics, there has not been any obvious swell of public support for it, either. One may surmise that the ECB seems a relatively remote institution to the average European citizen, one that has yet to mobilize much emotion in them.

While the ECB can rest assured that there are no direct challenges to its independence in the EU at the moment, it also does not see any looming on the horizon. As long as the ECB is not blamed for Europe's economic problems, the central bank is unlikely to face threats to its autonomy or policy strategy.

NOTES

1. "Tietmeyer Urges Quick ECB Decision," *Financial Times*, 8–9 November 1997.

2. This deal seemed to have been cast into doubt in 2001, when Trichet was indicted by a French court for his involvement with a scandal concerning his work at the French Treasury and the finances of a then government-owned bank, Credit Lyonnais. Trichet was cleared of the charges in the summer of 2003, allowing him to take over the ECB presidency that year.

3. Duisenberg later claimed that he had made no promise to step down after four years. "Duisenberg Will Not Quit Mid-term as ECB President," *Financial Times*, 31 December 1998.

4. "Chirac Laughs Off Suggestions of Farce," *Financial Times*, 4 May 1998.

5. It was widely assumed that the French argued to the German government that making a Frenchman president of the ECB was in compensation for headquartering the ECB in Frankfurt. Some claimed that the French government looked at the position as compensation for giving up the presidency of the European Bank for Reconstruction and Development, which had been led by Jacques de Larosière.

See "Kohl Calls for an End to Dispute on Central Bank Chief," *Financial Times*, 24 November 1997.

    6. "ECB Row Points to Problems for EMU," *Financial Times*, 10 November 1997.

    7. "The Quiet Men Who Are Changing the Euro-11 Group," *Financial Times*, 8 February 2000.

    8. The French government made an attempt in February 2000 to make the Eurogroup a formal subgroup of Ecofin, thus giving it substantially more power. This idea has not found widespread support among Eurozone governments and is particularly resisted by the United Kingdom, Sweden, and Denmark, countries that belong to the EU but not EMU. See "Moves Afoot to Overhaul the Eurogroup," *Financial Times*, 9 February 2000.

    9. "France to Seek Bigger Euro-11 Say on Single Currency," *Financial Times*, 2 June 2000.

    10. The "growth" part of the title was included to assuage the fears of some governments that it sounded like they were concerned only with fiscal balance and not economic growth. Nothing in the agreement commits governments to growth measures.

    11. "Brussels May Ease Stability Pact Rules," *Financial Times*, 11 July 2002.

    12. "How Europe's Stability and Growth Pact Buckled under Slowing Growth and Political Resistance to Budget Discipline," *Financial Times*, 25 September 2002.

    13. "Commission Powerless as Paris Defies Euro Rules," *Financial Times*, 4–5 October 2003; "France Given More Time to Pull Back Budget Deficit," *Financial Times*, 21 October 2003; "Paris Defies Brussels Compromise over Deficit," *Financial Times*, 22 October 2003.

    14. "Duisenberg Warns EU Ministers over Deficit Rules," *Financial Times*, 31 October 2003.

    15. "German Plan Could Be End of Stability Pact," *Financial Times*, 5 November 2003.

    16. "German Plan Could Be End."

    17. Deutsche Bundesbank, *Monthly Report*, November 2003.

    18. "German Plan Could Be End of Stability Pact," *Financial Times*, 5 November 2003.

    19. "Brüssel beschließt schärfere Sparauflagen gegen Berlin," *Handelsblatt*, 19 November 2003.

    20. "Ministers Conduct Late-Night Burial for EU Fiscal Framework," *Financial Times*, 26 November 2003.

    21. "Breaking the Pact: As France and Germany Abandon the Fiscal Rules, Divisions Widen over Europe's Future," *Financial Times*, 27 November 2003.

    22. ECB Press Release, "Statement of the Governing Council: Conclusions Regarding the Correction of Excessive Deficits in France and Germany," 25 November 2003.

    23. In an effort to salvage the Stability and Growth Pact, the ECB's Trichet called for changes in the implementation of the treaty so as to make it enforceable. In other words, it was better to have a watered down treaty than none in force at all.

    24. "EU Deficit Sanctions Decision 'Illegal,'" *Financial Times*, 14 July 2004; Court of Justice of the European Communities, Judgment of the Court of Justice in Case C-27/04, Press Release No. 57/04.

25. Court of Justice of the European Communities, Judgment of the Court of Justice in Case C-27/04, Press Release No. 57/04.

26. "EU Critics Claim 'Cop-out' as Prodi Eases Growth Pact," *Financial Times*, 4–5 September 2004.

27. "German Bank Hits at EU Pact Plan," *Financial Times*, 8 September 2004.

28. "Sweeping Rewrite of EU Stability Pact Agreed," *Financial Times*, 21 March 2005.

29. ECB Press Release, "Statement of the Governing Council on the ECOFIN Council's Report on Improving the Implementation of the Stability and Growth Pact," 21 March 2005.

30. "Bundesbank Chief Faces Calls to Quit over Hotel Stay," *Financial Times*, 5 April 2004.

31. "Bundesbank Chief Fights to Save Career," *Financial Times*, 7 April 2004.

32. "Berlin Denies Leaning on Bundesbank," *Financial Times*, 11 April 2003; "Eichel Faces Grilling over Welteke," *Financial Times*, 12 April 2004.

33. "Preisstabilität nicht meher als Ziel erwähnt," *Frankfurter Allgemeine Zeitung*, 14 October 2003. See, for example, ECB Press Release, "The European Central Bank Adopts an Opinion on the Draft Constitution," 22 September 2003.

34. *European Central Bank Monthly Bulletin*, August 2004, 63.

35. "Paris and Berlin Raise the Stakes over Failure to Ratify the Constitution," *Financial Times*, 13 May 2004.

36. While other sectors of the economy may also have an interest in the central bank's policies, such as manufacturing, agriculture, and labor interests, their interest in monetary policy is likely to be intermittent in comparison to that of the financial sector, and they are less likely to be mobilized to exert pressure to affect the selection of central bankers, as well as the image of their competence and policymaking independence, so as to shape their policies (Frieden 1991).

37. Interview with Executive Board member.

38. Interview with national central bank governor.

39. Interview with national central bank governor.

40. Interview with Executive Board member.

41. Interview with national central bank governor.

42. Interview with Executive Board member.

43. Interview with Executive Board member.

44. Interview with national central bank governor.

45. Interview with Eurozone multinational bank economist.

46. Interview with Eurozone multinational banker.

47. Interview with national central bank governor.

48. Interview with Executive Board member.

49. Interview with national central bank governor.

50. Interview with Executive Board member.

51. Interview with national central bank governor.

52. Interview with Executive Board member.

53. Interview with national central bank governor.

54. Interview with Executive Board member.

55. Interview with Executive Board member.

56. We know from Scheve (2004) that publics across countries do vary in their aversion to inflation based on relatively predictable factors, such as the level of unemployment.

57. Interview with Executive Board member.

58. Interview with national central bank governor.

59. Interview with national central bank governor.

60. Interview with national central bank governor.

61. Interview with member of the Bundesbank Central Bank Council.

5

The Exchange Rate Challenge

When the euro was launched as the common currency for the member states of European Monetary Union (EMU) on 1 January 1999, many financial-sector observers expected it to be a strong currency that would appreciate in value. Although the euro started out strong against the U.S. dollar, its main competitor, it was not long before the new European currency began to depreciate against the dollar. By early February 1999, the euro had lost 5 percent of its value against the dollar.[1] It is important to note that the European Central Bank (ECB) maintained an officially neutral position on the exchange rate. The Governing Council's only real position on the depreciation of the euro was that it was not warranted by the economic fundamentals in the Eurozone.

Then, in February 2000, the ECB changed its position toward the euro's depreciation and stated that the euro's loss in value was a matter of real concern (Duisenberg 2000a). By October 2000, the ECB had raised rates by 225 basis points since the same time the year before.[2] As the euro finally began to appreciate against the dollar in late 2000, the ECB began to play down the exchange rate. By the summer of 2001, the ECB had reverted to its earlier stance of neutrality toward the currency (Duisenberg 2000b).

In January 2004, the ECB changed its policy stance from one of neutrality back to one of activism. This time the problem was not the euro's unchecked depreciation but, rather, its continuing marked appreciation against the dollar. At this time, the members of the Governing Council started a short campaign of "talking down" the euro, which succeeded in lowering the currency's value in relation to the dollar. Thus, between 1999 and 2004, the ECB had come full circle, having adopted policies to retard euro appreciation and depreciation, as well as policies of neutrality toward the currency's external value.

What drove these external monetary policy stances on the part of the ECB? What factors shape the sources of exchange rate policy preferences among ECB decision-makers? This study seeks to solve this puzzle. The empirical question at hand is of primary importance for our understanding of the ECB and the politics of managing EMU and the euro.

This chapter creates a public-choice framework to explain the sources of exchange rate policy preferences among ECB decision-makers. There is no analytical framework in the economics or political science literature that explicitly focuses on the logic of independent central bank policy choice toward the exchange rate. The argument derived from this analytical framework is then evaluated against the empirical evidence to determine its validity.

This chapter rejects possible principal-agent explanations for understanding the ECB's external monetary policy. A principal-agent argument would posit that changes in the economic environment lead economic or political principals to demand certain policy changes from the central bank in order to meet new economic challenges. The public-choice argument developed here is grounded in the assumptions that independent central banks have very substantial autonomy to make policy and that they have a primary interest in appearing competent by providing economic outcomes of solid economic growth, low unemployment, and low inflation. Independent central banks will choose policy strategies that will maximize their interests in the existing economic environment. Thus, an independent central bank will enact a change in its policy when the economic environment affects the relative cost of maintaining that policy to the central bank's interests. In the case of the ECB's policy toward the euro-dollar exchange rate, a change in the economic environment and the way in which this change threatened the ECB's primary interest, namely, appearing competent, led to a change in policy. The change was not the result of the preferences of political or economic principals.

In the sections to follow, I assess what other scholars have to say about the sources of decision-makers' exchange rate policy preferences in independent central banks. Next, I outline an analytical framework that seeks to explain what factors shape the sources of decision-makers' external monetary policy preferences in an independent central bank. Then, I explore how well the argument developed here can explain the ECB's policy toward the external value of the euro. The chapter concludes with an assessment of what the findings mean for our understanding of the ECB, the EMU project, and the politics of central banking in general.

POSSIBLE EXPLANATIONS OF THE SOURCES OF EXCHANGE RATE POLICY PREFERENCES

No scholar has yet developed a framework for explaining the sources of independent central bankers' preferences toward the external value of the currency.[3] This is because, in almost all cases, government officials, not central bankers, are in charge of exchange rate policy, even in independent central banks. Central bankers have played a secondary role in exchange rate politics. The norm has been that finance ministers set the parameters of exchange rate policy, and central bankers execute it.

As the industrial countries have moved to floating exchange rates between the major currencies, the role of finance ministers has faded, and the responsibilities of central bankers have the potential to increase. Independent central bankers, in the absence of exchange rate targets provided by finance ministers, can use interest rates to affect the external value of the currency as they see fit. The ECB is an independent central bank that finds itself without an exchange rate mandate. As European finance ministers have not established exchange rate targets for the ECB, the central bank has discretion over how to manage the external value of the euro. The key question that thus arises is how we might expect an independent central bank to manage the external value of its currency in the absence of instructions from its government.

The principal-agent literature on central banks could aid in the development of a framework for understanding ECB policy toward the external value of the euro. Two branches of literature in economics and political science deal with central banking from a principal-agent standpoint. One focuses on why politicians would delegate authority to an independent central bank (Bernhard 1998; Goodman 1991; Maxfield 1997; Rogoff 1985). The other explores how political and economic principals dictate to legally independent central banks the types of policies they should pursue. This second branch of the literature on central banking is of interest here because it may shed light on what drives ECB exchange rate policy. Scholars in this branch of the literature have argued that independent central bankers are agents of two types of principals: politicians (Belden 1989; Chappell, Havrilesky, and McGregor 1995; Gildea 1990; Havrilesky 1988, 1993; Havrilesky and Gildea 1992; Lohmann 1998; Woolley 1984) and the financial sector (Frey and Schneider 1981; Neumann 1991).

This literature assumes that principals assign, either explicitly or implicitly, very constraining mandates for the central bank to perform. The scholars

who create political principal-agent analytical frameworks argue that central bankers act on behalf of the policy preferences of politicians because
politicians control the central bankers' payoffs for doing their jobs, such as
pay and perks. They argue that the central bank is an agent of financial
institutions because they control the payoffs that matter the most to central
bankers, such as prestige and future employment.

The principal-agent analytical frameworks of both varieties assume that
legally independent central bankers have nominal independence to create
policy according to their own preferences and are mere transmission belts
to achieve the policy preferences of their political or economic principals.

What would these political and economic principals want when it comes
to exchange rate policy? Jeffrey Frieden (1991, 1994, 1997) and C. Randall
Henning (1994) can provide some insights into what an independent central
bank making exchange rate policy according to a principal-agent analytical
framework would look like. Frieden (1991, 2002) has developed one of the
most prominent explanations of why certain economic interest groups have
different preferences concerning the exchange rate in a world of mobile
capital. He explains these different preferences by examining the groups'
exposure to international trade and capital movements. His work has been
a very useful resource for those trying to understand the politics of interest
groups attempting to influence exchange rate policy.[4]

Henning (1994) builds on Frieden in developing an analytical framework
of exchange rate policymaking that explains the variation in government
policy toward the exchange rate. He bases his framework on the premise
that the nature of the ties between industry and finance will shape the government's policies toward the external value of a currency. He argues that a
country with close industry-finance ties will pursue the goals of a competitively valued currency and a stable exchange rate. This policy preference
results from the fact that an industrial firm active in international markets
will want a low-valued currency to keep its goods price competitive and
exchange rate stability to lower the transaction costs of trade. Industry can
better make politicians heed its preferences if it is closely linked with finance, which has the closest ties to the policymakers who shape external
monetary policy.

Thus, based on the logic of the arguments made by the political and economic principal-agent analytical frameworks and Frieden's and Henning's
arguments, we can make predictions about the policy preferences of independent central banks, in this case the ECB, concerning the exchange rate.
First, it is important to note that the twelve member states of the EMU all
have strong bank-industry ties. None of them depends primarily on capital
markets for the financing of industry. They are also open, relatively export-
oriented economies. According to Henning's logic, both finance and the
government in these economies should be oriented toward a competitively

valued currency in order to boost exports; that is, in general, the political and economic principals of the ECB would want the central bank to keep the euro competitively valued relative to the dollar in order to help European exporters.

How would this literature explain the change in the ECB's stance toward the euro-dollar exchange rate between 1999 and 2002? It would argue that the ECB altered its stance in response to a change in economic circumstances that would have affected the interests of the central bank's political or economic principals. The economic interests of the ECB's supposed economic and political principals would lead us to surmise that those principals would have welcomed the depreciation of the euro in relation to the dollar as it would have helped them to boost exports and spur growth in the Eurozone. But we know that the ECB actually became actively engaged in trying to stem the fall of the euro vis-à-vis the dollar. The ECB would have thus been working against the interests of its supposed principals. This would lead us to reject the principal-agent explanation of the ECB's policy dynamics.

While the principal-agent literature on central banks can offer some helpful insights into where independent central bankers' exchange rate policy preferences may come from, I argue that none of these arguments is sufficient, on its own, to explain these preferences fully. The central banking literature says nothing about how independent central bankers themselves view the exchange rate. Even more importantly, the principal-agent central banking literature incorrectly assumes that independent central bankers are motivated primarily to make policy choices on behalf of political or economic principals. I argue in the next section, acting as the direct agent of some political principal is not in independent central bankers' interests.

The political economy literature that focuses on exchange rate politics deals with how politicians, not central bankers, manage exchange rates. I argue that independent central bankers have a very different incentive structure from politicians when it comes to making exchange rate policy. The analytical framework developed below seeks to explain the unique perspective independent central bankers have on exchange rate management.

EXCHANGE RATE POLICY PREFERENCE FORMATION IN INDEPENDENT CENTRAL BANKS

The next step is to explore the logic of what determines the exchange rate policy preferences of decision-makers in an independent central bank. The dependent variable is the central bank's policy toward the exchange rate vis-à-vis some other currency. Such a policy can be seen as occurring on a continuum: on one end, the central bank actively seeks the currency's depreciation, and on the other, it actively pursues the currency's appreciation.

At the midpoint between these ends, the central bank maintains a policy position of neutrality toward the exchange rate. This position would be the same as having no policy at all toward the external value of the currency. This analytical framework seeks to predict when an independent central bank will be close to one of these three general positions on the policy continuum.[5]

The place to start in exploring the exchange rate policy preferences of independent central bankers is to identify what matters to them most. Without identifying the microfoundations of independent central banker policy preferences, this analytical framework could not offer predictions of what policies the central bankers would choose. As in previous chapters, I argue that the most important things to an independent central banker, her interests, are her image of competence, a sense that she is doing a good thing for society, and her policymaking independence.[6]

Today, central bankers around much of the world, and certainly in the industrialized world, for the most part accept that maintaining price stability is the foundation for good general economic performance (Dyson 1994; Fratianni and Salvatore 1993; Maxfield 1997; Persson and Tabellini 1995). Without price stability, according to the prevailing economic thinking among central bankers, inflationary expectations will creep into the economy, and this will erode prospects for economic growth. This idea is a product of the example of the German Bundesbank's policy success since the 1950s, the lessons of inflation in the 1970s and 1980s, and the influence of monetarist thinking in the economics profession. Therefore, independent central bankers believe that it is in their best interest to focus policy on maintaining domestic price stability in order to maintain the health of the macroeconomy over the long run.

So, how would the exchange rate relate to this set of ideas about price stability? The exchange rate of a currency has potentially profound implications for an independent central bank's ability to achieve its goal of domestic price stability. In the best of all possible worlds for an independent central banker, she would not have to manage the exchange rate. The primary reason she would not want to make exchange rate management a priority is that it would constrain what she could do to manage the domestic monetary situation. It has become an accepted truth that you cannot have full capital mobility with a fixed exchange rate and domestic monetary autonomy (Cohen 1993; Mundell 1962). With capital mobility, which is the norm throughout much of the world today, a country can either have a fixed exchange rate or domestic monetary autonomy. Because central bankers need domestic monetary autonomy in order to make the policy choices to maintain domestic price stability, they have an incentive to oppose exchange rate management in favor of a fixed exchange rate.

This does not mean that independent central bankers have no reason to care about the exchange rate. In fact, the exchange rate is very important to them for two reasons. First, and most importantly, a depreciating currency can be a source of inflation in the central banker's country (Henning 1994, 65). With currency depreciation, imports into the country become more expensive, which can drive the aggregate price level higher. Therefore, central bankers have an incentive to make sure that the currency does not depreciate to a level at which it starts to threaten domestic price stability.

Second, and less importantly for the central bankers, the level of the currency can affect the competitiveness of exports to a large extent, depending on the level of trade dependence an economy experiences. As a general rule, if a currency is rapidly appreciating and threatening the competitive position of a trade-dependent economy, and there is no risk of accelerating inflation, the independent central bankers will want to arrest the currency's appreciation to forestall medium- to long-term damage to the macroeconomy. But, all things being equal, independent central bankers will never sacrifice price stability for export competitiveness.

Thus, to summarize, in times when the independent central bankers perceive the exchange rate as threatening domestic price stability, they will likely take measures to arrest the depreciation of the currency in foreign exchange markets. In times when they view the appreciation of the currency as threatening to the medium- to long-term health of the macroeconomy, and action will not threaten price stability, they will act to stop the currency's appreciation. The independent central bankers will take a position of policy neutrality (inaction) when neither price stability nor the export competitiveness of the economy is threatened.

This argument posits that it is the interests of central bankers, not political pressures from external sources, that orient their external monetary policy (or lack thereof) and shape monetary policy priorities. In fact, independent central bankers have an incentive to ignore outside sources of policy pressure regarding external monetary policy. Even though there may be short-term political payoffs for giving either politicians or financial-sector actors what they demand at any specific time regarding the exchange rate, doing so can jeopardize the central bank's image of competence over the medium and long term. This is because the groups that pressure the central bank generally have short-term goals. By focusing on those short-term goals, the central bank could quite possibly damage the prospect of maintaining price stability over the medium and long term, which is very important for guaranteeing a healthy economy. Central bankers know that the better they are able to maintain a healthy economy, the less likely they are to be pressured by the state or society. While it may not always be possible to resist pressure from state and societal actors, independent central bankers will try to do so as much as possible. Thus, those analytical frameworks that treat the central bank as an agent of political and societal principals do not take into account the huge incentive independent central bankers have to ignore outside pressure.

It is important to point out how this analytical framework differs from a principal-agent analytical framework. First, this analytical framework assumes much greater policy autonomy on the part of the central bank than the principal-agent analytical frameworks do. The principal-agent analytical frameworks posit that independent central banks make policy on behalf of narrow political or economic interests. The public-choice analytical framework developed here assumes that independent central banks make policy to satisfy what they think the broadest possible segment of society needs in terms of economic outcomes because catering to particularistic interests is a short-sighted and politically dangerous strategy for the central bankers. While we recognize that governments may sometimes give independent central banks mandates, those mandates are often very broadly defined and do not prescribe policy strategies.

To summarize the argument thus far, independent central bankers, armed with the prevailing strategies for monetary policy, would prefer not to have to manage the exchange rate as it constrains domestic monetary policy options, which could make it more difficult to pursue price stability, the independent central bank's primary priority. Thus, I hypothesize that independent central bankers will take a neutral stance toward the exchange rate in the absence of the threat of imported inflation. Likewise, I hypothesize that independent central bankers will try to appreciate the currency, in the absence of instructions from the government, only if the exchange rate threatens what the central bank defines as price stability. This set of hypotheses contrasts with the principal-agent argument's hypothesis that the independent central bank located in an export-oriented economy with strong bank-industry ties will not try to stem currency depreciation that improves the competitive position of industry in world markets.

THE TRAJECTORY OF ECB POLICY

Now let us examine the evidence to see if the argument presented above can explain the sources of the ECB's preferences concerning the euro-dollar exchange rate. For ease of analysis, I have divided the trajectory of ECB external monetary policy into four phases: (1) external monetary policy neutrality from January 1999 until February 2000, (2) external monetary policy activism from February 2000 until early 2001, (3) a return to policy neutrality from early 2001 until late 2003, and (4) policy activism for three months in 2003 into 2004.

The analytical framework described above would predict that the first instance of external monetary policy neutrality was caused by the absence of a threat from inflation imported through the exchange rate. It would also hypothesize that the period of external monetary policy activism was caused by concern about the importation of inflation through the exchange rate. The return to external monetary policy neutrality would result from the disappearance of the threat of inflation imported through the exchange rate. The policy to halt the appreciation of the euro would have been fostered by the central bank's perceived need to stem the damaging effects of the exchange rate on the prospects of Eurozone economic recovery.

How can these explanations be evaluated? The key to assessing their merit is to locate evidence to determine if the ECB's decision-makers' position on policy toward the exchange rate was motivated by concerns about importing inflation through the exchange rate or if other factors were more important.

First, we need to address the type of data to be used. Since we are searching for the motivations behind ECB policy, we must search for data that will provide insight into those motivations. One needs to be clear about the type of data that is not available: transcripts or voting records of Governing Council meetings. The ECB embargoes the transcripts of Governing Council meetings, and it consistently claims that no votes are taken in such meetings. Thus, there is no written record of what specifically is said in Governing Council meetings. Also, no Governing Council member will discuss the specifics of the council's meetings in interviews or press conferences.

Three sources of data are used in this analysis to shed light on policy motivations: (1) the editorial section of the *European Central Bank Monthly Bulletin*; (2) press releases from the ECB, including press conferences after Governing Council meetings, speeches by Governing Council members before various groups, and testimony of Executive Board members before the European Parliament; and (3) economic data on the Eurozone.

Editorials, public statements, and press conference data provide good insights into the thinking of Governing Council members. Using all three forms of position data reveals a richness of thinking that using just one form of data might not yield. Also, comparing all three allows one to check if the ECB is in fact consistent in how it thinks about exchange rate issues.

A final type of data, economic statistics, can provide a picture of the economic context in which positions were taken. Economic data can be particularly important in showing whether positions said to be taken for economic reasons actually correspond to economic realities.

The purpose of using these multiple types of data is to establish, as much as possible, the validity of each source used. The study aims to employ data that reveal true motivations for policy stances. By comparing multiple public statements, both across time by the same individual and across individuals involved with policymaking, we can surmise if their arguments and logic

are consistent. The more consistency there is, the more likely it is that true
motivations are being revealed. By comparing economic data to the stated
economic rationale for policy, we can judge if it does appear that economic
circumstances are driving policy.

Now, let us see how these various forms of data provide insights into the
motivations behind ECB external monetary policy.

EXTERNAL MONETARY POLICY NEUTRALITY

The ECB offered a glimpse into its thinking about the external value of the
euro soon after the common currency was launched in January 1999. In
March 1999, as the euro steadily lost value against the dollar, ECB president
Wim Duisenberg (1999) said in a speech,

> The primary objective of the single monetary policy is the maintenance of price
> stability. Monetary policy will always be geared to this objective. Consequently,
> the monetary policy strategy of the Eurosystem does not embody an implicit
> or explicit exchange rate target or objective, since gearing monetary policy
> decisions to maintaining such an exchange rate target may, at times, conflict
> with the goal of price stability.

In other words, the ECB was taking a stance of neutrality toward the exchange rate in order to avoid tying its hands in maintaining domestic price
stability. As the euro continued to slide in value relative to the dollar in
1999, Duisenberg (1999) provided more insight into how the central bank
thought about the exchange rate:

> The euro's low external value would matter in economic terms, only if it had
> a strong impact on euro-zone inflation. Does the actual movement give rise to
> concern? The answer is no. It doesn't matter very much.

A perusal of the editorial section of the *European Central Bank Monthly
Bulletin* from January 1999 to February 2000 shows that the ECB was closely
watching the euro-dollar exchange rate but did not see reason for concern.
The central bank was also explicit about its reasons for not being concerned.
In May 1999, the ECB mentioned the meaning of the exchange rate for the
central bank for the first time in its editorial: "The ECB closely monitors
exchange rate developments in the context of the broadly based assessment
of the outlook for price developments. In this context, it should be noted
that recent exchange rate developments have not yet indicated any risk for
future price stability."[7]

In the months following May 1999, the central bank discussed the euro-
dollar exchange rate in every editorial in the *Bulletin*. It noted that the rate

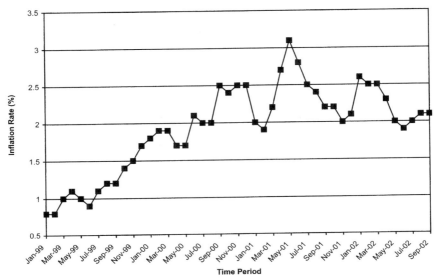

Figure 5.1.   Inflation (HICP), January 1999 to September 2002

did not give rise to concerns about imported inflation. This logic about the relationship between the exchange rate and domestic price stability was the expressed rationale behind the central bank's neutral external monetary policy stance.

The data from the Eurozone economic context support the ECB's claim to not be concerned about inflationary consequences of the exchange rate. We need to determine if, during the first six months of the euro, inflation was within the boundaries defined as price stability by the ECB, which is less than 2 percent annualized growth in consumer prices. Figure 5.1 shows the course of consumer price inflation, defined as the harmonized index of consumer prices (HICP), in the Eurozone from January 1999 to March 2003.

We find that inflation was running at 1.5 percent for the Eurozone in the last quarter of 1999. The growth of the monetary aggregate M3 was in line with the central bank's reference value, and there was little concern about its acceleration.[8] In none of the major economies of the Eurozone was inflation a growing problem. Only Ireland, Portugal, and, to a lesser extent, Spain were experiencing inflation above the central bank's price-stability level. As these are considered relatively minor economies in the Eurozone, they would not drive ECB policy. Germany and France, the two largest economies in the Eurozone, which together make up almost 70 percent of the Eurozone aggregate gross domestic product, had inflation rates of less than 1 percent.[9] Thus, from the standpoint of inflation, there was no concern at the Eurozone level over the negative economic effects of the euro's depreciation. On the contrary, the euro's depreciation was helping the export sectors of Eurozone economies. That the ECB's Governing Council voted to lower its main interest rate in April 1999 from 3.0 percent to 2.5 percent was a very clear sign that it felt little concern about the inflationary effects of the euro's depreciation.[10]

Taken together, the documentary and economic data indicate that, because the euro's relative depreciation would not threaten domestic Eurozone inflation, the Governing Council did not adopt a policy toward the euro vis-à-vis the dollar. This position on euro exchange rate policy in the economic context of the first year of the euro's existence complies with the predictions of the analytical framework. The evidence shows that these independent central bankers were satisfied that the euro's external value was not a threat to price stability, the central bank's primary mandate; thus, it did not give them reason to move to an activist policy toward the exchange rate.

THE MOVE TO EXTERNAL MONETARY POLICY ACTIVISM

As noted earlier, the ECB changed its stance toward the euro-dollar exchange rate in February 2000. The central bank raised its interest rate on its main refinancing operations by 25 basis points on 3 February. This move, coupled with the ECB's stated justification, marked the beginning of an activist phase in ECB policy toward the external value of the euro. The leadership of the ECB justified the policy move in a press conference announcing the interest rate move. President Duisenberg (2000a) stated the following:

> Developments in the exchange rate of the euro are becoming a cause for concern with regard to future price stability. At the end of January, the nominal effective exchange rate of the euro stood approximately 11.5% below its level in the first quarter of 1999. Given both the magnitude and the duration of the development, import prices can be expected to rise further, thereby increasing the risk that upward pressures on consumer price inflation might materialise in the medium term. . . . In conclusion, it is the responsibility of the Governing Council to maintain price stability, thereby contributing to sustainable growth in the euro area.

During the same press conference, Duisenberg and Christian Noyer, the ECB's vice president, were asked if it was solely the euro's exchange rate that pushed the ECB to raise rates. Duisenberg replied, "We carefully looked at the recent developments in the exchange rate as one of the main indicators which could have a lasting effect on future price developments and which we wanted to counteract" (2000a).

The official stance of the ECB Governing Council laid out in the editorial of the February 2000 *Monthly Bulletin* echoes Duisenberg's comments at the press conference. About the euro exchange rate, the statement reads,

> The continuous depreciation of the euro has contributed to increases in import prices. . . . Given the magnitude and duration of this development, the past movements of the exchange rate of the euro have become a cause for concern with regard to future price stability in view of their impact on consumer price inflation via increases in the prices of final and intermediate imported goods.[11]

Thus, the central bank was clearly justifying its tightening of monetary policy by pointing to the depreciation of the euro. The ECB gave further insight into the motivations behind its external monetary policy activism in a press conference in April 2000 following a meeting of the Governing Council. At the press conference, a journalist asked President Duisenberg about the link between the exchange rate and interest rate hikes. Duisenberg stated, "It is that factor—if those upward risks [to price stability] become stronger or if they do not abate—that would induce monetary policy reactions, not the exchange rate as such. The exchange rate as such is not our target."[12] This telling answer suggests that the ECB did not care inherently what the exchange rate of the euro was but only if it was causing inflation.

As the ECB continued to tighten policy in 2000, each time it pointed to the continued depreciation of the euro. In the fall of 2000, the ECB's steps to intervene in international currency markets were another clear sign of a policy of getting serious about the euro's slide in value. As with the rise in interest rates, the central bank pointed to the threat to domestic price stability brought on by the euro's depreciation. At a hearing before the Committee on Economic and Monetary Affairs of the European Parliament on 23 November 2000, Duisenberg (2000c) provided the following rationale for the series of interventions undertaken by the ECB in September and November 2000:

> The exchange rate of the euro has remained cause for concern. The depreciation of the euro during 1999 and 2000 has added upward pressures on consumer prices in the euro area. The exchange rate of the euro has remained out of line with economic fundamentals for a prolonged period of time. . . . In order to support the euro, concerted interventions by all G-7 members, on the initiative of the ECB, took place on 22 September, and the Eurosystem intervened several times in November.

A look at the economic data confirms the link between euro depreciation and the rise of inflation rates, particularly consumer price inflation. From January 1999 to February 2000, the price of imports into the Eurozone rose 20 percent.[13] This translated into consumer price increases because in February 2000, the rate of consumer price inflation rose to 2 percent, the ECB's stated ceiling for price stability. During the period from January 1999

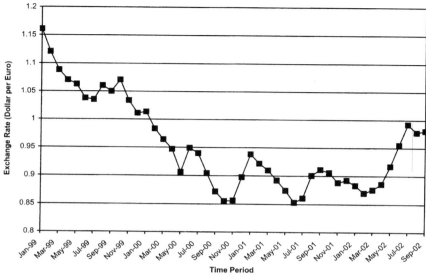

Figure 5.2.   Exchange Rate (dollar per euro), January 1999 to September 2002

to February 2000, the rate had been between 1 and 1.9 percent. As the consumer price inflation trend was due to increase in the months following February because of the passed-on costs of higher import prices, the ECB was almost forced to do something about the euro's depreciation or abandon its definition of price stability. See figure 5.2 for a view of the trajectory of consumer price inflation in the Eurozone. Taking these economic conditions into account, it is quite clear why the central bank moved to arrest the euro's slide.

Back to Neutrality

The ECB's interventions in the fall of 2000 proved relatively successful as they arrested the depreciation of the euro and, in fact, led to a gradual, yet uneven, appreciation trend for the common currency. Figure 5.2 shows the trajectory of the euro-dollar exchange rate from January 1999 to September 2002.

The ECB's stance following the beginning of the euro appreciation trend in November 2000, as shown in figure 5.2, was a neutral position on the exchange rate. There were no more interventions and no interest rate hikes based primarily on the depreciation of the euro. In fact, the ECB began to relax its monetary policy starting in the fall of 2000. It kept interest rates steady until the fall of 2001, when it began to lower rates, citing the medium-term outlook for lower inflation.[14]

Statements by the Governing Council throughout 2001 give insight into why the ECB had decided to move back to a more neutral stance vis-à-vis the euro's external value. The editorials in the *Monthly Bulletin* since December 2000 show a consistent theme. This statement in the editorial of the January 2001 *Monthly Bulletin* is indicative of the thinking of the central bank about the link between the exchange rate and inflation: "The subsequent significant fall in oil prices and the pronounced appreciation of the exchange rate of the euro which have occurred since late November should lead to a decline in annual consumer price inflation as from December 2000. However, some further gradual pass-through of earlier rises in oil and import prices via nonenergy HICP components should be expected."[15] In the months subsequent to that comment, the ECB maintained that while the previous depreciation of the euro had caused some persistent effects on consumer price inflation, these were diminishing, allowing for the relaxation of monetary policy. In his testimony before the Committee on Economic and Monetary Affairs of the European Parliament in December of 2001, ECB president Duisenberg (2001) gave insight into how the central bank was thinking about the euro exchange rate in 2001:

> We could then see that the shocks to the price level stemming from the increases in oil prices and the depreciation of the euro in 1999 and 2000, as well as from food price increases seen in early 2001, would have only temporary or one-off effects on consumer prices and were gradually falling out of the calculation of annual inflation rates. . . . It was therefore likely that inflationary pressures in the euro area would remain contained.

A very telling sign that the ECB was returning to a policy of neutrality toward the euro's external value was the fact that by the summer of 2001, the Governing Council did not discuss the exchange rate any longer in its editorials.

What do the economic data tell us about the ECB's rationale for a more relaxed policy toward the euro's external value? Since the ECB looks ahead when making monetary policy, we need to examine what the central bank thought inflation was going to look like in the medium term when it began its policy of relaxation toward the euro in early 2001. In late 2000 and early 2001, consumer price inflation was falling. It had been 2.8 percent in October 2000 and had fallen to 2.4 percent by March 2001. While the economic data indicated in early 2001 that inflation was not due to drop substantially in the medium term because of the lingering effects of earlier euro depreciation on consumer prices, these inflation effects were considered minor and temporary. These euro depreciation effects did have a noticeable impact on inflation in the euro area in the summer of 2001. As expected, inflation spiked, hitting nearly 3.5 percent in May and June 2001. Also, as expected, inflation quickly dropped off and continued to decline into 2002.

It was also obvious that the dollar was beginning a trend of depreciation vis-à-vis all of the major currencies of the world beginning in 2001. The general slowdown in the U.S. economy, deepened by the terrorist attacks of 11 September, made it apparent that the period of "dollar strength" was coming to an end. This would lead ECB decision-makers to think that the euro depreciation effects on inflation in the Eurozone were temporary and would not last long into 2001. Thus, it is perfectly consistent with the domestic inflation situation in the Eurozone economy that the ECB moved to a neutral position on the external value of the euro in 2001 and 2002.

Concerns about Euro Strength

The euro continued a trend of appreciation against the dollar in 2002 and into 2003. By the summer of 2003, when the euro had appreciated beyond parity with the dollar, market participants and observers began to wonder if the exchange rate was a growing problem for European exporters. Figure 5.3 shows the euro's exchange rate with the dollar from October 2002 to February 2004.

In fact, the euro appreciated by nearly 20 percent against the dollar over the course of 2003. It was widely known that the two largest economies

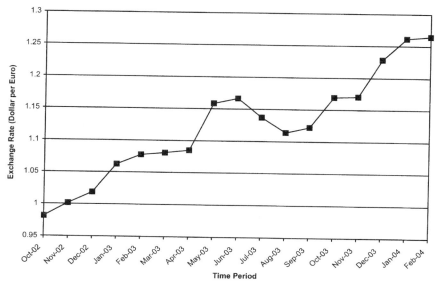

Figure 5.3.   Exchange Rate (dollar per euro), October 2002 to February 2004

in the Eurozone, France and Germany, which grew at anemic rates in 2002 and 2003, owed almost all of their growth to exports. Domestic demand was simply not going to drive those economies into sustained growth.

When asked in early 2003 if he was concerned about the euro's appreciation against the dollar, ECB president Duisenberg said,

> First of all, the euro has for some weeks now been fluctuating around a level against the dollar of around 1.08, which is slightly below the average level of the euro in the two years preceding the introduction of the euro. So it still reflects, we think, a healthy competitive position, which has not been undermined by the recent nominal appreciation. . . . Volatility is always bad. And we prefer stability to volatility. But I would emphasise that the behaviour of the exchange rate over recent months has not been all that volatile. Effectively, the movements have been quite limited. . . . Neither the speed and certainly nor the degree of so-called "volatility"—which was not much—is a cause of concern for us.[16]

Issues of the ECB's *Monthly Bulletin* in 2002 and into 2003 all pointed to the positive, inflation-reducing effect of the euro's appreciation. But as the euro continued to appreciate in 2003, market participants and the financial press in Europe began to wonder what would make the ECB worried about the euro's appreciation against the dollar. Public statements by members of the Governing Council indicated that the ECB had no plans to intervene by any policy means to halt the euro's appreciation in the short term.[17]

As the euro inched closer to $1.20 to the euro, chief economists at major European corporations and banks began to predict a halt to any Eurozone recovery if the $1.20 threshold in the exchange rate was breached. As the French and German economies hovered near recession, and any and all growth was coming from exports, these countries' firms, as well as their governments, were beginning to have serious worries about the ECB's policy of neutrality toward the euro's rise.[18]

The ECB began to change its policy toward the euro-dollar exchange rate in December 2003. It moved to a strategy of actively "talking down" the euro against the dollar; that is, the Governing Council members decided to show the public that they did not welcome any further appreciation of the euro against the dollar. By stating this, the ECB was notifying the currency markets that they did not intend to allow the appreciation to go unchecked. It was no longer a safe bet that the euro would be allowed to rise in value against the dollar.

Members of the Governing Council began to change their policy on the euro's external value primarily because, while the threat of inflation in the Eurozone was very low, the threat posed by the high-valued euro to its fragile economic recovery was real.[19] In November 2003, the HICP in the Eurozone was running at 2.2 percent, but the ECB projected that it was on a trajectory of 2 percent for the coming year. The ECB expected a "gradual recovery" in Eurozone economic growth in the medium term but acknowledged risks to that scenario.[20] But the euro had appreciated almost 20 percent against the dollar from the beginning of 2003 to December of that year.[21] The main risk, in the short term, was the exchange rate.[22]

In late December 2003, Belgian central bank governor Guy Quaden and Dutch governor Nout Wellink stated that the appreciation of the euro was starting to hurt the Eurozone economy.[23] At the 8 January press conference following the Governing Council's fortnightly meeting, ECB president Jean-Claude Trichet, who had just recently replaced Duisenberg, made a rather indirect attack on the euro's external value when he said,

> We have a stake in financial stability. By this I mean stability in general, and it is clear that we do not particularly like excessive volatility or excessive turbulence. So we are not particularly satisfied with what I called the excessive volatility or excessive turbulence of excessive shifts in general.[24]

Trichet heightened his rhetoric of concern about the euro-dollar exchange rate a few days later when he stated at a Bank of International Settlements meeting in Basel, Switzerland, that the "brutal moves of the dollar" against the euro were a problem. He continued by saying that the exchange rate situation was "not welcome and not appropriate."[25] Trichet was joined in his "talking down" attack on the euro-dollar exchange rate by others in the Governing Council, such as Otmar Issing, the chief economist, and several national central bank governors.[26]

Another plank in the ECB's strategy to reverse the appreciation of the euro was to have other Group of Seven (G-7) nations signal to markets that the euro-dollar exchange rate was unacceptable. Prior to a G-7 meeting in February 2004, some Governing Council members began to pressure their non-European counterparts to signal publicly to markets that euro appreciation would not be welcomed.[27] Klaus Liebscher, governor of the Austrian central bank, stated, "We live in a world of interdependencies.... [T]he US also has an interest in stable markets."[28] The Governing Council was also supported by the finance ministers in the Eurozone, who established a joint position on the need for a G-7 signal on euro appreciation.[29]

The ECB was able to issue the following joint statement from the G-7 meeting in the United States: "Excess volatility and disorderly movements in exchange rates are undesirable for economic growth."[30] This statement, along with further comments to talk down the euro by Governing Council members in February and March 2004, brought an end to the euro's appreciation against the dollar (although there was no large depreciation) by April of that year.[31] Beginning in April 2004, the ECB moved back to a policy of neutrality on the euro's exchange rate with the dollar.

LESSONS LEARNED

The policy trajectory recounted above indicates what the policy priorities of the ECB in regard to the external value of the euro were. An independent central bank will have an inherent desire not to manage the exchange rate as that function could impede the central bank's ability to manage monetary policy aimed at maintaining price stability. An independent central bank would only want to engage in exchange rate management when the exchange rate threatened to spark domestic inflation through higher import prices or when perceived excessive appreciation seriously threatened growth prospects. Thus, if an independent central bank is not under orders from the government to manage an exchange rate target, if there is no threat of imported inflation through the exchange rate, and if the exchange rate is not threatening growth prospects, the central bank will want to maintain a neutral stance toward the exchange rate.

We can see from the policy story presented here that the ECB's stance toward the euro-dollar exchange rate held very well to these predictions. The ECB maintained a neutral stance toward the euro's external value from its launch in January 1999 until February 2000, when the ECB began to voice concern over the currency's value. The central bank also began to justify a tightened monetary policy and currency market interventions because of the depreciating euro. The ECB explicitly stated that the central bank was concerned about the euro's slide in external value because of its inflationary effects in the Eurozone economies. The ECB stopped talking about the euro's value and justifying policy actions in terms of the exchange rate when the exchange rate no longer threatened to import inflation into the Eurozone. Thus, the ECB only cared about the drop in the euro's value against the dollar when it threatened domestic price stability.

The ECB only began to react to the appreciation of the euro when it was clearly adding to the momentum leading the two largest economies in the Eurozone into recession by choking off their ability to export their way into growth. It must be noted, however, that it took nearly two years of euro appreciation and its reaching a very high level relative to the dollar to trigger the ECB to act to stem the common currency's rise in value. When it did act, the ECB did so by talking down the euro and not by taking more drastic measures, such as adjusting interest rates or intervening in the currency markets. Clearly, the ECB is not given to moving quickly or aggressively to stem the euro's value in order to please European governments or market participants.

The ECB's policy toward the external value of the euro clearly shows that the central bank prioritizes price stability. The drop in the value of the euro in international currency markets was by no means unpopular with all Europeans. In fact, it was greeted enthusiastically by some very powerful forces in European politics.[32] European exporters saw a major increase in their exports as the euro declined in value relative to the dollar.[33] This was particularly true in Germany, an economy that, recently, has depended on exports for economic growth.[34] Despite the economic advantage offered by euro-led export growth in the Eurozone, the ECB took the potentially unpopular measure of counteracting the euro's drop in external value in order to protect price stability in the Eurozone. It would hardly seem that the ECB was acting as an agent of European industry and its bank allies.

Nor did all of Europe's politicians lament the euro's drop in value. In fact, the national politician most vocal on the euro's external value was Gerhard Schröder, the German chancellor, who stated that the euro's slide was a good thing for Europe because it boosted exports. Despite this argument from one of Europe's most powerful politicians, the ECB took measures that cut into Europe's exports. This also seems to belie any notion that the ECB was acting as an agent of politicians.

The actions and rationales of the ECB for those actions seem to indicate that the central bank conforms to the notion that it is managed by a technocratic leadership, which sees maintaining price stability as the central bank's primary mission. The editorials, speeches, and public comments of the ECB's Governing Council all show a very clear picture of a central bank that is serious about holding to the central bank's price-stability mandate. At no time did any single member of the Governing Council express a view indicating that there were factors other than concern for price stability motivating policy toward the exchange rate.

CONCLUSION

This chapter has sought to explain the sources of the external monetary policy preferences of ECB decision-makers. I have argued that the independent central bankers' policy preferences on exchange rate management are a result of the central bank's focus on domestic price stability. Unless the exchange rate threatens domestic price stability, the independent central bank would prefer to stay out of the business of exchange rate management.

The results of this study should be both hopeful and worrisome to proponents of a common European monetary policy. The hopeful result is that the ECB is a truly independent central bank that takes its price-stability mandate seriously. Some had feared that the ECB would not be able to operate as the Bundesbank had because there might not have been as much support for central bank independence in the Eurozone as there is in Germany.

The worrying aspect for some may be the above-mentioned independence. Some would say that the ECB is a collegium of technocratic inflationphobes, as evidenced by their fixation on price stability. But one could argue, as the central bank itself does, that the ECB is following its mandate, which was created by democratically elected European politicians. It seems unlikely that the central bank will change its attitude about the relationship between the exchange rate and price stability unless it receives a new mandate. As was the case with the Bundesbank, if the ECB can continue to deliver good economic outcomes, no politician will dare touch its independence.

NOTES

1. The most important cause of the euro's decline against the dollar was the relative strength of the American economy vis-à-vis the less robust economies of the Eurozone, particularly the sluggish German economy. The high-growth, low-inflation American economy was a more attractive investment opportunity than the Eurozone with its low growth rates and signs of a lack of political will among major Eurozone governments to liberalize labor markets, which is considered a major impediment to growth.

2. Several excellent studies of the politics of EMU touch on ECB policy. Among them are Dyson (2000), Frieden and Jones (1998), Neal and Barbezat (1998), and Verdun (2002). None of these explicitly deal with the logic behind the ECB's external monetary policy.

3. One of the classic empirical works on the politics of exchange rate policy-making in the United States is Destler and Henning (1989).

4. Please note that the analytical framework does not seek to predict the instrument of policy, such as currency market interventions, interest-rate increases, or public comments on the currency.

5. These goals are not listed in any particular order. The order of importance of these things may differ across central bankers and across time for individual central bankers.

6. In the editorial section of the *Monthly Bulletin*, the ECB explains the rationale behind its policy decisions. All of these materials can be accessed through the ECB's website at www.ecb.int.

7. *European Central Bank Monthly Bulletin,* May 1999, 5.

8. *European Central Bank Monthly Bulletin,* February 1999, 7.

9. *Bundesbank Monthly Bulletin,* February 1999, 7.

10. The exceptions to the ECB's general passiveness about the euro's depreciation were Bundesbank president Hans Tietmeyer and his successor, Ernst Welteke. By June 1999, Tietmeyer and Welteke were publicly stating their frustration with the common currency's unchecked depreciation. This German concern with the depreciation of the euro was a product of the large amount of political capital expended by the Bundesbank to convince the skeptical German public that the euro would be as strong as the deutsche mark had been. But the weakening of the euro was, in fact, good for the German economy as it helped boost exports. See "Tietmeyer

Describes Euro's Slide as Not Good News," *Financial Times*, 4 June 1999; "Weak Euro Strengthens German Export Hopes," *Financial Times*, 8 June 1999. The German public's worries about the euro's weakness were so pronounced that in 2000 Duisenberg felt compelled to appeal to the Eurozone publics to have faith in the ECB's monetary policy. "ECB Chief Appeals to Public in Bid to Boost Support for Euro," *Financial Times*, 6–7 May 2000.

11. *European Central Bank Monthly Bulletin*, February 2000, 5.

12. ECB Press Conference, 13 April 2000.

13. *European Central Bank Monthly Bulletin*, June 2000, 27.

14. *European Central Bank Annual Report 2001*, 9.

15. *European Central Bank Monthly Bulletin*, January 2001, 6.

16. ECB Press Conference, 6 February 2003; Testimony before the Committee on Economic and Monetary Affairs of the European Parliament, 12 June 2003.

17. "ECB Unlikely to Intervene to Halt the Euro's Climb against the Dollar," *Financial Times*, 6 October 2003; "ECB Plays Down Effect of Stronger Euro on Growth," *Financial Times*, 10 October 2003.

18. "Eurozone Revival Hopes Fade as Fresh Data Show Too Much Hangs on Exports," *Financial Times*, 21 November 2003; "Euro's Record High against Dollar Raises Recovery Fears," *Financial Times*, 29–30 November 2003; "Euro Erodes Germany's Role as an Industrial Powerhouse," *Financial Times*, 13 January 2004; "Euro Still a Threat to German Economy," *Financial Times*, 16 January 2004.

19. "Dollar Sorgen," *Frankfurter Allgemeine Zeitung*, 20 November 2003.

20. ECB Press Conference, 4 December 2003; "Der Aufschwung hat längst begonnen," *Wirtschaftswoche*, 11 December 2003.

21. "Nothing Fails Like Success at the ECB," *Wall Street Journal Europe*, 6 January 2004.

22. "Cautious Trichet Reaffirms ECB Pursues a Strong Euro," *Wall Street Journal Europe*, 18 December 2003.

23. "ECB Fears Strength of Euro Will Undermine Recovery," *Financial Times*, 29 December 2003.

24. ECB Press Conference, 8 January 2004.

25. "Europe Central Bank Chief Concerned by 'Brutal' Effect of Dollar's Decline," *Financial Times*, 13 January 2004.

26. "Bank Chiefs Drive Euro Down from Record High against the Dollar," *Financial Times*, 17–18 January 2004.

27. "EuroTower: Trichet pflegt Euro-Diplomatie," *VWD-Finanz und Witschaftsspiegel*, 9 January 2004; "Für den Euro ist es nicht zu spät," *Die Welt*, 14 January 2004.

28. "ECB Seeks Support on Exchange Rate Stability," *Financial Times*, 19 January 2004.

29. "Ministers Signal Sharp Rise of Euro Must End," *Financial Times*, 20 January 2004.

30. "Ministers Warn over Currency Volatility," *Financial Times*, 9 February 2004.

31. The leveling out of the euro's value was welcomed by exporting European industries. Surveys showed that worry about the effect of the euro's exchange rate was no longer a particular concern for European firms. See "Unternehmen können

mit starkem Euro leben," *Handelsblatt*, 5 February 2004; "Stark und Schwach," *Süddeutsche Zeitung*, 13 February 2004.

32. "Schröder Exposes Rift over Euro Exchange Rate Policy," *Financial Times*, 5 September 2000; "Germans at Odds over Weak Euro," *Financial Times*, 6 September 2000.

33. *European Central Bank Annual Report 2001*, 56.

34. *Bundesbank Annual Report 2001*, 3.

6

European Monetary Union Enlargement and the European Central Bank

One of the greatest challenges looming for the European Central Bank (ECB) is the enlargement of the European Union (EU). In 2004, the EU expanded from fifteen to twenty-five members. Cyprus, the Czech Republic, Estonia, Hungary, Latvia, Lithuania, Malta, Poland, the Slovak Republic, and Slovenia were all accepted into the EU. Romania and Bulgaria are expected to join soon if new member negotiations are completed as planned. Turkey has applied for membership and is currently in negotiations.

There are also three present members of the EU that are not part of the Eurozone (Denmark, Sweden, and the United Kingdom), but they are considering joining. Thus, if all of the countries that can join European Monetary Union (EMU) actually do, this will expand EMU's size tremendously.

The addition of new member countries to EMU presents a series of critical issues for ECB decision-makers to consider. All of the new EU member countries are obliged to join EMU as soon as they meet the criteria for membership. There is no EMU opt-out option for these countries. Of obvious concern is how to bring relatively poorer and less advanced economies into EMU without negative consequences. In addition, there are the older EU members that opted out of EMU, namely, Denmark and the United Kingdom, as well as Sweden, which did not opt out but has not yet taken the necessary steps to join the Eurozone. Also of central concern is how the addition of so many new members will affect decision-making structures in the central bank. Finally, there is the issue of how the central bank governors of the new EMU member states will fit into the general consensus on monetary policy strategy that exists among the present Governing Council members. How will all of these countries affect monetary policymaking at the ECB when and if they join the Eurozone?

This chapter explores these questions. I argue that the expansion of the EU is indeed a challenge for the ECB that will require a possibly difficult process of coordinating the operations of so many new entrants, some of which have a somewhat different operational culture from the ECB, particularly the British. There is also the issue of different economic conditions and problems in the Central European countries, giving rise in their central banks to different interests from those in their Western European counterparts.

Despite these challenges, EMU expansion poses no serious challenges to the smooth operation of the ECB in the Eurozone. Divisions within the ranks of the Governing Council over monetary policy priorities and strategies could potentially undermine the ECB's image of competence and weaken the central bank's political support, but it is much more likely that the new member state governors will be cooperative participants in the policymaking of the ECB. All of the potential entrants into EMU have come to accept the ECB's price-stability culture. It is also likely that the British, Danes, and Swedes will acquiesce to the prevailing monetary policy strategy in the ECB.

This chapter begins with an overview of the new member countries' economies and monetary arrangements to give the reader a sense of what the context of expansion will look like for the ECB. The chapter then explores the need to restructure the decision-making rules in the Governing Council in the light of ten new central banks' joining the Eurosystem. The chapter concludes with a discussion of the problems that may result from the potential new member countries' central bankers' having different norms about monetary policy from those held by their Western European counterparts.

WHY JOIN EMU?

The potential member countries' governments want to join EMU as soon as they can for several reasons. First, adopting the common currency means that the new member countries will not face exchange rate risk with their very important trade partners in the EU. This would save trading firms a great deal of money as they would not have to hedge to protect themselves from currency volatility. These gains would benefit both new EU member countries and the opt-outs.

Second, doing away with currency volatility would reduce the costs of borrowing in European capital markets as firms would not be forced to hedge the value of their debts because of exchange rate risk. This could help spark growth in the new member and candidate countries' economies as the lower costs of capital would make it easier to raise capital in those economies.

Third, the end of exchange rate volatility could mean lower interest rates. Interest rates could be lowered as international investors become comfortable with domestic assets being denominated in euros as opposed to the old national currencies. Thus, the EMU new member countries would not have to pay as high a risk premium on capital through high interest rates to keep investors in their economy. This could also help stimulate growth.

Fourth, there is the rather intangible, yet still very important, issue of prestige for the new EU member states. Being part of EMU would be a very large boost to the prestige of the new member and candidate country governments. Those governments could claim that they had made their countries part of the club of the rich, successful European countries. This may help those governments at the polls.

Clear public-opinion evidence indicates that joining EMU is quite popular in the vast majority of the ten new EU members. Table 6.1 shows the percentages of respondents in the ten new EU member states who think membership in EMU would be a positive versus a negative thing.

In the table, we can see that seven out of the ten countries' populations think the consequences of joining the Eurozone would be more positive than negative. Only in Poland, Latvia, and Malta are the citizens negatively predisposed toward the introduction of the euro. Thus, in these countries, politicians must be wary of the potential political backlash from introducing the common currency when the public is more worried than enthused about the prospect.

If we look at the public-opinion picture in the older EU members that are not part of the Eurozone, we see a much greater degree of skepticism

Table 6.1.   Citizen Attitudes toward the Consequences of Joining the Eurozone
Question: Do you think the introduction of the euro would have positive or negative consequences for [your country]?

Country	Positive Consequences (%)	Negative Consequences (%)	Do Not Know/Not Applicable (%)
Slovenia	56	32	12
Hungary	54	32	13
Cyprus	49	39	12
Slovakia	49	38	13
Czech Republic	45	42	14
Lithuania	45	41	14
Estonia	44	40	16
Poland	41	44	16
Latvia	38	41	21
Malta	35	44	21

about joining the Eurozone. In the United Kingdom, a large majority, steady at around 70 percent, opposes joining the Eurozone. In 2003, in Sweden, a referendum on joining the Eurozone led to a no vote of 56 percent opposed to 42 percent in favor of joining. Public opinion has remained hostile since then. In Denmark, there has been a majority of around 60 percent in favor of joining since the failed referendum of 2000. Most Danish politicians view this as an unstable majority, however, because a new referendum campaign would likely stoke anti-EU sentiment, as it did during the last referendum.[1] Thus, in the older member states, politicians do not face a political bonus by trying to join the Eurozone. In fact, doing so may entail significant domestic political costs for them.

The fifth reason for joining, one that is important for all potential members, is the political clout states seek to gain within the EU by being part of monetary union. The idea is that if you are not part of the Eurozone, you will have less sway in the direction of economic integration in general. An official at the Swedish Riksbank had this to say:

> Proponents of membership are going towards the benefits of a political nature, saying that if you are not a member of the monetary union, you will also be marginalized in all other kinds of discussion about economic policy in Europe. People are willing to say we will probably have a reasonably good economic development even if we stay out. But we will have much smaller possibility to influence what the other countries are doing.[2]

The sixth reason why EMU would benefit new members applies more to the United Kingdom than to the other countries. EMU membership would make domestic capital markets in London more attractive to foreign borrowers. While there are already some euro transactions now in London capital markets, having everything denominated in euro would lower the costs of borrowing for other Eurozone economies. But there is no strong push from the City to join the euro; nor is there strong opposition as the City can do well in- or outside the Eurozone. A Bank of England official put it this way:

> If we were clearly seen as an "in" part of the Eurozone, then I guess, on balance, we'd expect to get a greater absolute amount of business. . . . Would London be damaged if we were outside of the euro? Our conclusion from actual experience is we haven't been damaged.[3]

It is important to note that all of these benefits have accrued to some of the older members of EMU. The economic benefits of EMU membership are almost universally true for all of the EMU member states. The issue of gaining prestige from EMU membership was much more important for those EU countries with histories of economic difficulties, such as the southern European countries. For Italy, Spain, Portugal, and Greece, being part of

EMU signaled that they had set their economic houses in order and were in the same league as the richer northern European states. All of the new EU member country governments could gain from showing their electorates that they had reached the ranks of the advanced industrial democracies of Europe.

THE DRAWBACKS OF EMU MEMBERSHIP FOR POTENTIAL JOINERS

While the potential gains of EMU membership seem like good reasons to try to be admitted as soon as possible, there are some potential drawbacks for new member and candidate states. Just as joining EMU carried risks for all of the present members, the same is the case for countries that have just joined and those poised to join.

Perhaps most importantly, being part of EMU for any economy means losing monetary policymaking autonomy. Monetary policy can no longer be fashioned to fit specific national conditions. Rather, it will have to deal with the economic situation in the Eurozone as a whole. The more a country's economic conditions differ from those in the critical mass of Eurozone economies, the less that country will want monetary policy to be made by those critical mass countries.

In the case of the transition economies, this one-size-fits-all monetary policy is a particular concern. As later sections of this chapter discuss further, the post-Communist transition economies have much lower per capita incomes than the present members of the EMU. Thus, the transition economies have a strong interest in economic growth in order to catch up with their Western European neighbors. A monetary policy geared toward containing inflation in the major Western European economies in EMU could constrain Central and Eastern European hopes for catching up economically.

EMU membership could also lead to significant seignorage losses for some new member and candidate countries. Most new member countries make about 1 to 2 percent of their gross domestic product (GDP) from seignorage from issuing local currency. Such a loss would not be a large economic problem in the face of the gains from EMU, however.

The UK government faces a relatively unique problem when it comes to joining EMU. The British pound sterling is an important international currency and a symbol of global economic prestige to the British populace. To many Brits, the pound is a central aspect of Britain's great power status. Thus, of all the governments facing EMU membership, the British government has the most to fear in terms of potential domestic political backlash. The British government knows it has an uphill battle to fight to convince the British public to support joining EMU.[4]

Despite these potential disadvantages, potential member country governments have clearly decided that the potential benefits of joining EMU outweigh the potential costs, or they would not push so hard to join. EMU is
viewed as a means both to improve domestic economic conditions and, in
the case of transition economies, to give the government prestige by seeming to enter the ranks of the wealthy advanced economies.

But the desire to join EMU is only one part of actually joining. There is
also the precondition called for in the Maastricht Treaty on European Union
that there be significant real, as well as nominal, economic convergence.
As we shall see, these convergence processes offer substantial hurdles for
potential member countries to enter EMU.

THE ISSUE OF ECONOMIC CONVERGENCE

The ten new member states that joined the EU in 2004 are not a homoge-
neous group. Among them are Central and Eastern European post-Socialist
transition economies, as well as two southern European states, Cyprus
and Malta. The transition economies clearly face different problems than
the two small economies, but there is one commonality across the new
EU member countries: they are all poorer than the present EU member
average.

Table 6.2 shows the breakdown of per capita income for the new member
countries. If we examine the per capita incomes of the new EU members,
country by country, we find that only Cyprus is in the same general range

Table 6.2.   GDP per Capita

Country	Index
Czech Republic	62
Denmark	113
Estonia	40
Cyprus	77
Latvia	35
Lithuania	39
Hungary	53
Malta	69
Poland	41
Slovenia	69
Slovakia	47
Sweden	105
United Kingdom	107

Source: Eurostat 148 (2003).
Note: EU 15 = 100; data are from 2002.

of per capita income as the present EU members. The opt-outs, Denmark and the United Kingdom, are quite wealthy within the group and exceed the EU average income, as does Sweden. The other transition economies are much poorer than the Western European economies. Thus, there is a serious wealth divide between the Western European and post-Communist members of the EU. This divide matters because those in the transition economies are looking to catch up in terms of income with the Western European member states in the EU. This desire to catch up with their richer neighbors has policy implications. It means that there will be a strong public preference for growth-oriented policies that will foster income increases. Thus, the public-opinion context is different in the transition economies, where the emphasis will be on growth, from that in the advanced industrialized economies, where there is generally more tolerance for stability-oriented monetary policies.

There has been an encouraging amount of economic growth in the new member countries in the last several years. In general, their economies are growing faster than those of the present fifteen member states. Table 6.3 shows the economic growth rates for the older EU members and the ten new member states.

The Baltic three, Latvia, Lithuania, and Estonia, have growth rates roughly twice the average of the fifteen older members of the EU. The Western European new EU member states have the slowest economic growth rates of the group. This pattern is due to the success of privatization in the Baltic economies and their ability to attract investment relative to the other

Table 6.3. GDP Growth Rate

Country	Percentage
Czech Republic	3.4
Denmark	0
Estonia	4.6
Cyprus	2.2
Latvia	7.3
Lithuania	8.8
Hungary	2.9
Malta	1.9
Poland	3.9
Slovenia	2.3
Slovakia	8.8
Sweden	2.0
United Kingdom	2.8
Eurozone	0.4

Source: *ECB Monthly Bulletin,* March 2004.
Note: Data are from 2003.

Table 6.4. Unemployment Rate

Country	Percentage
Czech Republic	8.0
Denmark	6.1
Estonia	9.5
Cyprus	4.7
Latvia	7.3
Lithuania	8.8
Hungary	5.9
Malta	8.8
Poland	19.1
Slovenia	6.4
Slovakia	16.6
Sweden	6.0
United Kingdom	4.9
Eurozone	12.3

Source: ECB Monthly Bulletin, March 2004.
Note: Data are from 2003.

transition economies. The transition economies, in general, are growing faster than the Western European economies because they are still making high returns on new investment in services and production compared to the more advanced Western European economies. The opt-outs, on the average, are growing slightly faster than the Eurozone average.

While growth may generally be higher in the transition economies, the unemployment figures are mixed. This is a central issue in some of the transition economies as they struggle to find work for those left unemployed by the closing of uncompetitive state enterprises. Table 6.4 shows the unemployment rates for the new EU member countries and the the opt-outs, and the average for the present twelve members of the Eurozone.

The unemployment picture is quite serious in countries such as Poland (19.1 percent) and the Slovak Republic (16.6 percent). The rest of the new EU member states together have a rate below the average Eurozone unemployment rate of 12.3 percent. The lowest rate of unemployment among the transition economies is in Hungary, which has a 5.9 percent unemployment rate. The opt-outs also have a much more positive unemployment picture than the Eurozone average would indicate.

Achieving a rough convergence of incomes and employment prospects is thus an important goal for European political leaders in order to create a working EMU that includes the transition economies. Without real economic convergence between the advanced industrialized and transition economies, a common monetary policy for the broader Europe would be very difficult to achieve.

MEETING THE EMU CRITERIA

Aside from the real economic convergence that will be necessary for the new member countries to join EMU, nominal convergence criteria as set out in the Maastricht Treaty must also be met. These include convergence criteria for price stability, long-term interest rates, stable exchange rates, and deficit and debt limits. The central banks of EMU states must also be legally independent of government instruction. The price-stability criteria says that the inflation rate in each potential EMU member state must be no more than 1.5 percent higher than the average of the inflation rates of the three member countries with the lowest inflation rates. The long-term interest rate in the potential EMU member state can be no more than 2 percent higher than the EMU average. The stable exchange rate criterion mandates that the potential EMU member must be part of the new exchange rate mechanism (ERM II) system for at least two years before being allowed to join EMU. Finally, the deficit criterion says that a potential EMU member's budget deficit cannot exceed 3 percent of GDP, and the amount of outstanding government debt may not exceed 60 percent of GDP.

The inflation story in the new member countries is, with a few exceptions, improving, but it is not where it needs to be for all those countries that want to join EMU. Table 6.5 shows the inflation rates in the ten new member countries as well as the opt-outs and the Eurozone.

It is apparent from the table that only Hungary, Latvia, Poland, Slovenia, and Slovakia are having problems with price stability. The rest of the

Table 6.5.   Inflation Growth (HICP)

Country	Percentage
Czech Republic	2.6
Denmark	0.9
Estonia	3.0
Cyprus	1.9
Latvia	6.2
Lithuania	1.1
Hungary	6.8
Malta	2.7
Poland	3.6
Slovenia	3.6
Slovakia	7.4
Sweden	1.0
United Kingdom	1.3
Eurozone	2.1

Source: ECB Monthly Bulletin, February 2005.
Note: Data are from 2004.

potential EMU members seem to be safely within or close to the limits of the price-stability boundaries established by the Maastricht Treaty.

The data show a positive situation for three of the new EU member states when it comes to membership in the ERM II. Estonia, Lithuania, and Slovenia joined the ERM II in the summer of 2004.[5] The ERM II allows for 15 percent movement above and below the agreed-upon bilateral peg to the euro. Of the opt-outs, only Denmark is a member of the exchange rate mechanism (ERM).[6] Thus, only Denmark, Estonia, Lithuania, and Slovenia are within two years of joining the Eurozone, as the Maastricht Treaty stipulates a two-year minimum ERM II membership period.

There are significant dangers to joining the ERM II for some of the potential EMU joiners. The ERM II offers speculators an opportunity to target the currencies of ERM members. Because the currencies are in a fixed-rate regime, speculators have a more stationary target to bet on in the currency markets, which lowers their risk of betting incorrectly on currencies' movements. This raises the speculators' propensity to engage in market operations that can have a large impact on the value of the currencies. This is why the ERM failed in 1992–1993, and it is the principal reason why the Swedes and British are reluctant to join the ERM II. In fact, the British, who are hoping to join the Eurozone at some point, say that they have no intention of joining the ERM II before entering EMU.[7]

The data picture is mixed concerning government deficits. The following pattern seems to develop in the data: the larger economies among the new member countries, for the most part, are exceeding their allowed deficit limits, and the smaller economies are keeping within those limits. The Czech Republic, Hungary, Malta, and Poland all have deficits significantly greater than the limit of 3 percent of GDP. The Czech Republic's was quite far off the mark at 12.9 percent in 2003. This will be a difficult situation for the Czech government to rectify in the short run.

The scenario for government long-term debt is brighter for the new member and candidate countries. As of 2003, all of the new EU member countries, as well as the EMU opt-outs, had debt levels below the limit of 60 percent of GDP. Only Cyprus and Malta were above the debt limits established by the Maastricht Treaty.

The pattern of new EU member countries' and EMU opt-outs' enacting the secondary legislation necessary to join EMU is, for the most part, quite positive. All of the countries have either central banks that are legally independent of government instructions or currency boards. In both forms of monetary authority, the government does not have a say over monetary policy.

Despite the enactment of legislation in the new member countries to make their central banks independent, there have been some examples of backsliding. In the Czech Republic, Poland, and Hungary, politicians have attempted to limit the autonomy of their central banks in order to increase their power over economic policy and thus help their electoral prospects. In the Czech Republic, it took the Constitutional Court to block legislative measures to limit central bank autonomy. There was a parliamentary attempt in Poland in 2002 to amend the central bank law to make it responsible for promoting growth. There was also an attempt in 2001 to expand the size of the Monetary Policy Council to make government control easier. Hungary has also seen similar legislative attempts to limit the independence of its central bank.

These attempts to undermine the independence of the central banks in new member countries show that some new member country governments have not agreed with the norm widely held in Western Europe that price stability is the foundation of sustainable economic growth. This seeming lack of agreement with this norm has attracted serious concern within the ECB over the commitment of some new member governments to the institutional basis of EMU. This may make it harder for the ECB to back these countries' entries into the monetary union.

There has been good progress among the new member and candidate countries on legislation that denies the government access to central bank credits and prohibits favored access by the public sector to financial institutions. But, there is still work to be done in this area in some of the new member countries, Poland being a salient example. It is one of the principal laggards in such legislation.

HOW EMU EXPANSION WILL AFFECT THE OPERATIONS OF THE ECB

The decision-makers in the ECB must face three key issues when new EU entrants join EMU. First, as noted above, the ECB must manage an economic space with very divergent circumstances, particularly in terms of per capita incomes. This means that it will be dealing with national publics that may have quite different expectations about what it should provide in terms of monetary policy. Second, the predicted growth of the EU to twenty-eight members by 2007 means that a restructuring of the institutions of the ECB is a paramount concern. A Governing Council of over thirty members would be far too inefficient and cumbersome a body for effective policymaking. The proposed new structure of the Governing Council was dealt with in chapter 2. Third, there is the issue of whether the monetary policy views of the central bankers from the original fifteen will be congruent with those of the new entrants. With little exposure to Western economic thinking, one may wonder if the central bankers from the transition economies conceptualize the goals and strategies of monetary policy the same way as their

Western European counterparts. These issues could have a profound impact
on how the ECB operates, and each warrants specific attention.

Divergent Economic Interests in EMU

The biggest concern is that the major income difference that exists between the new EU members and the older members will lead to divergent
political pressures in the two groups of countries. Specifically, central bank
governors from the new EU member countries may face very strong pressure
from their publics to spur economic growth in order to raise incomes. In
fact, publics in the new member countries may very well expect significant
income increases as a benefit of being part of EMU. They will look to their
national central bank (NCB) governors to make sure that the ECB delivers
on that expectation.

If we consider what the central bankers cherish most, their image of competence and policymaking independence, the central bankers in the new
member countries find themselves in a very uncomfortable position, with
domestic publics counting on them to bring their living standards up to
Western European levels, which will take some time. Furthermore, tight
monetary policies focused on price stability in the broader Eurozone could
make this task all the harder. But most of the new EU members are growing
at a faster rate than the present members of the Eurozone. Thus, there may
be more incentive among the present EMU-member central bankers to push
for looser monetary policy than among the potential Eurozone joiners.

How important is it that there may be differences as to what to prioritize
in the Governing Council? Does the American Federal Reserve, for example,
not have battles within the Federal Open Market Committee (FOMC) over
the correct direction for monetary policy? Such differences would be much
more important in the ECB than in the American Federal Reserve for one
principal reason. In the Fed, the members of the FOMC do not have clearly
distinguishable constituencies. In the ECB, an NCB governor represents his
or her country. Thus, battles over monetary policy in the ECB can be issues
of one nation's interests versus another's. If central bankers were to take
their positions public, decision-making could be politicized in a way that
would not likely happen in the American Federal Reserve.

It is imperative that two things happen in order to avoid such a scenario. One, real economic convergence between the rich Western European
economies and the transition economies must progress further before a common monetary policy is feasible between them. Second, the members of the
Governing Council must stick to the norm that policy matters discussed in
their meetings are not to be mentioned in public. While public airing of
policy differences has happened infrequently, there is a precedent for such

behavior. Monetary policy positions must not take on national tones, or the work of the ECB will be severely hampered.

New EU Member Countries and the Stability Culture

As we have seen, all of the new member and candidate governments have committed themselves to the goal of joining EMU, and all have agreed to the norms held among the present EMU central banks as to what the goals and strategies of monetary policy should be. A crucial question is, why do the independent central bankers in the potential Eurozone countries agree with the ECB's monetary policy model?

The potential joiners agree with the ECB's monetary policy model, first and foremost, because it has proven over time to be successful. Although the ECB has not been in operation for a very long time, the central bank it was modeled on, the German Bundesbank, was viewed as a hugely successful central bank for decades. The ECB monetary policy model is one that has proven its merit and is considered best-practice central banking, particularly in the new member states of the EU.

Thus, if the central bankers from countries set to join EMU want to produce a monetary policy that will make them appear competent and generate political support, it makes sense to agree to the ECB model.

Some may think there are reasons to doubt that the central bankers in the new member and candidate countries would share the same monetary policy norms as their Western European counterparts. First, the academic training of the majority of the transition economy central bank governors would have been conducted in Communist university systems, where their economics training would have been very different from that of their Western counterparts. If one peruses the curriculum vitae of the governors of the central banks of the ten new members and the two candidate countries, it becomes obvious that there is a mixed picture in terms of exposure to the ideas of economic management in Western Europe. While a majority has had some training or work experience in Western Europe, a sizable minority received training only under the Socialist system and has not had work experience in the West. In theory, these individuals would possibly not accept the ECB's stability-culture thinking as readily as those trained in economics in Western Europe or the United States.

Second, the new member and candidate country governors would not have had the lengthy period of exposure to the German model of monetary policymaking that the former members of the European Monetary System had. Only recently have the transition economy central bankers had the opportunity to travel and interact with central bankers from Western Europe.

While Central European central bankers have been exposed to the ECB monetary policy model and its Bundesbank predecessor for a relatively short time, it did not take long for them to accept the ECB's norms of monetary policy. In fact, some of the Central European central bankers have become more orthodox in their monetarist orientation than most on the Governing Council. As one member of the Executive Board says, "Some of them [Central European central bankers] have gone from one extreme to the other."[8] Among the opt-outs and Sweden, there can be no doubt that their central bankers give price stability the same top priority as the ECB does; they may simply differ with some at the ECB as to the best tactics for achieving price stability.

The Governing Council of the ECB has made a concerted effort to expose the new member country governors to the ECB's operations and modes of thinking as much as possible. Once a year, the governors and deputy governors of the new member country central banks meet with the ECB's General Council in order to discuss the issues of joining EMU. Officials of the ECB and the new member country national central banks have also held several bilateral meetings. Aimed at helping the national central banks with the technical issues related to becoming part of the Eurozone, these meetings are also intended to lead to a convergence of perspectives on monetary issues among ECB officials and their new member country counterparts.

The Relative Economic Size of the New EU Member States

While all of the issues mentioned above merit consideration in the run-up to EMU expansion, one should not lose sight of the simple fact that the new EU members have very small economies compared to the present members of the EU. In fact, the combined GDP of the ten new joiners in 2004 represents only 7 percent of the total GDP of the present Eurozone. Thus, the new EU states are economic dwarves compared to almost all of the present EMU members. Their combined GDP does not even exceed that of the Netherlands, a relatively small Eurozone country.

Why does it matter that these are small economies? First, what happens in these economies will have little impact on the whole Eurozone. If one of these small economies has economic problems, they will be very unlikely to have any noticeable contagion effect in the Eurozone. This means that the Governing Council will not give these economies' conditions the same consideration when making monetary policy as they would the larger economies.

Second, the new structure of the Governing Council's operations gives more voting weight to the countries with the largest economies. Gone is the system where Luxembourg would always have the same say as Germany. Thus, the new EU members will have relatively less say in the deliberations of the Governing Council than the bigger economies of the Eurozone. This is not true, however, of the opt-outs and Sweden, which have relatively large economies compared to the ex-Socialist economies.

The Opt-outs, Sweden, and the Stability Culture

The new member countries are not the only future entrants into EMU that may have difficulty agreeing completely with the German-inspired stability culture that dominates the ECB's monetary policy strategy. The Danish and Swedish governments and central banks will not likely offer a challenge to the status quo of ECB operations because these are relatively small economies, and their monetary policy strategies are already similar to those of the ECB. Of the opt-outs, the United Kingdom presents possibly the greatest challenge to the existing monetary policy strategy for several reasons.

First, the finance system of the United Kingdom is capital market based rather than bank based; that is, the Bank of England deals with economic actors that depend on the more short-term-oriented stock-and-bond markets than on bank loans. Thus, the Bank of England's monetary policy strategy has always been more sensitive to the ups and downs of the capital markets than that of their Continental European counterparts, where financial markets play a limited role. If the Bank of England were to become part of the Eurozone, it would want more emphasis on the health of the capital markets in the United Kingdom than the bank-based-system NCB governors would.

Second, the British have operated under a different monetary policy strategy than the ECB. The British, as well as the Swedish, engage in inflation targeting rather than monetary targeting, which is the ECB's strategy. This strategy consists of the British Parliament's setting an inflation target and the Bank of England's shaping policy in order to keep prices below that target level. The Bank of England insists that this is a superior system to the ECB's strategy of controlling the size of the money supply by a set amount in order to keep prices stable. The Bank of England voiced its criticism of the ECB's strategy when it was first formulated in 1998–1999 and will probably revisit the matter when the British government commits the United Kingdom to EMU membership.[9]

The Swedes plan to raise the issue of the monetary policy strategy when they join EMU. A Swedish Riksbank official states,

> I would not over-state the differences, but I think we'll lean, on some issues, in a little different direction than they [the ECB] are leaning. But we would be able to live with that. We would go in trying to get the thinking moving in a direction that is good for the euro area, which is closer to where we are today, I think.[10]

But the Swedes are realistic about their chances to remold the monetary policy strategy of the ECB. They are aware that their biggest weakness is their small size relative to many of the Western European members of the Eurozone. A Riksbank official says, "I suppose the political argument [for joining] is important because we are a small country, in any case. Even if we argue that we would lose political influence if we don't join the monetary union, the political influence that we would have as members would be pretty small anyway."[11]

While the Swedes may raise the monetary policy strategy issue in the ECB, the British governor is the one who will receive the most attention. Britain is a very large and important member of the EU, with the third largest economy. It also has a long and proud tradition of economic management. For these reasons, it is unlikely that the Bank of England will sit by as the ECB operates in a fashion inconsistent with its ideas about competent policymaking. Thus, while it may be good to bring the large and healthy British economy into the Eurozone, including the Bank of England in the deliberations of the Governing Council may also challenge the ECB's policymaking status quo.

It is important to note that it is unlikely that the Bank of England could seriously threaten the monetary policy strategy status quo in the ECB. While the British central bank could raise new issues in the Governing Council, it likely would not be able to form a coalition that could destabilize the existing strategy model. Not enough countries within the Eurozone would agree with the British model of monetary policymaking as the majority of EU member states have bank-based financial systems and, most importantly, are committed to the successful German model.

CONCLUSION

This chapter has explored what the expansion of the Eurozone will likely mean for the operations of the ECB. EMU enlargement could present ECB decision-makers with challenges to the monetary policy strategy status quo. Some new member states and the United Kingdom have definite economic interests in, at the least, altering the ECB's monetary policy strategy at the margins. It is unlikely, however, that these countries will be able to sway the group of central bankers who represent the ECB status quo from their position on the central bank's monetary policy strategy. The group of large Western European central bankers is not about to change the policy model status quo simply because their poorer neighbors have been admitted into EMU.

There is one factor that could lead to policy change: the prospect of deflation. In an era of slow growth in the advanced industrialized economies, the fear of inflation has been, to some extent, replaced by a concern about deflation. Steadily falling prices could lead the European economies into recessions that could be difficult to overcome. While this has not occurred yet, it is a distinct possibility in the Eurozone, where growth is anemic and monetary policy remains quite tight.

The experience of deflation in the Eurozone could add political impetus to calls from the new member countries for the ECB to rethink its sole emphasis on price stability as its policy goal. It could bring some within the present core of supporters of the ECB's policy strategy status quo over to the side of new member country critics of that policy model. This would probably be contingent on how deep and long-lasting the period of deflation was.

It is important to note that any attempt to change the ECB's monetary policy model could be very divisive politically at the European level. It could pit EU government against EU government as they attempt to chart the future course of the ECB's monetary policy. The key to whether intergovernmental political conflict will develop is whether a public battle between the central bankers unfolds. If the central bankers within the ECB keep their disagreements private, as they did in the run-up to the launch of EMU, then the issue of what to do about monetary policy likely will not attract governmental intervention. But if the arguments over strategy become public, they could become a source of public concern, and thus draw politicians into the fray. This would be particularly true in the United Kingdom, where there is a great amount of skepticism about the operations of the ECB as it is. If the British public becomes convinced that the ECB is working against its interests, it would only be a matter of time before the ECB became a rallying cry for elected British politicians.

Thus, the key to a smooth enlargement of EMU is to convince the new member central bankers that present monetary policy works well for all members. This will likely succeed if economic conditions in the new member states, at the least, do not deteriorate after they join EMU. It will also take adroit diplomacy on the part of the established ECB central bankers to convince the new member central bankers and their publics that the ECB is a catalyst for, not an obstacle to, good economic outcomes in Europe.

NOTES

1. "Staying Cool—Sweden, Denmark, UK Keep Their Distance to the Euro," *Credit Suisse Economic and Policy Consulting*, August 2003.

2. Interview with Swedish Riksbank official.

3. Interview with Bank of England official.

4. Interview with Bank of England official.

5. Lithuania is linked to the ERM in a unilateral arrangement, a currency board.

6. Denmark's bands in the ERM II are 2.5 percent above and below the agreed bilateral krona-euro exchange rate.

7. A Bank of England official, when asked about ERM II membership as a criterion for EMU membership, said that the Maastricht Treaty was referring to the first ERM arrangement and, thus, ERM II is not a valid part of the Maastricht Treaty criteria for joining EMU. He conceded that not everyone in Europe would agree with that interpretation, but he said that it was also unlikely, as he saw it, that present EMU members would keep the United Kingdom out of monetary union over the matter of ERM II membership. He said that Britain is simply too important as a potential member of the Eurozone to exclude over something so trivial.

8. Interview with ECB Executive Board member.

9. Interview with Bank of England official.

10. Interview with Swedish Riksbank official.

11. Interview with Swedish Riksbank official.

Conclusion

This book has been a study of the determinants of monetary policy in the European Central Bank (ECB), the most powerful supranational institution in the European Union (EU). Not only does it have very significant policy-making powers, but it also has a great deal of autonomy to make the kind of policies it believes right for the citizens of the Eurozone. The ECB is not only a major actor in international monetary and economic affairs, but it is also a very important factor in the trajectory of European integration. The operations of the ECB could catalyze further integration, particularly in areas such as fiscal and economic policy coordination and the development of a common external position on monetary and economic issues.

This study has attempted to identify the factors that determine the sources of the ECB's monetary policy strategy. It developed a theory of the sources of independent central bank policymaking that put politics at the center of the process. The core argument of this book is that independent central bankers are concerned, first and foremost, with their image of competence in their societies and their operational independence. Thus, they will make policies that they believe will maximize these two interests.

It is these interests that drove the decision-makers in the ECB to emulate the monetary policy strategy of the Bundesbank. The Bundesbank strategy model was chosen because it was viewed as the best available model of central banking practices in the world, one that would ensure bankers' image of competence and their operational independence. It was a model that the

165

decision-makers in the ECB were also very familiar with because of their long years of experience working with the German central bank. Also, the Germans were highly credible advocates of their model of monetary policy. Because of their record of perceived economic success, when German central bankers argued on behalf of their way of looking at monetary policy, they were the most persuasive central bankers in Europe. It must be noted that if the same discussion about which monetary model to adopt were held today, the profound economic problems Germany faces would make it difficult for the Bundesbank to argue that Germany serves as a model of economic success. But when the monetary blueprint for the EU was being considered in the 1980s and 1990s, Germany stood out as a clear example of how to have low inflation, low unemployment, and solid growth.

The Bundesbank's monetary policy strategy was also an efficient way to buy the ECB a high degree of quick credibility with the markets. As the ECB was seemingly created more out of a political calculus than any economic necessity, European policymakers correctly worried that markets might be anxious about the future of financial stability in the EU. The Bundesbank had been a very trusted institution among actors in the European financial markets. With the plan for European Monetary Union, Europe was giving up the Bundesbank's leadership of European monetary affairs for a completely new and untried institution. This new institution, it must be made clear, would be comanaged by European nationals from some countries with dubious monetary and economic policy records. It was not unthinkable that markets would react to the nascent ECB with a great deal of trepidation, having negative financial and economic consequences down the line. Copying the monetary policy strategy of the Bundesbank would reassure markets by advertising the new central bank as the continuation of the Bundesbank, if not in institutional form, at least in practice. Thus, by replicating the monetary policy strategy of the Bundesbank, the ECB was protecting its interests by going with best practices, and it also bought the ECB's policymakers a degree of instant credibility.

This book has also noted that the ECB has modified the Bundesbank model of monetary policy. The ECB has given slightly different emphasis to the relative roles of money supply growth and general economic indicators in guiding its monetary policy. It has also changed, albeit slightly, the definition of price stability that the central bank employs. Neither of these changes should be interpreted as abandonment of the Bundesbank-based policy strategy. Rather, they indicate marginal strategy changes brought on by the experience with monetary policy operations that the ECB has had since its launch in 1999. Because the ECB operates in a different environment than the Bundesbank did prior to the establishment of monetary union, it is to be expected that the ECB would need to mold its strategy and tactics to fit its unique environment.

OPERATING IN A CONTEXT OF NATION-STATES

The ECB's operational environment is unique compared to any other central bank in the world. The ECB makes monetary policy not for a single, unified national economy and polity but for twelve separate national economies and political systems. This adds a level of complexity to the operations of the ECB that few central banks in the world even come close to facing. The ECB faces disparate national financial systems, political systems, and general publics. Each one of these on its own is a serious challenge to the central bank.

Due to the lack of a single, unified European financial system, the ECB has to tailor its monetary policy to keep the various systems liquid and healthy, even though they may need different things at different times. Thus, the ECB must try to balance the needs of the national financial sectors to keep all of them sound. While there has been a good deal of economic convergence among the members of the monetary union, there is still enough variation in national economic conditions to make the balancing act a constant challenge for the central bank.

The lack of a unified European financial sector also has political implications for the ECB. In most industrialized democracies with independent central banks, the financial sector is a natural political ally of the central bank. While the financial sector may not be universally pleased with the central bank's policies at all times, it prefers that the central bank have operational independence rather than be under the thumb of the politicians. That the European financial sectors are still organized along national lines may hinder the various financial institutions in Europe from providing much of a unified front to protect the ECB from any serious political challenges that it may face.

The political context in which the ECB operates is challenging, to say the least. The central bank faces a myriad of political actors, all with an interest in its operations and the ability to affect how efficacious those operations are. The ECB faces twelve national governments, many with very different attitudes about the proper goals of economic and monetary policy. Also, the ECB faces a string of EU-level institutions, foremost among them the European Commission and the European Parliament, which have limited control over the context in which the central bank operates. No other central bank operates in such a complex political environment.

This array of political actors that it must deal with makes it difficult for the ECB to influence the political and policy environment in which it operates. Who represents the political will of the EU? The various member governments? The EU institutions, such as the European Commission or the European Parliament? Henry Kissinger used to ask, if he wanted to call Europe, whom would he call? One may ask, if the ECB wants to talk to the

Eurozone's political leadership, whom does it call? This matter of the diffusion of political authority has come to a head with the Stability and Growth Pact. As the ECB faces a growing list of defectors from the pact, the central bank finds itself having to enter into contentious dialogue with several national governments. This lack of a centralized political authority makes it much harder for the ECB to influence the policy environment that impacts its own operations. If the EU's various political entities, national and supranational, pull in different directions, this is problematic for the central bank. For this reason, we can expect the ECB to advocate for increasing centralization of policy authority over issues that affect the policy environment in which the central bank finds itself, while not jeopardizing its independence.

Another aspect of the fractious environment in which the ECB operates is the Eurozone's general public. In fact, it is incorrect to refer to a Eurozone general public as there are, as of this writing, twelve separate national publics, each of which has a different historical experience and different attitudes about the European project. Thus, it is very difficult, if not impossible, for the ECB to gauge what the Eurozone general publics think about specific policy issues. While this may not be problematic in that the ECB is not going to look to the publics for cues on how to formulate monetary policy, it is problematic for the central bank in gauging the level of political support it has. The ECB, like every other independent central bank in the world, must be assured that it has public support in order to maintain its operational independence. If publics reduce their support for the central bank, we can assume with a fair degree of confidence that politicians will try to lessen its operational independence. Thus, the ECB has to count on the Eurozone publics to support it, at least passively.

However, the lack of a unified public could also be a benefit for the ECB. Several large countries' publics would have to turn against the ECB to create the momentum for politicians to infringe on the operational independence of the central bank, either by changing the treaty that establishes the ECB's powers and duties or by pressuring it politically. Thus, the inherent difficulties of grassroots mobilization across the Eurozone could actually help the ECB.

THE ECB IN COMPARATIVE PERSPECTIVE

At this point in the study, it may be instructive to say a few words about how the ECB seems to be operating in relation to its two closest relatives, the German Bundesbank and the American Federal Reserve System. I refer to these central banks as the ECB's closest relatives because they were, to varying degrees, the institutional models for the ECB. The Bundesbank was based on the model of the American Fed, and the ECB was based on the model of the Bundesbank. So, what is similar and what is different about how the ECB operates in relation to these other important central banks?

As I have stated many times in this study, the ECB is directly based on the Bundesbank's institutional and strategy model. This near-replication of the Bundesbank was based on a conscious set of decisions by Europe's politicians and central bankers. But while the ECB has much in common with the Bundesbank, some important differences from the German central bank have impacted its operations.

First, the ECB has a much more specific and institutionally protective mandate than the Bundesbank. As was made clear in chapter 2, the ECB's protocol is clearer than the Bundesbank Law as to what the ECB is supposed to focus on in making its policies. Also, because the independence of the ECB is protected by a treaty, changing which would require unanimity among its signatories, the ECB is much better protected by the law than the Bundesbank was. The Bundesbank could have its independence altered by a simple act of the German Parliament. Thus, institutionally, the ECB is much more secure than the Bundesbank ever was.

But, politically, the ECB is much less protected than the Bundesbank was. No German politician seriously entertained the idea of threatening the independence of the German central bank. There was no consensus among German politicians and certainly not in the German public that such a move would be warranted. The Bundesbank had a very high degree of societal support that placed it off limits for serious political pressure.

In the environment in which the ECB operates, political support for its independence is much weaker than that the Bundesbank enjoyed in Germany. Major European politicians, such as French president Jacques Chirac, have publicly stated their desire to restrict the independence of the ECB. It is unlikely that the French public, with its short history of an independent central bank, would try to restrain its politicians from taking on the ECB's independence. And the French government is not the only Eurozone government with misgivings about the independence of the ECB.

What does this mean for the independence of the ECB? It means that the ECB faces a much less secure political environment than the Bundesbank did. While the institutionalized independence of the ECB is not threatened, there are ways to pressure the ECB other than changing its mandate and protocol. For example, if European politicians were to create a "political counterweight" to the ECB, as some in France have demanded, the ECB could find itself under intense pressure to heed politicians' preferences on monetary policy. Thus, copying the Bundesbank's institutions and monetary policy strategy does not guarantee that it will be able to follow on the same path as the German central bank. Political context matters, and the ECB faces a much more challenging political environment than the Bundesbank ever did.

In many ways, the ECB's political environment is closer to that faced by the American Federal Reserve. The Fed operates in a political environment where elements of elite and public opinion contest its operational independence and its stated monetary policy goals. Also, the United States better approximates the diversity of the economic environment in the Eurozone than the much smaller Federal Republic did. Thus, the ECB may have more to learn from the American case than the German one.

What is instructive about the Fed's experience for the ECB? In the absence of historical traumas like the German hyperinflation of 1923–1924 and the German Currency Reform of 1948, it is generally not as easy for all elements of society to come to accept an operationally independent central bank with a strict price-stability mandate. It has taken the Fed decades to think of itself as protected from serious political attacks, and the same may be the case for the ECB. The better the economic outcomes the Eurozone experiences over the years, the more easily detractors of the ECB will come to terms with its independence and mandate.

Also, based on what we know from Fed monetary policy deliberations, it is clear that the Fed must gear its monetary policy toward influencing those sectors and regions of the country that it deems most consequential to the overall macroeconomic picture in the United States. While the Bundesbank had to do that, too, as all central banks must do, the larger and more heterogeneous the economy a central bank manages, the more regional and sectoral trade-offs it must make. As this study has illustrated, the ECB has been doing this since its inception, giving larger weight to the bigger economies, like those of Germany, France, and Italy. With the announced changes to the ECB's decision-making procedure, where the countries' relative voting weights will now be based explicitly on the size of their economies, the ECB is moving more toward the Fed model, where the New York Fed is given more weight than the other banks in the system.

At the same time, aspects of the environment in which the ECB operates are more similar to the Bundesbank's environment than the Fed's. One such aspect is the financial environment in which the central bank operates. The bank-based financial systems of the Eurozone are generally much more like the German financial system than the U.S. capital market system. The emphasis on bank loans rather than securities trading means that the ECB's monetary policy time horizon is longer term than that of the Fed, which must weigh the short-term impact of its decisions on the capital markets, which are much more fluid and reactive.

Another significant difference between the Fed and the ECB is found in the central banks themselves: the locus of decision-making authority. In the American Federal Reserve, the most important person in terms of decision-making power is the chairperson of the Federal Open Market Committee. She or he is the primus inter pares. In the ECB, as it was in the Bundesbank, the president is one among equals and does not have the power to direct the central bank's policy, either formally or informally. Each of the members of the Governing Council, who have voting rights, has an equal say in policy. It is also unlikely, given the sensitivities that persist in the EU about national representation, that a norm in which the president has more say than the others on the council will develop.

Thus, in general, we can say that the ECB shares similarities and differences with both the Bundesbank and the American Federal Reserve. It is important to point out that the ECB is, in fact, facing a unique operational environment and set of political pressures; thus, making predictions about the ECB based on the American and German cases will always be an imperfect business. The ECB will develop its place within its political environment as no other central bank in the world has.

POSSIBLE FUTURE SCENARIOS

One of the questions that observers of the ECB have is, where does the central bank go from here in terms of its political role in the EU and its ability to maintain its policy independence? One can envision three potential future scenarios for the ECB. Each of these will be explored separately below.

In the first scenario, the ECB maintains its status quo position within the EU political economy. The ECB operates in a somewhat murky political environment, where threats to its independence exist, and it faces a complex set of political authorities. In this scenario, the basic operational independence of the central bank is not under serious challenge, and the bank can operate according to its defined mandate as it sees fit.

The continuation of this scenario would have the following consequences. European financial markets would be left relatively undisturbed by changes to the ECB. Also, the political status quo, either at the European level or the national level, would not be altered by any modifications to the way the ECB makes policy. This means, in concrete terms, that European financial markets would remain stable, yet fragmented, and that the ECB would not have much influence on the limited momentum for economic liberalization in Europe.

In the second scenario, the ECB comes under increasing pressure to shape its monetary policy according to the preferences of European politicians. Politicians at the nation-state level, rather than in the EU's supranational institutions, would likely be the ones to exert pressure as it is difficult to imagine those supranational institutions ever getting the amount of power necessary, independent of actions by national governments, to control the ECB. In this scenario, the Eurogroup or some similar body would likely be given significant powers to provide guidance to the ECB on monetary policy matters. This scenario would require a very high degree of agreement among Eurozone member governments in order to create a body that could exert that type of pressure.

The consequences of this scenario would be profound. First, it would likely be very unsettling for European financial markets for the ECB to be pressured as this scenario envisions. It would also cause, at least to some extent, a certain amount of political disquiet as some politicians, even sub-national politicians, would raise concerns about the wisdom of politicizing the monetary policymaking process. Also, if this scenario were to come to pass, it would probably be accompanied by a concomitant slowdown in the economic liberalization process as those who oppose central bank in-dependence would also likely oppose taking significant steps to liberalize their domestic economies.

In the third scenario, the power of the ECB to influence the course of events in Europe would be significantly increased. For this scenario to be realized, several things would need to happen. First, the challengers to the ECB's policymaking power in the EU would have to give up their quest to rein in the ECB. Second, the ECB would have to face a more central-ized political authority in Europe at the supranational level that was firmly committed to neoliberal economic principles.

This scenario would stabilize financial markets, potentially even leading to a boom in investment in the Eurozone. Also, this scenario would mean an increase in the move toward economic liberalization in the Eurozone, some-thing that a strengthened ECB would certainly advocate. But this scenario could also be destabilizing to the political status quo in some member states. If politicians lost control over more of the tools of economic management, they would be increasingly at the mercy of the ECB during the election cy-cle. Also, the losers of economic liberalization would likely try to challenge the process, potentially disrupting domestic politics in the member states.

Which of these scenarios is most likely to come to be? Based on the config-uration of political power of the various players in the context surrounding the ECB, it seems likely that the status quo will be preserved for the fore-seeable future. It is difficult to imagine that the challengers to the ECB's operational independence would be able to overcome the resistance within the ranks of the European national leadership to the idea of infringing on the independence of the central banks. Most of the European governments made a principled commitment to an independent central bank modeled on the institutions of the Bundesbank when they signed the Treaty on Mone-tary Union. There is little reason, at present, to expect them to abandon that commitment.

It is also difficult to imagine that European political leaders would discount the reaction of financial markets to moves to impinge on the independence of the ECB. Just as the French government had to abandon moves to add significantly expansive elements to its economic policy in 1982 because of the reaction of the financial markets, we can expect the same kind of backtracking on attempts to rein in the ECB. Some governments may take steps in that direction, but they will not get very far.

Nor should we expect that the ECB will see its relative power in the Eurozone appreciably increased in the near term. It is highly unlikely that European national politicians are going to give power to a supranational EU authority that will effectively strip them of their ability to control fiscal policy. Proof of this can be found in the way several European governments have behaved in regard to the Stability and Growth Pact. There is a persistent reticence to give up control over economic policy that would leave policymakers at the complete mercy of EU officials. It is not happening now, and there is little reason for it to happen anytime soon.

THEORETICAL INSIGHTS

What do this study's findings mean for our understanding of the sources of policy for independent central banks? First, they clearly show that independent central banks are political institutions. Although one of the rationales, even the most important one, for creating an independent central bank is to remove it from politics, this is impossible. An independent central bank cannot be apolitical. The simple reason for this is that the policies these institutions make are too important for groups in a polity not to try to influence them. Politicians and the financial community have an incentive to try to shape monetary policy. Politicians want to shape it to stay in office. Participants in the financial sector want to shape it to maximize profits. Each of these groups' ability to influence monetary policy is determined by its ability to engage in collective action. If a group cannot engage in collective action because it cannot converge on a particular policy preference, it will not have much say over the parameters of acceptable monetary policy.

The second major implication for our understanding of the sources of policy in independent central banks is that while the policy ideas of central bankers are the key to understanding their policy choices, the central bankers have a constrained ability to determine policy. Their policy ideas must fit within the parameters of acceptable policy determined by the most powerful policy source group in the polity. But policy ideas are not the only things that determine the monetary policy orientation of the central bank. For example, the ECB's strict stability-oriented monetary policy orientation was not solely a product of monetarist thinking in the central bank. The ECB's policy came from the policy ideas held by its decision-makers and the political and economic context that set the demands for certain types of policies. The fact that the Eurozone is dominated by bank-based financial markets means that the ECB should make monetary policy that is long term and stability oriented. Thus, the policy ideas are not created in a vacuum. They must fit the circumstances the bank faces if there is any hope for them to be successful.

The third, very significant implication of the findings is that independent central banks are not as inherently undemocratic as many would argue. Contrary to some opinions, independent central bankers are not technocrats who experiment with society. Decision-makers in an independent central bank must heed the policy preferences of the most powerful groups in society when making policy. This is exactly what a legislature or executive does when it makes policy. It is true that decision-makers in an independent central bank are not elected, but if independent central bankers care about their image of competence and public support for their operational independence, then they will seek a societal consensus on the goals and strategy of monetary policy. A polity that has developed a consensus about the type of monetary policy that it wants is going to get that policy because central bankers will not last long by making policy that goes against the societal consensus. This is as true in the ECB as it is in any independent central bank. The members of the Governing Council are very aware of the importance of societal support for their policies and try to cultivate it at every available opportunity.

POLICY IMPLICATIONS

What do the findings of this study imply for the creation of central bank institutions or policies? One very important implication for policymakers who advocate an anti-inflation monetary policy is that legal central bank independence alone will not guarantee such an outcome. Many scholars and policy advocates have argued that making the central bank independent of government instructions is the best way to ensure low inflation outcomes. The thinking that backs much of this advocacy is that an independent central bank will produce anti-inflationary monetary policies because all central bankers will want to do so because of their background in financial matters. This study has shown that the institutions of central banking do not dictate policies; politics does. An anti-inflation policy, or any other type of monetary policy, is not the product of institutions or rules. It is the result of policy ideas held by the policymakers and the societal support for such policies. Thus, trying to institutionalize a certain policy direction without taking into account the policy norms held by the central bankers and without the support of the most powerful societal groups is futile.

This means that the key for advocates of a particular monetary policy direction is to bring the central bankers and the most powerful societal groups around to their position by convincing either the general public or the financial community that the monetary policy advocated will bring the societal groups substantial rewards. One could use the media to spread the message about the policy being advocated, but it would also be useful to use the central bank itself as a conveyor of the message. This could be accomplished by appointing central bankers who share a preference for the advocated policy and then entrusting those central bankers to go out and try to convince the public and financial community of the benefits of the advocated policy course.

This course of action would likely be more successful among the general public than within the financial community because the financial community has relatively clear and stable interests in particular policy outcomes. Also, the financial community is a reservoir of significant expertise in monetary matters and is not very susceptible to arguments from policy advocates. The general public, which may not have very clearly defined interests and may have a weaker understanding of the mechanisms of monetary policy than the financial community, should be easier to sway into supporting a particular policy direction.

The second major policy implication to draw from this research is that shifting policy directions to meet new challenges may be very difficult in polities where the financial sector opposes such a change in direction. This may produce a situation where the central bankers know both that a change in policy direction is necessary to keep the aggregate economy healthy and that there is not political support for such a change in policy direction. Thus, central bankers may end up continuing with a policy that they know will bring long-term harm to the economy.

How can this situation be overcome? Central bankers must be made more independent of not just government but society. Yet, is it possible for a central bank to be truly independent of both government and society? I would argue that it is impossible. The stakes of monetary policy are too high for all potential governmental and societal actors to be agnostic on monetary policy. A central bank only has the policymaking power that its society, particularly the financial sector, has given to it. Most financial sectors in advanced industrialized economies will have the power to define the parameters of the central bank's acceptable monetary policies. So, a major change in the orientation of monetary policy can only come when the financial sector will not oppose that change. This explains why some independent central banks in lesser developed countries continue policies that produce inflation, which damages the economy over the long run. In such cases, the financial sectors are not powerful enough to defend the central bank from the interference of politicians in the policymaking process.

NEED FOR FURTHER RESEARCH

This study has answered some questions, yet it has raised others and suggests many avenues of further research. First, we have little existing research on public attitudes toward central banks and monetary policy. Most scholars of central banking and political economy assume that the public is not competent or engaged enough to form opinions on such matters. But as this research shows, the public's views on monetary policy are important to the operational independence of the central bank. We need to know much more about the formation and change of public attitudes toward monetary policy. We also need to know more about how signals from the public about monetary policy preferences are interpreted by politicians and central bankers.

Another important avenue of further research concerns the policy preferences and political role of the financial sector in monetary policymaking. This research found many of the existing arguments about these matters in the literature on central banking inadequate. Financial sectors are not the bastions of pro-price-stability policies that many scholars assume they are. The complexity of finance today has made the financial sectors in advanced industrialized economies increasingly heterogeneous. Multiple forms of financial institutions exist, performing different types of financial services. The result is a sector of the economy characterized more by cleavages than cohesion of interests. We need to understand better how this affects the politics of advanced industrialized democracies.

Finally, it is very important that we understand how globalization is affecting the policymaking process in independent central banks. Are global markets diminishing the importance of domestic political processes to the way independent central banks make policy decisions? Is globalization creating a global culture of central banking as ideas flow ever more freely between countries? Does that mean that the ideas used within the acceptable parameters of monetary policy will come to be dominated by a global economic elite? The answers to these questions may give us a very good idea of where the central banks of the advanced industrialized economies are heading in the future.

References

Alesina, Alberto. 1988. "Macroeconomics and Politics." In *NBER Macroeconomic Annual*, ed. Stanley Fischer. Cambridge: Cambridge University Press.

Alesina, Alberto, and Lawrence Summers. 1993. "Central Bank Independence and Macroeconomic Performance: Some Comparative Evidence." *Journal of Money and Banking* 25 (May): 151–62.

Allen, Christopher. 1989. "The Underdevelopment of Keynesianism in the Federal Republic of Germany." In *The Political Power of Economic Ideas: Keynesianism across Nations*, ed. Peter Hall. Princeton, NJ: Princeton University Press.

Andrews, David. 2003a. "Building Capacity: The Institutional Foundations of EMU." Unpublished manuscript, European University, Florence.

———. 2003b. "The Committee of Central Bank Governors as a Source of Rules." *Journal of European Public Policy* 10, no. 6 (December): 956–73.

Antenbrink, Fabian. 1999. *The Democratic Accountability of Central Banks: A Comparative Study of the European Central Bank*. Oxford: Hart Publishing.

Apel, Emmanuel. 2003. *Central Banking Systems Compared: The ECB, the Pre-Euro Bundesbank and the Federal Reserve System*. London: Routledge.

Barro, Robert, and David Gordon. 1983. "Rules, Discretion, and Reputation in a Model of Monetary Policy." *Journal of Monetary Economics* 12, no. 1: 101–20.

Baun, Michael J. 1995. "The Maastricht Treaty as High Politics: Germany, France and European Integration." *Political Science Quarterly* 110, no. 4: 605–34.

———. 1996. *An Imperfect Union: The Maastricht Treaty and the New Politics of European Integration*. Boulder, CO: Westview Press.

———. 1998. *A Wider Europe: The Process and Politics of European Union Enlargement.* Lanham, MD: Rowman & Littlefield.

Bearce, David H. 2003. "Social Preferences, Partisan Agents, and Monetary Policy Outcomes." *International Organization* 57 (Spring): 373–410.

Begg, David, Paul De Grauwe, Francesco Giavazzi, H. Uhlig, and Charles Wyplosz. 1998. "The ECB: Safe at Any Speed?" *Monitoring the European Central Bank.* London: Centre for Economic Policy Research.

Belden, Susan. 1989. "Policy Preferences of FOMC Members as Revealed by Dissenting Votes." *Journal of Money, Credit, and Banking* 41: 432–41.

Belke, Ansgar, and Daniel Gros. 1999. "Estimating the Costs and Benefits of EMU: The Impact of External Shocks on Labor Markets." *Weltwirtschaftliches Archiv* 135, no. 1: 1–47.

Berger, Helge, and Jakob de Haan. 2002. "Are Small Countries Too Powerful within EMU?" *Atlantic Economic Journal* 30, no. 3: 1–20.

Berger, Helge, Jakob de Haan, and Robert Inklaar. 2004. "Should the ECB Be Restructured and If So, How?" Working paper, University of Groningen.

Berman, Sherri, and Kathleen McNamara. 1999. "Bank on Democracy—Why Central Bankers Need Public Oversight." *Foreign Affairs* (March/April): 2–8.

Bernhard, William. 1998. "A Political Explanation of Variations in Central Bank Independence." *American Political Science Review* 92, no. 2: 311–28.

Blinder, Alan. 1998. *Central Banking in Theory and Practice.* Cambridge, MA: MIT Press.

Bofinger, Peter. 2003. "Consequences for the Modification of the Governing Council Rules." Briefing Paper for the Committee for Monetary and Economic Affairs (ECON) of the European Parliament.

Brentford, Phillip. 1998. "Constitutional Aspects of the Independence of the European Central Bank." *International and Comparative Law Quarterly* 47, no. 1: 75–116.

Buiter, Willem. 1999. "Alice in Euroland." *Journal of Common Market Studies* 37, no. 2: 181–209.

Bundesbank Annual Reports, various issues.

Bundesbank Monthly Reports, various issues.

Calvert, Randall L., Matthew D. McCubbins, and Barry R. Weingast. 1989. "A Theory of Political Control and Agency Discretion." *American Journal of Political Science* 33, no. 3: 588–611.

Campanella, Miriam. 2000. "The Battle between ECOFIN-11 and the European Central Bank: A Strategic Interaction Perspective." In *The State of the European Union*, ed. M. Green Cowles and M. Smith, 110–26. Vol. 5. Oxford: Oxford University Press.

Canzoneri, Matthew B., Vittorio Grilli, and Paul R. Masson, eds. 1992. *Establishing a Central Bank: Issues in Europe and Lessons from the U.S.* Cambridge: Cambridge University Press.

Carr, Jonathon. 1985. *Helmut Schmidt: Helmsman of Germany.* New York: St. Martin's Press.

Chappell, Henry, Thomas Havrilesky, and Rob Roy McGregor. 1995. "Policymakers, Institutions, and Central Bank Decisions." *Journal of Economics and Business* 47: 113–36.

Clark, William Roberts. 1993. "The Sources of Central Bank Independence in Developing Countries." Paper prepared for the annual meeting of the American Political Science Association, Washington, DC.

Cohen, Benjamin. 1993. "The Triad and the Unholy Trinity: Problems of International Monetary Cooperation." In *Pacific Economic Relations in the 1990s: Cooperation or Conflict?* ed. Richard Higgott, Richard Leaver, and John Ravenhill. Boston: Allen and Unwin.

———. 1994. "Beyond EMU: The Problem of Sustainability." In *The Political Economy of European Monetary Unification*, ed. Barry Eichengreen and Jeffrey Frieden, 149–65. Boulder, CO: Westview Press.

Collignon, Stephan, and Daniela Schwarzer. 2002. *The Power of Ideas: The Contribution to the Euro by the Association for the Monetary Union of Europe*. London: Routledge.

Craig, Paul. 1999. "EMU, the European Central Bank and Judicial Review." In *Legal Framework of the Single European Currency*, ed. Paul Beaumont and Neil Walker, 95–119. Oxford: Hart.

Crouch, Colin, ed. 2001. *After the Euro: Shaping Institutions for Governance in the Wake of European Monetary Union*. Oxford: Oxford University Press.

Crowley, Patrick. 2001. "The Institutional Implications of EMU." *Journal of Common Market Studies* 39, no. 3: 385–404.

Cukierman, Alex. 1992. *Central Bank Strategy, Credibility, and Independence*. Cambridge, MA: MIT Press.

Cukierman, Alex, Steven Webb, and Filin Neyapti. 1992. "Measuring the Independence of Central Banks and Its Effect on Policy Outcomes." *World Bank Economic Review* 6: 353–98.

De Haan, Jakob. 1997. "The European Central Bank: Independence, Accountability and Strategy: A Review." *Public Choice* 93: 395–426.

———. 2000. *History of the Bundesbank: Lessons for the European Bank*. London: Routledge.

Demertzis, Maria. 2001. "Can the ECB Be Truly Independent?" In *Challenges for Economic Policy Coordination within European Monetary Union*, ed. Andrew Hallett, Peter Mooslechner, and Martin Schürz, 105–27. Boston: Kluwer Academic Press.

Destler, I. M., and C. Randall Henning. 1989. *Dollar Politics: Exchange Rate Policy-making in the United States*. Washington, D.C.: Institute for International Economics.

Deutsche Bundesbank. 1989. *The Deutsche Bundesbank*. 3rd ed. Frankfurt: Deutsche Bundesbank.

———, ed. 1999. *Fifty Years of the Deutsche Mark*. London: Oxford University Press.

Dornbusch, Rudiger, Carlo Favero, and Francesco Giavazzi. 1998. "Immediate Challenges for the European Central Bank." In *EMU: Prospects and Challenges for the Euro*, ed. David Beggs, Charles Wyplosz, Klaus Zimmerman and Georges de Meuil, 15–64. Oxford: Blackwell.

Downs, Anthony. 1957. *Inside Bureaucracy*. Boston: Little, Brown, and Company.

Duisenberg, Wim. 1999. "The Euro, the Dollar and National Economic Policies: What Room for Manoeuvre?" Speech given at the Euro J+80 Conference, March 25.

———. 2000a. ECB Press Conference, 3 February 2000, Frankfurt, Germany, available at www.ecb.int.

———. 2000b. ECB Press Conference, 14 December 2000, Frankfurt, Germany, available at www.ecb.int.

———. 2000c. "Hearing before the Committee on Economic and Monetary Affairs of the European Parliament," 23 November 2000, Frankfurt, Germany, available at www.ecb.int.

———. 2001. "Hearing before the Committee on Economic and Monetary Affairs of the European Parliament," 18 December 2001, Brussels, Belgium, available at www.ecb.int.

Dutzler, Barbara. 2003. *The European System of Central Banks: An Autonomous Actor? The Quest for an Institutional Balance in EMU*. New York: Springer Verlag.

Dyson, Kenneth. 1994. *Elusive Union*. London: Longman.

———. 1999. "Benign or Malevolent Leviathan? Social Democratic Governments in a Neo-liberal Euro Area." *The Political Quarterly* 70, no. 2 (April–June): 195–209.

———. 2000. *The Politics of the Euro-Zone: Stability or Breakdown?* Oxford: Oxford University Press.

———, ed. 2002. *European States and the Euro: Europeanisation, Variation, and Convergence*. Oxford: Oxford University Press.

Dyson, Kenneth, and Kevin Featherstone. 1999. *The Road to Maastricht: Negotiating Economic and Monetary Union*. Oxford: Oxford University Press.

Dyson, Kenneth, Kevin Featherstone, and George Michalopoulos. 1995. "Strapped to the Mast: EC Central Bankers between Global Financial Markets and the Maastricht Treaty." *Journal of European Public Policy* 2, no. 3 (September): 465–87.

Eichengreen, Barry. 1998. "European Monetary Unification: A Tour d'Horizon." *Oxford Review of Economic Policy* 143, no. 3 (Autumn): 24–40.

Eijffinger, Sylvester, and Jakob de Haan. 2000. *European Monetary and Fiscal Policy*. Oxford: Oxford University Press.

Elgie, Robert. 2002. "The Politics of the European Central Bank: Principal-Agent Theory and the Democratic Deficit." *European Public Policy* 9, no. 2 (April): 186–200.

Elgie, Robert, and Helen Thompson. 1998. *The Politics of Central Banks*. London: Routledge.

Emerson, Michael, Daniel Gros, Alexander Italianes, Jean Pisani-Ferry, and Horst Reichenbach. 1992. *One Market, One Money: An Evaluation of the Potential Benefits and Costs of Forming an Economic and Monetary Union*. Oxford: Oxford University Press.

European Central Bank (ECB). 2001. *The Monetary Policy of the ECB*. Frankfurt: ECB.

———. 2004. *The Monetary Policy of the ECB*. Frankfurt: ECB.

European Central Bank Annual Report, various issues.

European Central Bank Monthly Bulletin, various issues.

Favero, Carlo, Torsten Persson, and Charles Wyplosz. 2000. *One Money, Many Countries: Monitoring the European Central Bank 2*. London: CEPR.

Financial Times, various issues.

Financial Times Deutschland, various issues.

Frankfurter Allgemeine Zeitung, various issues.

Franzese, Robert. 1999. "Partially Independent Central Banks, Politically Responsive Governments, and Inflation." *American Journal of Political Science* 43, no. 3: 681–706.

Fratianni, Michele, and Dominick Salvatore, eds. 1993. *Monetary Policy in Developed Economies*. Westport, CT: Greenwood.

Frey, Bruno, and Friedrich Schneider. 1981. "Central Bank Behaviour: A Positive Empirical Analysis." *Journal of Monetary Economics* 9: 291–315.

Frieden, Jeffrey. 1991. "Invested Interests: The Politics of National Economic Policies in a World of Global Finance." *International Organization* 45: 425–51.

———. 1994. "Exchange Rate Politics: Contemporary Lessons from American History." *Review of International Political Economy* 1: 81–103.

———. 1997. "The Politics of Exchange Rates." In *Mexico 1994: Anatomy of an Emerging Market Crash*, ed. Sebastian Edwards and Moises Naim, 81–94. Washington, DC: Carnegie Endowment for International Peace.

———. 2002. "Real Sources of European Currency Policy: Sectoral Interests and European Monetary Integration." *International Organization* 56, no. 4 (autumn): 831–60.

Frieden, Jeffrey, and Erik Jones, eds. 1998. *The Political Economy of European Monetary Union*. Boulder, CO: Westview Press.

Friedman, Milton. 1960. *A Program for Monetary Stability*. New York: Fordham University Press.

Friedman, Milton, and Anna Schwartz. 1963. *A Monetary History of the United States, 1867–1960*. Princeton, NJ: Princeton University Press.

Gildea, John. 1990. "Explaining FOMC Members' Votes." In *The Political Economy of American Monetary Policy*, ed. Thomas Meyer. New York: Cambridge University Press.

Goldstein, Judith. 1993. *Ideas, Interests, and American Trade Policy*. Ithaca, NY: Cornell University Press.

Goldstein, Judith, and Robert Keohane, eds. 1993. *Ideas and Foreign Policy: Beliefs, Institutions, and Political Change*. Ithaca, NY: Cornell University Press.

Goodman, John. 1991. "The Politics of Central Bank Independence." *Comparative Politics* 23, no. 3: 329–49.

———.1992. *Monetary Sovereignty: The Politics of Central Banking in Western Europe*. Ithaca, NY: Cornell University Press.

Gormley, Laurence, and Jakob de Haan. 1996. "The Democratic Deficit of the European Central Bank." *European Law Review* (April): 95–112.

Grahl, John. 1997. *After Maastricht: A Guide to European Monetary Union*. London: Lawrence and Wishart.

Greider, William. 1987. *Secrets of the Temple: How the Federal Reserve Runs the Country*. New York: Simon and Schuster.

Grieco, Joseph M. 1995. "The Maastricht Treaty, Economic and Monetary Union and the Neo-realist Research Programme." *Review of International Studies* 21: 21–40.

Groeneveld, Johannes M. 1998. *Inflation Patterns and Monetary Policy: Lessons for the European Central Bank*. Northampton, MA: Edward Elgar Publishing.

Gros, Daniel. 1998. "External Shocks and Labor Mobility: How Important Are They for EMU?" In *The New Political Economy of EMU*, ed. Jeffrey Frieden, Daniel Gros, and Erik Jones, 53–81. Lanham, MD: Rowman & Littlefield.

———. 2003. "Reforming the Composition of the ECB Governing Council in View of Enlargement: An Opportunity Missed." *CEPS Policy Brief* 32, April.

Gros, Daniel, and Niels Thygesen. 1998. *European Monetary Union*. 2nd ed. New York: Addison-Wesley Longman.

Haas, Peter. 1990. *Saving the Mediterranean: The Politics of International Environmental Cooperation*. New York: Columbia University Press.

———. 1992. "Introduction: Epistemic Communities and International Policy Coordination." *International Organization* 46: 1–35.

———. 1997. *Knowledge, Power, and International Policy Coordination*. Columbia: University of South Carolina Press.

Hall, Peter, ed. 1986. *The Political Power of Economic Ideas: Keynesianism across Nations*. Princeton, NJ: Princeton University Press.

———. 1994. "Central Bank Independence and Coordinated Wage Bargaining: Their Interaction in Germany and Europe." *German Politics and Society* 31: 1–23.

Hall, Peter A., and Robert Franzese Jr. 1998. "Mixed Signals: Central Bank Independence, Coordinated Wage Bargaining, and European Monetary Union." *International Organization* 52, no. 3 (Summer): 505–35.

Handelsblatt, various issues.

Hanrieder, Wolfram. 1982. *Helmut Schmidt: Perspectives on Politics*. Boulder, CO: Westview Press.

Hasse, Rolf. 1990. *The European Central Bank*. Gütersloh: Bertelsmann Foundation.

Havrilesky, Thomas. 1988. "Monetary Policy Signaling from the Administration to the Federal Reserve." *Journal of Money, Credit, and Banking* 20: 83–101.

———. 1993. *The Pressures on American Monetary Policy*. Boston: Kluwer Academic Publishers.

Havrilesky, Thomas, and John Gildea. 1992. "Reliable and Unreliable Partisan Appointees to the Board of Governors." *Public Choice* 73: 397–417.

Havrilesky, Thomas, and Thomas Granato. 1993. "Determinants of Inflationary Performance: Corporatist Structures vs. Central Bank Autonomy." *Public Choice* 76: 249–61.

Heisenberg, Dorothee. 1999. *The Mark of the Bundesbank*. Boulder, CO: Lynne Rienner Press.

Henning, C. Randall. 1994. *Currencies and Politics in the United States, Germany, and Japan*. Washington, DC: International Institute of Economics.

———. 1997. *Cooperating with Europe's Monetary Union*. Washington, DC: Institute for International Economics.

———. 2000a. "External Relations of the Euro Area." In *The Euro as a Stabilizer in the International Economic System*, ed. Robert Mundell and Armand Clesse, 35–46. London: Kluwer Academic Publishers.

———. 2000b. "U.S.-EU Relations after the Inception of the Monetary Union: Cooperation or Rivalry?" In *Transatlantic Perspectives on the Euro*, ed. C. Randall Henning and Pier Carlo Padoan, 5–63. Washington, DC: Brookings Institution Press for the European Community Studies Association.

Henning, C. Randall, and Pier Carlo Padoan. 2000. *Transatlantic Perspectives on the Euro*. Pittsburgh, PA: ECSA.

Hosli, Madeleine O. 1998. "The EMU and International Monetary Relations: What to Expect for International Actors?" In *The European Union in the World Community*, ed. Carolyn Rhodes, 165–91. Boulder, CO: Lynne Rienner Press.

Howarth, David, and Peter Loedel. 2003. *The European Central Bank: The New European Leviathan?* London: Palgrave Macmillan.

Issing, Otmar, Vitor Gaspar, Ignazio Angeloni, and Oreste Tristani. 2001. *Monetary Policy in the Euro Area: Strategy and Decision-Making at the European Central Bank.* Cambridge: Cambridge University Press.

Iversen, Torben. 1998a. "Wage Bargaining, Central Bank Independence, and the Real Effects of Money." *International Organization* 52: 469–504.

———. 1998b. *Contested Economic Institutions: The Politics of Macroeconomics and Wage Bargaining in Advanced Democracies.* Cambridge: Cambridge University Press.

Johnson, Peter A. 1998. *The Government of Money—Monetarism in Germany and the United States.* Ithaca, NY: Cornell University Press.

Jones, Erik. 1998. "Economic and Monetary Union: Playing with Money." In *Centralization or Fragmentation? Europe Facing the Challenges of Deepening, Diversity, and Democracy,* ed. Andrew Moravcsik, 59–93. Washington, DC: Brookings.

———. 2002. *The Politics of Economic and Monetary Union: Integration and Idiosyncrasy.* Oxford: Rowman & Littlefield.

Jones, Erik, Jeffrey Frieden, and Francisco Torres, eds. 1998. *Joining Europe's Monetary Club: The Challenges for Smaller Member States.* New York: St. Martin's Press.

Kaelberer, Matthias. 2001. *Money and Power in Europe: The Political Economy of European Monetary Cooperation.* Albany: State University of New York Press.

Kaltenthaler, Karl. 1998. *Germany and the Politics of Europe's Money.* Durham, NC: Duke University Press.

Kaltenthaler, Karl, and Christopher Anderson. 2001. "Europeans and Their Money: Explaining Support for the Common European Currency." *European Journal of Political Research* 40: 139–70.

Kapstein, Ethan. 1992. "Between Power and Purpose: Central Bankers and the Politics of Regulatory Convergence." *International Organization* 46: 265–87.

Katzenstein, Peter. 1987. *Policy and Politics in West Germany.* Philadelphia: Temple University Press.

Kaufman, Henry M. 1995. "The Importance of Being Independent: Central Bank Independence and the European System of Central Banks." In *The State of the European Union. Building a European Polity?* ed. C. Rhodes and S. Mazey, 267–92. Boulder, CO: Lynne Rienner Press.

Kees, Andreas. 1987. "The Monetary Committee of the European Community." *Kredit und Kapital* 20, no. 2: 258–67.

———. 1994. "The Monetary Committee as Promoter of European Integration." In *Monetary Stability through International Cooperation,* ed. A. Bakker, H. Boot, O. Sleipen and W. Vanthoor. Dordrecht, Netherlands: Kluwer.

Kennedy, Ellen. 1991. *The Bundesbank: Germany's Central Bank in the International Monetary System.* New York: Council on Foreign Relations Press.

Kettl, Donald. 1986. *Leadership at the Fed.* New Haven, CT: Yale University Press.

Kyland, Finn, and Edward Prescott. 1977. "Rules Rather Than Discretion: The Inconsistency of Optimal Plans." *Journal of Political Economy* 85: 473–91.

Lannoo, Karel. 1999. "Financial Supervision in EMU." Brussels: Centre for European Policy Studies, January.

Levitt, Malcolm, and Christopher Lord. 2000. *The Political Economy of Monetary Union.* London: Macmillan.

Loedel, Peter. 1999. *Deutsche Mark Politics*. Boulder, CO: Lynne Rienner Press.

Lohmann, Susanne. 1998. "Federalism and Central Bank Independence: The Politics of German Monetary Policy, 1957–1992." *World Politics* 50: 401–46.

Lommatzsch, Kirsten, and Sabine Tober. 2002. "Monetary Policy Aspects of the Enlargement of the Euro Area." Research Note 4, Deutsche Bank Research, August.

———. "2003: Zur Reform der Abstimmungsregeln im EZB-Rat nach der Erwiterung des Euroraumes." *DIW-Wochenbericht* 5.

Ludlow, Peter. 1982. *The Making of the European Monetary System*. London: Butterworth Scientific.

Lupia, Arthur. 1998. *The Democratic Dilemma: Can Citizens Learn What They Need to Know?* Cambridge: Cambridge University Press.

Magnette, Paul. 2000. "Towards 'Accountable Independence'? Parliamentary Controls of the European Central Bank and the Rise of a New Democratic Model." *European Law Journal* 6, no. 4 (December): 326–40.

Maier, Philipp. 2002. *Political Pressure, Rhetoric and Monetary Policy: Lessons for the European Central Bank*. Northampton, MA: Edward Elgar Publishing.

Mangano, Gabriel. 1999. "Monetary Policy in EMU: A Voting-Power Analysis of Coalition Formation in the European Central Bank." Working paper, London School of Economics.

March, James, and Herbert Simon. 1958. *Organizations*. New York: Wiley.

Marcussen, Martin. 2000. *Ideas and Elites: The Social Construction of Economic and Monetary Union*. Aalborg, Denmark: Aalborg University Press.

Marsh, David. 1992. *The Bundesbank: The Bank That Rules Europe*. London: Heinemann and Sons.

Marshall, Matt. 1999. *The Bank: The Birth of Europe's Central Bank and the Rebirth of Europe's Power*. London: Random House Business Books.

Masson, Paul R., and Mark P. Taylor. 1993. "Fiscal Policy within Common Currency Areas." *Journal of Common Market Studies* 31, no. 1 (March): 29–44.

Maxfield, Sylvia. 1994. "Financial Incentives and Central Bank Authority in Industrializing Countries." *World Politics* 46, no. 4: 556–89.

———. 1997. *Gatekeepers of Growth: The International Political Economy of Central Banking in Developing Countries*. Princeton, NJ: Princeton University Press.

Mayes, David G. 1998. "Evolving Voluntary Rules of the Operation of the European Central Bank." *Current Politics and Economics of Europe* 8, no. 4: 357–86.

McNamara, Kathleen. 1998. *The Currency of Ideas: Monetary Politics in the European Union*. Ithaca, NY: Cornell University Press.

———. 2001. "Where Do Rules Come From? The Creation of the European Central Bank." In *The Institutionalization of Europe*, ed. Neil Fligstein, Wayne Sandholtz, and Alec Stone Sweet. Oxford: Oxford University Press.

———. 2002. "Rational Fictions: Central Bank Independence and the Social Logic of Delegation." *West European Politics* 25, 1: 47–76.

McNamara, Kathleen, and Sophie Meunier. 2002. "Between National Sovereignty and International Power: What External Voice for the Euro?" *International Affairs* 78, no. 4: 849–68.

Moravcsik, Andrew. 1993. "Preferences and Power in the European Community: A Liberal Intergovernmentalist Approach." *Journal of Common Market Studies* 31, no. 4 (December): 473–524.

————. 1998. *The Choice for Europe*. Ithaca, NY: Cornell University Press.

Mundell, Robert. 1962. "Capital Mobility and Stabilization Policy under Fixed and Flexible Exchange Rates." *Canadian Journal of Economics and Political Science* 29: 475–85.

Naudin, Francois. 2000. *The European Central Bank: A Bank for the 21st Century*. London: Kogan Page.

Neal, Larry, and Daniel Barbezat. 1998. *The Economics of the European Union and the Economies of Europe*. London: Oxford University Press.

Neumann, Manfred. 1991. "Precommitment by Central Bank Independence." *Open Economics Review* 2: 95–112.

Niskanen, William. 1971. *Bureaucracy and Representative Government*. Chicago: University of Chicago Press.

Oatley, Thomas. 1997. *Monetary Politics: Exchange Rate Cooperation in the European Union*. Ann Arbor: Michigan University Press.

Padoa-Schioppa, Tomasso. 1999. "EMU and Banking Supervision." Lecture at the London School of Economics, Financial Markets Group, February 24.

————.2003. "Central Banks and Financial Stability." Speech, Jakarta, Indonesia, July 7.

————.2004. "The Evolving European Financial Landscape: Integration and Regulation." Speech at the colloquium organized by Groupe Caisse des Dépôts/KfW, Berlin, March 22.

Persson, Torsten, and Guido Tabellini, eds. 1995. *Monetary and Fiscal Policy*. Cambridge, MA: MIT Press.

Pollack, Mark A. 1997. "Delegation, Agency, and Agenda-Setting in the European Community." *International Organization* 51, no. 1: 99–134.

Posen, Adam. 1993. "Why Central Bank Independence Does Not Cause Low Inflation." In *Finance and the International Economy: The AMEX Bank Review Prize Essays in Memory of Robert Marjolin*, ed. Richard O'Brien. Vol. 7. Oxford: Oxford University Press.

————. 1995. "Declarations Are Not Enough: Financial Sector Sources of Central Bank Independence." In *NBER Macroeconomics Annual 1995*, ed. B. Bernanke and J. Rotemberg. Cambridge, MA: MIT Press.

Rogoff, Kenneth. 1985. "The Optimal Degree of Commitment to an Intermediate Monetary Target." *Quarterly Journal of Economics* 100 (November): 1169–89.

Sandholtz, Wayne. 1993. "Choosing Union: Monetary Politics and Maastricht." *International Organization* 47, no. 1 (Winter): 1–39.

Scheve, Kenneth. 2004. "Public Inflation Aversion and the Political Economy of Macroeconomic Policymaking." *International Organization* 58 (Winter): 1–34.

Schmidt, Helmut. 1989. *Men and Powers*. New York: Random House.

Shepsle, Kenneth. 1979. "Institutional Arrangements and Equilibrium in Multidimensional Voting Models." *American Journal of Political Science* 23: 27–59.

Sheridan, Jerome. 1996. "The Déjà Vu of EMU: Considerations for Europe from Nineteenth Century America." *Journal of Economic Issues* 30, no. 4 (December): 1143–61.

Sikkink, Kathryn. 1991. *Ideas and Institutions: Developmentalism in Brazil and Argentina*. Ithaca, NY: Cornell University Press.

Smaghi, Lorenzo Bini, and Daniel Gros. 2000. *Open Issues in European Central Banking.* Basingstoke, United Kingdom: Palgrave Macmillan.

Smyser, W. R. 1993. *The German Economy.* 2nd ed. New York: St. Martin's Press.

Soskice, David, and Torben Iversen. 1998. "Multiple Wage-Bargaining Systems in the Single European Currency Area." *Oxford Review of Economic Policy* 14, no. 3 (Autumn): 110–24.

Story, Jonathon. 1988. "The Launching of the EMS: An Analysis of Change in Foreign Economic Policy." *Political Studies* 36: 397–421.

Suzuki, Motoshi. 1993. "Domestic Determinants of Inflation." *European Journal of Political Research* 23: 245–59.

Taylor, Christopher. 2000. "The Role and Status of the European Central Bank: Some Proposals for Accountability and Cooperation." In *After the Euro: Shaping Institutions for Governance in the Wake of European Monetary Union,* ed. Colin Crouch, 179–202. Oxford: Oxford University Press.

Toma, Eugenia, and Mark Toma, eds. 1986. *Central Bankers, Bureaucratic Incentives, and Monetary Policy.* Boston: Kluwer.

Tsoukalis, Loukas. 1997. *The New European Economy Revisited.* Oxford: Oxford University Press.

Vaubel, Roland. 1993. "Eine Public Choice Analyse der Deutschen Bundesbank und ihre Implikationen für Europäische Währungsunion." In *Europa vor dem Eintritt in die Wirtschafts- und Währungsunion,* ed. Dieter Duwendag and Jürgen Siebke. Berlin: Duncker and Humblot.

Van Oudenaren, John. 2000. *Uniting Europe: European Integration and the Post–Cold War World.* Lanham, MD: Rowman & Littlefield.

Verdun, Amy. 1996. "An 'Asymmetrical' Economic and Monetary Union in the EU: Perceptions of Monetary Authorities and Social Partners." *Journal of European Integration* 20, no. 1 (Fall): 59–81.

———. 1998. "The Institutional Design of EMU: A Democratic Deficit." *Journal of Public Policy* 18, no. 2: 107–32.

———. 1999. "The Role of the Delors Committee in Creating EMU: An Epistemic Community?" *Journal of European Public Policy* 4, no. 2: 308–28.

———. 2000a. "Governing by Committee the Case of Monetary Policy." In *Committee Governance in the European Union,* ed. T. Christiansen and E. Kirchner, 132–44. Manchester, England: Manchester University Press.

———. 2000b. "Monetary Integration in Europe: Ideas and Evolution." In *The State of the European Union,* ed. M. Green Cowles and M. Smith, Vol. 5, 91–109. Oxford: Oxford University Press.

———, ed. 2002. *The Euro: European Integration Theory and Economic and Monetary Union.* Lanham: Rowman & Littlefield.

Verdun, Amy, and T. Christiansen. 2000. "Policies, Institutions and the Euro: Dilemmas of Legitimacy." In *After the Euro: Shaping Institutions for Governance in the Wake of European Monetary Union,* ed. C. Crouch, 162–78. Oxford: Oxford University Press.

Von Hagen, Jürgen. 1999. "A New Approach to Monetary Policy." In *Fifty Years of the Deutsche Mark,* ed. Deutsche Bundesbank. London: Oxford University Press.

Walsh, James. 2000. *European Monetary Integration and Domestic Politics.* Boulder, CO: Lynne Rienner Press.

Woolley, John. 1984. *Monetary Politics.* Cambridge: Cambridge University Press.

Wyplosz, Charles. 1997. "EMU: Why and How It Might Happen." *Journal of Economic Perspectives* 11, no. 4 (Fall): 3–21.

Zilioli, Chiara, and Martin Selmayr. 2001. *The Law of the European Central Bank.* Oxford: Hart.

Zysman, John. 1983. *Governments, Markets, and Growth: Financial Systems and the Politics of Industrial Change.* Ithaca, NY: Cornell University Press.

Index

Amato, Giuliano, 20
anchor currency, 12, 17, 18, 50, 53, 115
Austria, 89n25, 93, 100, 114, 118, 140

Balladur, Eduoard, 20
Balladur memorandum, 20
bank-based finance, 77, 106, 107, 161, 162, 170, 173
Bank deutscher Länder (BdL), 38, 44, 45, 46, 48, 54
Bank for International Settlements (BIS), 48, 49, 55
bank loans, 77, 117, 161, 170
Barre, Raymond, 14
Barre Report, 14
BDI. *See Bundesverband der Deutschen Industrie*
Belgium, 114, 118
bonds, 106, 161
Brandt, Willy, 14, 15, 17
Britain. *See* United Kingdom
Bundesbank: credibility, 3, 12, 22, 31, 32, 44, 58, 166; and the EMS, 11, 12, 14, 18, 19, 20, 31; and EMU, 15, 16, 20, 22, 25, 26; establishment, 35, 45; independence, 6, 22, 32, 38, 46, 70, 73, 83, 113, 118, 119, 142, 169, 170; public support, 22; and the "Snake," 31
Bundesbank Law, 35, 45, 46, 70, 71, 83, 89n16
Bundesbank model, 3, 10, 12, 20, 26, 32, 35–59, 61, 62, 65, 72, 88, 128, 159, 165, 166, 169, 172
Bundesverband der Deutschen Industrie (BDI), 22n2, 23n10, 23n12, 100

CAP. *See* Common Agricultural Policy
capital market-based finance, 77, 106, 107, 109, 170
Carter, Jimmy, 17
CBC. *See* Central Bank Council
Central Bank Council (CBC), 47, 56, 65, 67, 95, 122n61
commercial banks, 106, 107
Committee of Central Bank Governors, 21, 39, 48–50

Common Agricultural Policy (CAP), 12,
    14–15, 16, 17
convergence criteria, 23, 26, 29, 155–57
Council of Ministers, 49, 80, 96, 98
currency market intervention, 63, 80,
    135, 141, 143n4
currency reform (Germany), 44
Cyprus, 147, 149, 152, 153, 154, 155, 156
Czech Republic, 147, 149, 152, 153, 154,
    155, 156, 157

Delors, Jacques, 12, 21, 22, 31, 33n6, 38,
    51, 52
Delors Committee, 21, 22, 23, 26, 38,
    39, 44, 51–54
Delors Report, 23, 26, 52
democratic deficit, 174
Denmark, 120n8, 147, 150, 152, 153,
    154, 155, 156, 163n1, 163n6
deutsche mark, 16, 17, 18, 19, 25, 27,
    28, 44, 50, 53, 63, 80, 100, 113, 115,
    143n10
directorate (Bundesbank), 47, 59n5, 67,
    83
dollar, 2, 13, 14, 16, 18, 50, 80, 123, 124,
    127, 130, 132, 134, 136, 138, 139,
    140, 141, 142, 143n1
Duisenberg, Wim: appointment, 29, 30,
    93–94, 119n3; policy statements,
    63–64, 123, 132, 134, 135, 139, 140,
    144n10
Dutch central bank, 29, 64, 93, 140
Dyson, Kenneth, 11, 15, 16, 18, 20, 21,
    22, 25, 26, 33n6, 38, 39, 50, 52, 97,
    128, 143n2

East Germany, 15, 23
Ecofin. *See* Economic and Financial
    Affairs Council
Economic and Financial Affairs Council
    (Ecofin), 20, 96, 98, 100, 101, 120n8,
    121n29
Economic and Monetary Union (EMU):
    first attempt, 13, 14, 15, 16, 17, 18,
    21, 22; launch, 27–31; negotiations,
    23, 24, 25–26, 52–54; second attempt,
    19, 20, 21, 22, 31, 32, 38, 40, 50, 52

economic government, 96, 97
"economists," 26
Eichel, Hans, 99, 100, 101, 121n32
EMI. *See* European Monetary Institute
EMS. *See* European Monetary System
EMU. *See* Economic and Monetary
    Union
EP. *See* European Parliament
epistemic community, 39, 58
equities, 106
Erhard, Ludwig, 45
ERM. *See* exchange rate mechanism
ESCB. *See* European System of Central
    Banks
Estonia, 147, 149, 152, 153, 154, 155,
    156
EU. *See* European Union
Eucken, Wilhelm, 45
euro: appreciation, 123–43;
    depreciation, 123–43; launch, 85
Eurogroup, 82, 96–97, 120n8, 171
European Central Bank (ECB):
    accountability, 70–72; appointments,
    64, 82–85, 92–95; chief economist,
    54–58, 64, 65, 140; decision-making
    process, 62–67; independence,
    70–72, 94, 95–97, 102, 106, 113, 118,
    119, 121n36, 165, 176; instruments of
    policy, 77–78; mandate, 72–73;
    monetary policy strategy, 35–59,
    73–77; political pressure, 95–97;
    president's role, 62–67; staff, 54,
    82–85
European Commission, 38, 51, 68, 80,
    167
European Court of Justice, 100
European economy, 115–18
European industrial relations,
    104–5
European finance sector, 105–10
European Monetary Institute (EMI),
    27–31, 38, 54
European Monetary System (EMS):
    asymmetry, 17–19, 50, 53, 54, 80, 83;
    crises, 17, 26–27; negotiations, 18,
    19, 38, 49; political consequences,
    19, 50

European Parliament (EP), 68, 131, 135, 137, 144n16, 167

European public opinion, 110–15

European System of Central Banks (ESCB), 36, 53, 54, 62, 65, 70, 78, 84, 89n18, 101, 103

European Union (EU), 1, 2, 3, 5, 10, 37, 38, 55, 62, 64, 68, 69, 74, 78, 79, 80, 81, 85, 88n1, 89n14, 92, 95, 96, 98, 101, 102, 103, 116, 119, 165, 166, 167, 168, 171, 173

exchange rate mechanism (ERM): ERM I, 27, 80, 89n22; ERM II, 80, 156, 163n5, 163n6, 163n7

exchange rate policy: central bank interests in, 125–30; ECB exchange rate policy, 79–81, 123–43

exchange rate targeting, 80

Executive Board, 53, 54, 55, 59n8, 92, 95, 108, 110, 111, 112, 131

exports, 117, 118, 126, 127, 129, 130, 134, 139, 141, 142, 143n10, 144n13, 144n18

Federal Reserve Bank, 4, 6, 66, 67, 77, 95, 113, 158

Federation of German Industry. *See* Bundesverhand der Deutschen Industrie (BDI)

finance system: interests, 74–77; oversight, 78–79; structure, 74–77

Finland, 100, 114, 118

franc, 19, 27

France: and economic government, 82, 169; and the EMS, 21; EMU negotiations, 15, 26, 33n4; and the Stability and Growth Pact, 33n15, 98–101

Frankfurt: location decision, 28, 119n5

Frieburg School, 46–47

Frieden, Jeffry, 4, 5, 121n36, 126, 143n2

G-7. *See* Group of Seven

General Council, 88n1

Genscher, Hans-Dietrich, 20, 21

Genscher memorandum, 20, 24

Germany: currency reform, 44, 170; Finance Ministry, 14, 15, 16, 18, 20, 25, 98; Foreign Ministry, 20, 21; hyperinflation, 44, 45, 170; Nazism, 45; relations with Eastern Europe, 15; relations with France, 15, 17, 26, 28; public opinion, 24; reunification, 19–26; and Stability and Growth Pact, 29, 33n8, 33n15

Giscard D'Estaing, Valéry, 12, 18, 20, 31, 63, 103

Governing Council: background of members, 82–83; decision-making process, 39, 52, 53, 54, 56, 57, 58, 62–67; membership, 62–67; powers, 62–67; reform, 67–70, 170

government debt, 26, 29, 99, 101, 106, 155, 156

government deficits, 22, 29, 96, 99, 100, 101, 120n22, 155, 156

Greece, 114, 150

Group of Seven (G-7), 48, 135, 140

Hague summit, 14

Hannover summit, 21

Heisenberg, Dorothee, 4, 38, 50, 52

Henning, Randall, 5, 16, 20, 46, 77, 105, 106, 126, 129, 143n3

HICP (inflation measure), 73, 74, 85, 86

ideational model, 2, 8, 40, 53, 173, 176

IGC. *See* Intergovernmental Conference

image of competence, 40, 42, 63, 106, 107, 108, 110, 111, 121n36, 128, 129, 148, 158, 165, 174

IMF. *See* International Monetary Fund

imported inflation, 50, 97, 98, 129, 130, 131, 133

inflation: and growth, 42, 46, 72

inflation targeting, 37, 41, 56, 57, 161

Intergovernmental Conference (IGC), 25, 26, 28

International Monetary Fund (IMF), 81, 82, 89n23, 89n24

interview strategy, 8–9

Ireland, 66, 113, 114, 118, 133

Issing, Otmar: at the Bundesbank, 30, 36; at the ECB, 30, 56–58, 65, 71, 89n21, 140
Italy, 4, 27, 33n15, 98, 102, 113, 114, 118, 150, 170

Jenkins, Roy, 18

Kohl, Helmut, 20, 24, 25, 28, 38, 120n5

Lamfalussy, Alexandre, 28, 55
Land Central Bank (LCB), 47, 59n6
Latvia, 147, 149, 152, 153, 154, 155
LCB. *See* Land Central Bank
liberalization of capital controls, 22
Liebscher, Klaus, 140
Lithuania, 147, 149, 152, 153, 154, 155
Loedel, Peter, 4, 5, 28, 50, 70, 89n20, 89n23
Lombard loans, 77
London: and the euro, 150
Luxembourg, 16, 49, 82, 96, 114, 160

Maastricht summit, 1, 26
Maastricht Treaty, 1, 2, 26, 28, 29, 32, 35, 63, 70, 71, 72, 73, 78, 82, 95, 98, 103, 111, 152, 155, 156, 164n7
Madrid summit, 23
Malta, 147, 149, 152, 153, 155, 156
Marjolin, Robert, 13
Marshall, Matt, 5, 57
McNamara, Kathleen, 2, 4, 38, 39, 40, 51, 81
Mitterrand, François, 33n4
monetarism, 46, 47, 48
"monetarists," 26
Monetary Committee, 48–51
money supply targeting, 36, 37, 46, 47, 55, 56, 57, 59n2, 75, 76, 77, 161
Monnet, Jean, 13
Moravcsik, Andrew, 4, 11, 16, 20, 33n11, 38, 52
"Mr. Euro," 81–82, 88n3, 89n25, 89n26, 96
Müller-Armack, Alfred, 45

national central bank (NCB): background, 83; governors, 62, 66, 67, 83, 88, 92, 108, 109, 110, 111, 112, 118, 158, 161; powers, 62, 66, 68, 69, 83, 84
NCB. *See* National Central Bank
Netherlands, 63, 93, 98, 100, 114, 115, 118, 160
Noyer, Christian, 134

OECD. *See* Organization for Economic Cooperation and Development
oil crisis, 16, 17, 51
opt-outs, 147, 148, 153, 155, 156, 160, 161
Organization for Economic Cooperation and Development (OECD), 81
Ostpolitik, 15

Padoa-Schioppa, Tommaso, 33n6, 79
Pöhl, Karl-Otto, 22–23, 31–32, 52–53
Poland, 147, 149, 152, 153, 154, 155, 156, 157
policy autonomy, 15, 41, 49, 52, 59, 71, 88, 92, 119, 124, 128, 130, 151, 157, 165
Portugal, 99, 114, 118, 133, 150
Posen, Adam, 40, 77, 105, 106
price stability: Bundesbank definition, 36, 47, 73–77; change in definition, 75–77; ECB definition, 35, 73–77
principal agent theory, 41, 124, 125, 127, 130

rational action, 40
Romania, 147
Röpke, Wilhelm, 45

Schlesinger, Helmut, 47, 55, 56, 65
Schmidt, Helmut, 12, 17, 18, 19, 20, 31, 32n1, 38
Schröder, Gerhard, 142
Slovakia, 149, 152, 153, 154, 155
Slovenia, 147, 149, 152, 155, 156
"snake," 16, 17, 18, 19, 48, 49, 50, 80

Spain, 100, 113, 114, 118, 133, 150
Stability and Growth Pact, 29, 33n15, 97–102, 168, 173
Stoltenberg, Gerhard, 21
Strasbourg summit, 25
Sweden, 41, 120n8, 147, 150, 152, 153, 154, 155, 160, 161, 163n1

Thatcher, Margaret, 21
theory of persuasion, 43
Tietmeyer, Hans, 93, 119n1, 143n10
treaty on European Union. *See* Maastricht Treaty
Trichet, Jean-Claude, 30, 33n16, 64, 82, 88n6, 94, 95, 101, 119n2, 120n2

Turkey, 147
two pillar strategy, 74–77

unemployment, 3, 4, 7, 42, 116, 117, 122n56, 124, 154, 166
United Kingdom: and the EMS, 27; and EMU, 13, 31; and Eurozone expansion, 147–63, 164n7

Verplaetse, Alfons, 57

Wellink, Nout, 140
Welteke, Ernst, 66, 102, 121n32, 143n10
Werner, Pierre, 16, 21, 49
Werner Report, 16, 49

About the Author

Karl Kaltenthaler is faculty fellow in the Bliss Institute for Applied Politics at the University of Akron. He also teaches in the Department of Political Science at Case Western Reserve University.